P9-DGI-082

COMPLETE
MANDARIN
CHINESE
THE BASICS

Written by
Janet Lai

Edited by
Christopher A. Warnasch
Shaina Malkin

www.livinglanguage.com

Editors: Christopher A. Warnasch and Shaina Malkin
Production Editor: Carolyn Roth
Production Manager: Tom Marshall
Interior Design: Sophie Chin

First Edition

ISBN: 978-1-4000-2425-4

Library of Congress Cataloging-in-Publication Data available upon request.

This book is available at special discounts for bulk purchases for sales promotions or premiums. Special editions, including personalized covers, excerpts of existing books, and corporate imprints, can be created in large quantities for special needs. For more information, write to Special Markets/Premium Sales, 1745 Broadway, MD 6-2, New York, New York 10019 or e-mail specialmarkets@randomhouse.com.

PRINTED IN THE UNITED STATES OF AMERICA

10 9 8 7 6 5 4 3 2 1

ACKNOWLEDGMENTS

Thanks to the Living Language team: Tom Russell, Nicole Benhabib, Christopher Warnasch, Zviezdana Verzich, Suzanne McQuade, Shaina Malkin, Elham Shabahat, Sophie Chin, Denise DeGennaro, Linda Schmidt, Alison Skrabek, Lisbeth Dyer, Carolyn Roth, and Tom Marshall.

DEDICATION
To Wayne and Claire.

COURSE OUTLINE

Welcome to *Living Language Complete Mandarin Chinese: The Basics*! We know you're ready to jump right in and start learning Chinese, but before you do, you may want to spend some time familiarizing yourself with the structure of this course. It will make it easier for you to find your way around, and will really help you get the most out of your studies.

UNITS AND LESSONS

Living Language Complete Mandarin Chinese: The Basics includes ten *Units*, each of which focuses on a certain practical topic, from talking about yourself and making introductions, to asking directions and going shopping. Each Unit is divided into *lessons* that follow four simple steps:

1. *Words*, featuring the essential vocabulary you need to talk about the topic of the Unit;

2. *Phrases*, bringing words together into more complex structures and introducing a few idiomatic expressions;

3. *Sentences*, expanding on the vocabulary and phrases from previous lessons, using the grammar you've learned to form complete sentences; and,

4. *Conversations*, highlighting how everything works together in a realistic conversational dialogue that brings everything in the Unit together.

The lessons are each comprised of the following sections:

WORD LIST/PHRASE LIST/SENTENCE LIST/CONVERSATION
Every lesson contains two lists of words, phrases, or sentences, or two dialogues, one at the beginning and one about halfway through. The grammar and exercises will be based on these components, so it's important to spend as much time reading and rereading these as possible before moving on.

Notes

A brief section may appear after each list or dialogue to highlight any points of interest in the language or culture.

Nuts & bolts

This is the nitty-gritty of each lesson, where you'll learn the grammar of the language, the nuts and bolts that hold the pieces together. Pay close attention to these sections; this is where you'll get the most out of the language and learn what you need to learn to become truly proficient in Chinese. There are two Nuts & bolts in each lesson.

Practice

It's important to practice what you've learned on a regular basis. You'll find practice sections throughout each lesson; take your time to complete these exercises before moving on to the next section. How well you do on each practice will determine whether or not you need to review a particular grammar point before you move on.

Tip!

In order to enhance your experience, you'll find several tips for learning Chinese throughout the course. This could be a tip on a specific grammar point, additional vocabulary related to the lesson topic, or a tip on language learning in general. For more practical advice, you can also refer to the *Language learning tips* section that follows this introduction.

Culture note

Becoming familiar with the culture of Chinese-speaking countries is nearly as essential to language learning as grammar. These sections allow you to get to know these cultures better through facts about Chinese-speaking countries and other bits of cultural information. You'll also sometimes find links here to various websites you can visit on the internet to learn more about a particular country or custom, or to find a language learning tool that may come in handy.

UNIT ESSENTIALS

Finally, each Unit ends with a review of the most essential vocabulary and phrases. Make sure you're familiar with these phrases, as well as their structure, before moving on to the next Unit.

FURTHER REFERENCE

The coursebook also includes additional reference material to help you enhance your Chinese studies. *Chinese in action* offers more examples of Chinese in everyday use, from invitations to e-mails, using the vocabulary and grammar from all ten Units. The *supplemental vocabulary* lists include essential vocabulary by category, while the grammar summary can be used for a thorough review of key grammar points. The book also contains a list of *internet resources* where you can seek out more exposure to the language and information on Chinese-speaking countries.

Finally, you will find the first four conversations from the course written out in Chinese characters in *dialogues in Chinese characters*.

LEARNER'S DICTIONARY

If you've purchased this book as a part of the complete audio package, you also received a *Learner's Dictionary* with more than 10,000 of the most frequently used Chinese words, phrases, and idiomatic expressions. Use it as a reference any time you're at a loss for words in the exercises, or as a supplemental study aid. This dictionary is ideal for beginner or intermediate level learners of Chinese.

AUDIO

This course works best when used along with the four audio CDs included in the complete course package. These CDs feature all the word lists, phrase lists, sentence lists, and dialogues from each unit, as well as key examples from the Nuts & bolts sections and the Unit essentials. This audio can be used along with the book, or on the go for hands-free practice.

And it's as easy as that! To get even more out of *Living Language Complete Mandarin Chinese: The Basics,* you may want to read the *Language learning tips* section that follows this introduction. If you're confident that you know all you need to know to get started and prefer to head straight for Unit 1, you can always come back to that section for tips on getting more out of your learning experience.

Good luck!

If you're not sure about the best way to learn a new language, take a moment to read this section. It includes lots of helpful tips and practical advice on studying languages in general, improving vocabulary, mastering grammar, using audio, doing exercises, and expanding your learning experience. All of this will make learning more effective and more fun.

GENERAL TIPS

Let's start with some general points to keep in mind about learning a new language.

1. FIND YOUR PACE

The most important thing to keep in mind is that you should always proceed at your own pace. Don't feel pressured into thinking that you only have one chance to digest information before moving on to new material. Read and listen to parts of lessons or entire lessons as many times as it takes to make you feel comfortable with the material. Regular repetition is the key to learning any new language, so don't be afraid to cover material again, and again, and again!

2. TAKE NOTES

Use a notebook or start a language journal so you can have something to take with you. Each lesson contains material that you'll learn much more quickly and effectively if you write it down, or rephrase it in your own words once you've understood it. That includes vocabulary, grammar points and examples, expressions from dialogues, and anything else that you find noteworthy. Take your notes with you to review wherever you have time to kill—on the bus or train, waiting at the airport, while dinner is cooking, or whenever you can find the time. Remember—practice (and lots of review!) makes perfect when it comes to learning languages.

3. MAKE A REGULAR COMMITMENT

Make time for your new language. The concept of "hours of exposure" is key to learning a language. When you expose yourself to a new language frequently, you'll pick it up more easily. On the other hand, the longer the intervals between your exposure to a language, the more you'll forget. It's best to set time aside regularly for yourself. Imagine that you're enrolled in a class that takes place at certain regular times during the week, and set that time aside. Or use your lunch break. It's better to spend less time several days a week than a large chunk of time once or twice a week. In other words, spending thirty or forty minutes on Monday, Tuesday, Wednesday, Friday, and Sunday will be better than spending two and a half or three hours just on Saturday.

4. DON'T HAVE UNREALISTIC EXPECTATIONS

Don't expect to start speaking a new language as if it were your native language. It's certainly possible for adults to learn new languages with amazing fluency, but that's not a realistic immediate goal for most people. Instead, make a commitment to become "functional" in a new language, and start to set small goals: getting by in most daily activities, talking about yourself and asking about others, following TV and movies, reading a newspaper, expressing your ideas in basic language, and learning creative strategies for getting the most out of the language you know. Functional doesn't mean perfectly native fluent, but it's a great accomplishment!

5. DON'T GET HUNG UP ON PRONUNCIATION

"Losing the accent" is one of the most challenging parts of learning a language. If you think about celebrities, scientists, or political figures whose native language isn't English, they probably have a pretty recognizable accent. But that hasn't kept them from becoming celebrities, scientists, or political figures. Really young children are able to learn the sounds of any language in the world, and they can reproduce them perfectly. That's part of the process of learning a native language. As an adult, or even as an older child, this ability becomes reduced, so if you agonize over sounding like a native speaker in your new language, you're just setting yourself up for disappointment. That's not to say that you can't learn pronunciation well. Even adults can get pretty far through mimicking the sounds that they hear. So, listen carefully to the audio several times. Listening is a very important part of this process: you can't reproduce the sound until you learn to distinguish the sound. Then mimic what you hear. Don't be afraid of sounding strange. Just keep at it, and soon enough you'll develop good pronunciation.

6. Don't be shy

Learning a new language inevitably involves speaking out loud, and it involves making mistakes before you get better. Don't be afraid of sounding strange, or awkward, or silly. You won't: you'll impress people with your attempts. The more you speak, and the more you interact, the faster you'll learn to correct the mistakes you do make.

TIPS ON LEARNING VOCABULARY

You obviously need to learn new words in order to speak a new language. Even though that may seem straightforward compared with learning how to actually put those words together in sentences, it's really not as simple as it appears. Memorizing words is difficult, even just memorizing words in the short term. But long-term memorization takes a lot of practice and repetition. You won't learn vocabulary simply by reading through the vocabulary lists once or twice. You need to practice.There are a few different ways to "lodge" a word in your memory, and some methods may work better for you than others. The best thing to do is to try a few different methods until you feel that one is right for you. Here are a few suggestions and pointers:

1. Audio repetition

Fix your eye on the written form of a word, and listen to the audio several times. Remind yourself of the English translation as you do this.

2. SPOKEN REPETITION

Say a word several times aloud, keeping your eye on the written word as you hear yourself speak it. It's not a race—don't rush to blurt the word over and over again so fast that you're distorting its pronunciation. Just repeat it, slowly and naturally, being careful to pronounce it as well as you can. And run your eye over the shape of the word each time you say it. You'll be stimulating two of your senses at once that way—hearing and sight—so you'll double the impact on your memory.

3. WRITTEN REPETITION

Write a word over and over again across a page, speaking it slowly and carefully each time you write it. Don't be afraid to fill up entire sheets of paper with your new vocabulary words.

4. FLASH CARDS

They may seem childish, but they're effective. Cut out small pieces of paper (no need to spend a lot of money on index cards) and write the English word on one side and the new word on the other. Just this act alone will put a few words in your mind. Then read through your "deck" of cards. First go from the target (new) language into English—that's easier. Turn the target language side face up, read each card, and guess at its meaning. Once you've guessed, turn the card over to see if you're right. If you are, set the card aside in your "learned" pile. If you're wrong, repeat the word and its meaning and then put it at the bottom of your "to learn" pile. Continue through until you've moved all of the cards into your "learned" pile.

Once you've completed the whole deck from your target language into English, turn the deck over and try to go from English into your target language. You'll see that this is harder, but also a better test of whether or not you've really mastered a word.

5. MNEMONICS

A mnemonic is a device or a trick to trigger your memory, like "King Phillip Came Over From Great Spain," which you may have learned in high school biology to remember that species are classified into kingdom, phylum, class, order, family, genus, and species. They work well for vocabulary, too. When you hear and read a new word, look to see if it sounds like anything—a place, a name, a nonsense phrase. Then form an image of that place or person or even nonsense scenario in your head. Imagine it as you say and read the new word. Remember that the more sense triggers you have—hearing, reading, writing, speaking, imagining a crazy image—the better you'll remember.

6. GROUPS
Vocabulary should be learned in small and logically connected groups whenever possible. Most of the vocabulary lists in this course are already organized this way. Don't try to tackle a whole list at once. Choose your method—repeating a word out loud, writing it across a page, etc., and practice with a small group.

7. PRACTICE
Don't just learn a word out of context and leave it hanging there. Go back and practice it in the context provided in this course. If the word appears in a dialogue, read it in the full sentence and call to mind an image of that sentence. If possible, substitute other vocabulary words into the same sentence structure ("John goes to the *library*" instead of "John goes to the *store*.") As you advance through the course, try writing your own simple examples of words in context.

8. COME BACK TO IT
This is the key to learning vocabulary—not just holding it temporarily in your short-term memory, but making it stick in your long-term memory. Go back over old lists, old decks of flashcards you made, or old example sentences. Listen to vocabulary audio from previous lessons. Pull up crazy mnemonic devices you created at some point earlier in your studies. And always be on the lookout for old words appearing again throughout the course.

TIPS ON USING AUDIO

The audio in this course doesn't only let you hear how native speakers pronounce the words you're learning, but it also serves as a second kind of "input" to your learning experience. The printed words serve as visual input, and the audio serves as *auditory* input. There are a few different strategies that you can use to get the most out of the audio. First, use the audio while you're looking at a word or sentence. Listen to it a few times along with the visual input of seeing the material. Then, look away and just listen to the audio on its own. You can also use the audio from previously studied lessons as a way to review. Put the audio on your computer or an MP3 player and take it along with you in your car, on the train, while you walk, while you jog, or whenever you have free time. Remember that the more exposure you have to and contact you have with your target language, the better you'll learn.

TIPS ON USING DIALOGUES

Dialogues are a great way to see language in action, where it's used by people in realistic situations. To get the most out of a dialogue as a language student, think of it as a cycle rather than a linear passage. First read through the dialogue once in the target language to get the gist. Don't agonize over the details just yet. Then, go back and read through a second time, but focus on individual sentences. Look for new words or new constructions. Challenge yourself to figure out what they mean by the context of the dialogue. After all, that's something you'll be doing a lot of in the real world, so it's a good skill to develop! Once you've worked out the details, read the dialogue again from start to finish. Now that you're very familiar with the dialogue, turn on the audio and listen to it as you read. Don't try to repeat yet; just listen and read along. This will build your listening comprehension. Then, go back and listen again, but this time pause to repeat the phrases or sentences that you're hearing and reading. This will build your spoken proficiency and pronunciation. Now listen again without the aid of the printed dialogue. By now you'll know many of the lines inside out, and any new vocabulary or constructions will be very familiar.

TIPS ON DOING EXERCISES

The exercises are meant to give you a chance to practice the vocabulary and structures that you learn in each lesson, and of course to test yourself on retention. Take the time to write out the entire sentences to get the most out of the practice. Don't limit yourself to just reading and writing. Read the sentences and answers aloud, so you'll also be practicing pronunciation and spoken proficiency. As you gain more confidence, try to adapt the practice sentences by substituting different vocabulary or grammatical constructions, too. Be creative, and push the practices as far as you can to get the most out of them.

TIPS ON LEARNING GRAMMAR

Each grammar point is designed to be as small and "digestible" as possible, while at the same time complete enough to teach you what you need to know. The explanations are intended to be simple and straightforward, but one of the best things you can do is to take notes on each grammar section, putting the explanations into your own words, and then copying the example sentences or tables slowly and carefully. This will do two things. It will give you a nice clear notebook that you can take with you so you can review and practice, and it will also force you to take enough time with each section so that it's really driven home. Of course, a lot of grammar is memorization—verb endings, irregular forms, pronouns, and so on. So a lot of the vocabulary learning tips will come in handy for learning grammar, too:

I. AUDIO REPETITION

Listen to the audio several times while you're looking at the words or sentences. For example, for a verb conjugation, listen to all of the forms several times, reading along to activate your visual memory as well.

2. SPOKEN REPETITION

Listen to the audio and repeat several times for practice. For example, to learn the conjugation of an irregular verb, repeat all of the forms of the verb until you're able to produce them without looking at the screen. It's a little bit like memorizing lines for a play—practice until you can make it sound natural. Practice the example sentences that way as well, focusing of course on the grammar section at hand.

3. WRITTEN REPETITION

Write the new forms again and again, saying them slowly and carefully as well. Do this until you're able to produce all of the forms without any help.

4. FLASH CARDS

Copy the grammar point, whether it's a list of pronouns, a conjugation, or a list of irregular forms, on a flashcard. Stick the cards in your pocket so you can practice them when you have time to kill. Glance over the cards, saying the forms to yourself several times, and when you're ready to test yourself, flip the card over and see if you can produce all of the information.

5. GRAMMAR IN THE WILD

Do you want to see an amazing number of example sentences that use some particular grammatical form? Well, just type that form into a search engine. Pick a few of the examples you find at random, and copy them down into your notebook or language journal. Pick them apart, look up words you don't know, and try to figure out the other grammatical constructions. You may not get everything 100% correct, but you'll definitely learn and practice in the process.

6. COME BACK TO IT

Just like vocabulary, grammar is best learned through repetition and review. Go back over your notes, go back to previous lessons and read over the grammar sections, listen to the audio, or check out the relevant section in the grammar summary. Even after you've completed lessons, it's never a bad idea to go back and keep the "old" grammar fresh.

HOW TO EXPAND YOUR LEARNING EXPERIENCE
Your experience with your new language should not be limited to this course alone. Like anything, learning a language will be more enjoyable if you're able to make it a part of your life in some way. And you'd be surprised to know how easily you can do that these days!

1. USE THE INTERNET
The internet is an absolutely amazing resource for people learning new languages. You're never more than a few clicks away from online newspapers, magazines, reference material, cultural sites, travel and tourism sites, images, sounds, and so much more. Develop your own list of favorite sites that match your needs and interests, whether it's business, cooking, fashion, film, kayaking, rock climbing, or . . . well, you get the picture. Use search engines creatively to find examples of vocabulary or grammar "in the wild." Find a favorite blog or periodical and take the time to work your way through an article or entry. Think of what you use the internet for in English, and look for similar sites in your target language.

2. CHECK OUT COMMUNITY RESOURCES
Depending on where you live, there may be plenty of practice opportunities in your own community. There may be a cultural organization or social club where people meet. There may be a local college or university with a department that hosts cultural events such as films or discussion groups. There may be a restaurant where you can go for a good meal and a chance to practice a bit of your target language. Of course, you can find a lot of this information online, and there are sites that allow groups of people to get organized and meet to pursue their interests.

3. FOREIGN FILMS

Films are a wonderful way to practice hearing and understanding a new language. With English subtitles, pause, and rewind, they're practically really long dialogues with pictures! Not to mention the cultural insight and experience they provide. And nowadays it's simple to rent foreign DVDs in the store or online or even access whole films online. So, if you're starting to learn a new language today, rent yourself some movies that you can watch over the next few weeks and months.

4. MUSIC

Even if you have a horrible singing voice, music is a great way to learn new vocabulary. After hearing a song just a few times, the lyrics somehow manage to plant themselves in the mind. And with the internet, it's often very easy to find the entire lyric sheet for a song online, print it out, and have it ready for whenever you're alone and feel like singing . . .

5. TELEVISION

If you have access to television programming in the language you're studying, including of course anything you can find on the internet, take advantage of that! You'll most likely hear very natural and colloquial language, including idiomatic expressions and rapid speech, all of which will be a healthy challenge for your comprehension skills. But the visual cues, including body language and gestures, will help. Plus, you'll get to see how the language interacts with the culture, which is also a very important part of learning a language.

6. FOOD

A great way to learn a language is through the cuisine. What could be better than going out and trying new dishes at a restaurant with the intention of practicing your newly acquired language? Go to a restaurant, and if the names of the dishes are printed in the target language, try to decipher them. Then try to order in the target language, provided of course that your server speaks the language! At the very least you'll learn a few new vocabulary items, not to mention sample some wonderful new food.

1. PĪNYĪN ROMANIZATION

The Chinese language does not have an alphabet. Each word is represented by a character, which may be composed of just one stroke (line) or as many as several dozen. To represent Chinese sounds for those who do not read characters, various systems of romanization have been devised. *Living Language Complete Mandarin Chinese: The Basics* uses **pīnyīn,** the standard system used in China and the one most commonly used in the United States, in both its coursebook and dictionary.

Each syllable in Chinese has an initial consonant sound and a final vowel sound. There are twenty-three initial sounds (consonants) and thirty-six final sounds (vowels or combinations of vowels and consonants). Here is how each sound is written in **pīnyīn,** with its approximate English equivalent. As you will see, the sound values of some **pīnyīn** letters are different from the sound values of their equivalents in English.

INITIAL SOUNDS

Pīnyīn	English	Examples
b	*b* in <u>b</u>ear	**bāng** *(to help)*, **bù** *(not)*, **bàn** *(half)*
p	*p* in <u>p</u>oor	**pán** *(plate)*, **pǔtōng** *(common)*, **pēn** *(to spray)*
m	*m* in <u>m</u>ore	**mǐ** *(rice)*, **mén** *(door)*, **māma** *(mother)*
f	*f* in <u>f</u>ake	**fēng** *(wind)*, **fá** *(to punish)*, **fāxiàn** *(to discover)*
d	*d* in <u>d</u>are	**dà** *(big)*, **dài** *(to bring)*, **dānchē** *(bicycle)*
t	*t* in <u>t</u>ake	**tiān** *(sky, day)*, **tiào** *(to jump)*, **tuī** *(to push)*
n	*n* in <u>n</u>ow	**nǐ** *(you)*, **nán** *(difficult)*, **niǎo** *(bird)*

l	*l* in *learn*	**lái** *(to come)*, **lěng** *(cold)*, **là** *(hot and spicy)*
z	*ds* in *yards*	**zuǒ** *(left)*, **zìjǐ** *(self)*, **zuò** *(to sit)*
c	*ts* in *its*	**cóng** *(from)*, **cuòwù** *(mistake)*, **cūn** *(village)*
s	*s* in *sing*	**sān** *(three)*, **sì** *(four)*, **suì** *(years old)*
zh	*dg* in *judge*	**zhuō** *(to catch)*, **zhū** *(pig)*, **zhú** *(bamboo)*
ch	*ch* in *church*	**chē** *(car)*, **chá** *(tea)*, **chī** *(to eat)*
sh	hard *sh* in *shhhh!*	**shìjiè** *(world)*, **shū** *(book)*, **shì** *(to try)*
r	*r* in *rubber*	**rén** *(person)*, **rè** *(hot)*, **rì** *(sun)*
j	*dy* in *and yet*	**jiù** *(old)*, **juān** *(to donate)*, **jiǔ** *(nine, wine)*
q	*ty* in *won't you*	**qián** *(money)*, **qù** *(to go)*, **qǐng** *(please)*
x	*sh* in *shoe*	**xièxie** *(thank you)*, **xīn** *(new)*, **xìng** *(last name)*
g	*g* in *get*	**gāo** *(tall)*, **gòu** *(enough)*, **gàosu** *(to tell)*
k	*k* in *keep*	**kāfēi** *(coffee)*, **kuài** *(fast)*, **kǒu** *(mouth)*
h	*h* in *help*	**hé** *(and)*, **hǎo** *(good)*, **huā** *(flower)*
y	*y* in *yes*	**yuè** *(moon, month)*, **yòu** *(again)*, **yòng** *(to use)*
w	*w* in *want*	**wǒ** *(I, me)*, **wū** *(house)*, **wèi** *(stomach)*

FINAL SOUNDS

Pīnyīn	English	Examples
a	*a* in *ma*	**bàba** *(father)*, **tā** *(he, she, it)*, **nà** *(that)*
ai	*y* in *my*	**zài** *(again)*, **mǎi** *(to buy)*, **tài** *(too)*

ao	*ou* in *p<u>ou</u>t*	gāo *(tall)*, hǎo *(good)*, yào *(medicine)*
an	*an* in *él<u>an</u>*	bàn *(half)*, fàn *(cooked rice)*, dānchē *(bicycle)*
ang	*ong* in *thr<u>ong</u>*	tāng *(soup)*, ràng *(to let)*, fāngbiàn *(convenient)*
o	*o* in *<u>or</u>*	bó *(thin)*, bōcài *(spinach)*, mó *(devil)*
ou	*oa* in *fl<u>oa</u>t*	yǒu *(to have)*, tōu *(to steal)*, ròu *(meat)*
ong	*ong* in *l<u>ong</u>*	tòng *(pain)*, kōng *(empty)*, gōnggòng *(public)*
e	*e* in *n<u>e</u>rve*	hē *(to drink)*, gēzi *(pigeon)*
ei	*ay* in *d<u>ay</u>*	bēizi *(cup)*, shéi *(who)*, měi *(pretty)*
en	*un* in *<u>un</u>der*	hěn *(very)*, rén *(person)*, fēn *(minute)*
eng	*ung* in *d<u>ung</u>*	péngyou *(friend)*, dēng *(light)*, zēngjiā *(to increase)*
i (after z, c, s, zh, ch, sh, r)	*r* in *thunde<u>r</u>*	chī *(to eat)*, shì *(matter)*, sǐ *(to die)*
i	*ee* in *s<u>ee</u>*	dī *(low)*, qí *(flag, to ride)*, bǐ *(pen)*
ia	<u>*yah*</u>	jiā *(home)*, jiàqian *(price)*, xiā *(blind)*
iao	*eow* in *m<u>eow</u>*	xiǎo *(small)*, tiào *(to jump)*, liáotiān *(to chat)*
ian	<u>*yan*</u>	diàn *(electricity)*, jiān *(shoulder)*, biàn *(to change)*
iang	<u>*yang*</u>	liǎng *(two)*, xiāng *(fragrant)*, jiāng *(ginger)*
ie	*ye* in *<u>yes</u>*	bié *(don't)*, xiě *(to write)*, jiē *(street)*
iu	*yo* in *<u>yo</u>-yo*	qiú *(ball)*, jiǔ *(nine, wine)*, liù *(six)*
iong	<u>*young*</u>	xiōng *(chest)*

in	*in* in s<u>in</u>	**xīn** *(heart)*, **qīnqì** *(relatives)*, **línjū** *(neighbor)*
ing	*ing* in s<u>ing</u>	**qǐng** *(please)*, **Yīngwén** *(English)*, **míngbai** *(to understand)*
u	*u* in fl<u>u</u>	**shū** *(to lose)*, **zú** *(foot)*, **tūrán** *(suddenly)*
ua	*ua* in s<u>ua</u>ve	**huā** *(flower)*, **shuā** *(brush)*, **zhuā** *(to grab)*
uai	*wi* in <u>wi</u>de	**shuài** *(handsome)*, **kuài** *(fast)*
uan	<u>wan</u>	**zhuānjiā** *(expert)*, **chuán** *(ship)*, **huán** *(to return)*
uang	<u>wong</u>	**chuāng** *(window)*, **shuāng** *(pair)*, **huángsè** *(yellow)*
uo	*wo* in <u>won</u>'t	**guójiā** *(country)*, **duō** *(many)*, **cuò** *(wrong)*
ui	<u>weigh</u>	**shuǐ** *(water)*, **huì** *(know how to)*, **zuǐ** *(mouth)*
un	*on* in <u>won</u> but with a shorter *o* sound	**cùn** *(inch)*, **kùnnan** *(difficult)*, **gǔn** *(to roll)*
ü (when ü combines with **j, q, x,** and **y,** the two dots above the letter can be omitted)	like *ee* in s<u>ee</u>, but with lips rounded into a pout (German h<u>ü</u>bsch, French t<u>u</u>.)	**qù** *(to go)*, **nǚ** *(female)*, **lǚguǎn** *(hotel)*

üan	like ü above with *an*	**quánlì** *(power)*, **yǔan** *(far)*, **juān** *(to donate)*
üe	like ü above with *e* in n*e*t	**juédìng** *(to decide)*, **xué** *(to study)*, **yuè** *(moon, month)*
ün	like ü above with *n* in a*n*	**xùnliàn** *(to train)*, **yùndòng** *(sports)*, **jūnduì** *(army)*
er	*are*	**ěrduo** *(ear)*

2. TONE MARKS

Each syllable in Mandarin Chinese must be pronounced with a tone. There are four tones in total, plus a neutral tone. Here are the tone marks as they are written in **pīnyīn**. They're written here over the vowel **a**, which is pronounced similarly to the vowel in *John*. Imagine saying the name John in the following contexts:

First tone	ā	High and neutral, no accent. Sing *"John."*
Second tone	á	From middle to high, as in asking a question. *"John? Is that you?"*
Third tone	ǎ	From middle to low, and then to high, as if stretching out a question: *"Jo-o-o-hn,* what do you think?"
Fourth tone	à	From high to low, as if answering a question. "Who's there?" *"John."*

Syllables pronounced with the neutral tone are unmarked. Common examples of words pronounced with a neutral tone include the Chinese particles **ma** and **ne**.

In Chinese, it is important to pronounce the correct tones. There are words which consist of all the same sounds, but differ in meaning depending on the tones used:

āi	*dust*	liū	*to skate*
ái	*cancer*	liú	*to flow*
ǎi	*short*	liǔ	*willow*
ài	*love*	liù	*six*

As you can see, the meaning of words can vary widely depending on which tone is pronounced.

When there are two syllables in a row in the third tone, the first syllable with a third tone is pronounced in the second tone. However, the tone is still written as a third tone in writing. For example:

Nǐ hǎo ma?

How are you?

In this phrase, **nǐ** would be pronounced in the second tone, although it is still written as a third tone.

The tones are placed over the final vowel sound of a syllable. In the case of compound vowels, such as **ai, uo, ao,** etc., the tone is placed over the primary vowel. The primary vowel is the vowel that is closer to the left end of the following vowel priority list: **a, o, e, i, u.** When **i** and **u** combine together to form a compound vowel, the tone marker is always placed over the second vowel. For example: **liù** *(six)* or **tuì** *(to withdraw).*

3. USE OF THE APOSTROPHE

When a syllable starting with **a, o,** or **e** immediately follows another syllable, an apostrophe is added to keep the two syllables separate and prevent any confusion of meaning.

dàng'àn   *file*
(**dàng + àn,** not
dàn + gàn)

Tiān'ānmén   *Tiananmen*
(**Tiān + ānmén,** not
Tiā + nānmén)

UNIT 1
Hello! How are you?

Nǐ hǎo! In Unit 1, you'll learn how to greet people, how to introduce yourself, how to tell people your name, your age and nationality, and how to use basic expressions of courtesy. You'll learn some very important basic grammar as well, such as personal pronouns, how to express plurals in Chinese, and how to ask and answer simple questions. Are you ready to begin?

——————————— Lesson 1 (words) ———————————

WORD LIST 1
Each Unit begins with a lesson that focuses on words. The words will be used throughout the Unit, so familiarize yourself with them. For advice on learning new vocabulary, consult the Language learning tips section at the beginning of this program.

shì	*to be, am, is, are, was, were*
bù	*not, no*
yě	*also*
hǎo	*good, well*
nǎ	*which*
guó(jiā)	*country*
lǎoshī	*teacher*
xuésheng	*student*
rén	*person, man*
guì	*honorable, expensive*
xìng	*last name*

| míngzi | *first name* |
| Zhōngwén | *Chinese language* |

NUTS & BOLTS 1
PERSONAL PRONOUNS

Personal pronouns are the pronouns that you use to refer to people in sentences, such as *I, you, we,* and so on. The Chinese personal pronouns are:

wǒ	*I*	wǒmen	*we*
nǐ/nín *(fml.)*	*you*	nǐmen *(pl.)*	*you, all of you*
tā	*he, she, it*	tāmen	*they*

The following abbreviations will be used in this course: *(pl.)* = plural, *(fml.)* = formal/polite, *(lit.)* = literally.

As you see, there are two ways to say *you* in Chinese. One is the polite form **nín**, which you would use in the case of a person for whom you want to show respect, such as your parents, your friend's parents, your teacher, your boss, or people who are generally older than you are. The other is the informal form **nǐ**, which you would use when addressing friends, colleagues, or people who are your own age or younger.

Note that the plural forms of both **nǐ** *(you)* and the polite **nín** *(you)* are **nǐmen. Nínmen** does not exist in Chinese. Also note that although the pronouns *he, she* and *it* are pronounced the same **(tā)**, their written characters are totally different: 他 *(he)*, 她 *(she)*, 它 *(it)*.

PRACTICE 1

Which Chinese pronoun would you use for the following people? There may be more than one correct answer.

1. Your friend David's mother

2. The CEO in your office (with whom you're talking)

3. Mary and John

4. Your friend Nancy

5. Yourself

WORD LIST 2

Měiguó	*America*
Zhōngguó	*China*
Yīngguó	*Britain*
Fǎguó	*France*
Xībānyá	*Spain*
Déguó	*Germany*
Yìdàlì	*Italy*
Rìběn	*Japan*
Àozhōu	*Australia*
xiānsheng	*Mr., husband, sir*
tàitai/fūrén *(fml.)*	*Mrs., wife*
xiǎojiě	*Miss, young lady*
yīshēng	*doctor*
hùshi	*nurse*
lùshī	*lawyer*
chūzūchē sījī	*taxi driver*
shāngrén	*business person*
yóukè	*tourist*

NUTS & BOLTS 2
NUMBERS 1–10
Now let's look at numbers in Chinese. Let's start with *one* through *ten*:

yī	*one*
èr	*two*
sān	*three*
sì	*four*
wǔ	*five*
liù	*six*
qī	*seven*
bā	*eight*
jiǔ	*nine*
shí	*ten*

Note that the number **yī** *(one)* changes tone depending on where and how it is used in a sentence. When **yī** is used in counting, in telling time, as part of a larger number, at the end of a word, or as an ordinal number, it is pronounced with a first tone.

yī, èr, sān, sì, wǔ . . .
one, two, three, four, five . . .

Otherwise, it changes to the second tone when it comes before a syllable in the fourth tone in a sentence, and to the fourth tone when it comes before a syllable in the first, second, or third tone.

yíqiè
everything

yìxiē
some

PRACTICE 2
Please translate the following numbers into Chinese:

1. four
2. six
3. one

4. five
5. ten

Culture note

In Chinese, the common titles of address are: **xiānsheng**, **tàitai/fūrén** and **xiǎojiě**. For example, use **xiānsheng** to address Mr. Wang. Use **xiǎojiě** to address Miss Wang. Finally, use **tàitai** or **fūrén** to address Mrs. Wang. Note that **tàitai** is commonly used in Hong Kong and Taiwan. **Fūrén** is commonly used in mainland China and is more formal and respectful than **tàitai**.

Also note that the placement of a person's last name before his or her title is the opposite of what is familiar to English speakers. For example, if you want to address Mr. Wang in Chinese, you need to say **Wáng xiānsheng**, instead of **xiānsheng Wáng**. Full names in Chinese are also placed in a different order than in the English tradition. In Chinese, the last name is put before the first name. In other words, if someone's first name is Yi and last name is Wang, then the correct order in Chinese would be Wang Yi.

ANSWERS
PRACTICE 1: 1. tā/nín; **2.** nín; **3.** tāmen/nǐmen; **4.** tā/nǐ; **5.** wǒ

PRACTICE 2: 1. sì; **2.** liù; **3.** yī; **4.** wǔ; **5.** shí

PHRASE LIST 1

The second lesson of each Unit moves from words to phrases. The following table lists some useful courtesy expressions found in daily conversation:

Nín/Nǐ hǎo.	*Hello.*
Nín/Nǐ hǎo ma?	*How are you?*
Nín/Nǐ hǎo ma?	*Good morning/afternoon/evening.*
Zǎo'ān.	*Good morning.*
Wǎn'ān.	*Good night.*
Jǐ suì?	*How old?*
Bú yàojǐn.	*It doesn't matter.*
Duìbuqǐ.	*Sorry./Excuse me.*
Búkèqì.	*You're welcome. (lit., Don't be polite.)*
Xièxie.	*Thank you.*
Zàijiàn.	*Goodbye.*

NUTS & BOLTS 1
PLURALS

In Chinese, the same form is used for both singulars and plurals. So, depending on the context, the nouns that you learned in Word list 1 could be translated as either singulars or plurals in English:

lǎoshī	*teacher, teachers*
xuésheng	*student, students*
rén	*person, people*

Remember that with pronouns, the ending **-men** is added onto the singulars to form the plurals:

wǒ *(I)*	**wǒmen** *(we)*
nǐ/nín *(you/you fml.)*	**nǐmen** *(you pl., all of you)*
tā *(he, she, it)*	**tāmen** *(they)*

Let's look at some examples:

Tāmen shì xuésheng.
They are students.

Wǒmen shì xuésheng.
We are students.

Nǐ shì xuésheng.
You are a student.

Notice that the form of *to be* doesn't change in Chinese—unlike English, Chinese doesn't have verb conjugation, which means that verbs don't change form based on subject or on when the action is taking place. Therefore, **shì** means *am, is, are, was,* or *were.* And finally, also notice that there are no articles (*the, a/an*) in Chinese. They are simply understood in the translation based on context.

PRACTICE 1
Please translate the following sentences into Chinese:

1. We are doctors.
2. She is a lawyer.
3. I am a doctor.
4. They are teachers.
5. He is a teacher.

PHRASE LIST 2

Here are some more phrases we'll be using later on in this unit.

Năguórén?	*What nationality?*
Měiguórén	*American*
Zhōngguórén	*Chinese*
Yīngguórén	*British*
Fǎguórén	*French*
Xībānyárén	*Spanish*
Déguórén	*German*
Yìdàlìrén	*Italian*
Rìběnrén	*Japanese*
Àozhōurén	*Australian*
Běijīngrén	*Pekingese*
Shànghǎirén	*Shanghaiese*
Xiānggǎngrén	*Hongkongese*
Nánjīngrén	*Nanjingese*
Guǎngdōngrén	*Cantonese*

NUTS & BOLTS 2

NATIONALITIES AND RÉN *(PERSON)*

As you can probably guess from the table above, nationality is expressed in Chinese by adding **rén** *(person)* after a country name, so that the combined form literally means a person born in a specific country. It's also very common in Chinese to add **rén** after a city or other place name to indicate where a person is from.

Tā shì Zhōngguórén.
He is Chinese.

Wǒmen shì Měiguórén.
We are American.

Tā shì Běijīngrén.
She is from Beijing.

PRACTICE 2

What nationalities are the following people? Answer in **pīnyīn**.

1. John is from London.

2. Jose is from Barcelona.

3. Yaeko is from Tokyo.

4. Joe is from Rome.

5. Mei is from Beijing.

Tip!

There are lots of ways to learn and memorize new vocabulary. Keep in mind that simply reading a word in a new language once or twice is not going to make it stick. You'll need to repeat the words, and practice several times before they stay in your memory. You could say the word aloud several times, or write it down several times as you say it. The more senses you activate the better. You could also make flashcards, writing the Chinese on one side of a little slip of paper, and the English on the other. As you're working through a Unit, carry flashcards of the vocabulary around with you so you can practice when you have "down time." First go from Chinese to English, and then when you're able to go through the whole "deck," reverse the order, and see if you can come up with the Chinese translations of the English words.

ANSWERS

PRACTICE 1: 1. Wǒmen shì yīshēng. **2.** Tā shì lùshī. **3.** Wǒ shì yīshēng. **4.** Tāmen shì lǎoshī. **5.** Tā shì lǎoshī.

PRACTICE 2: 1. Yīngguórén; **2.** Xībānyárén; **3.** Rìběnrén; **4.** Yìdàlìrén; **5.** Zhōngguórén

Lesson 3 (sentences)

SENTENCE LIST 1

The third lesson of each Unit moves on to sentences.

Wǒ shì yóukè.	*I am a tourist.*
Tā shì yīshēng.	*He/She is a doctor.*
Tā shì lǜshī.	*He/She is a lawyer.*
Wáng xiǎojiě shì hùshi. Tā shì Zhōngguórén.	*Miss Wang is a nurse. She is Chinese.*
Wáng xiānsheng shì chūzūchē sījī.	*Mr. Wang is a taxi driver.*
Nín shì lǎoshī ma?	*Are you (fml.) a teacher?*
Wǒ shì lǎoshī.	*I am a teacher.*
Wǒ bú shì lǎoshī.	*I am not a teacher.*
Wǒ shì Zhōngguórén.	*I am Chinese.*
Wǒ yě shì Zhōngguórén.	*I am also Chinese.*
Wǒ yě bú shì Zhōngguórén.	*I am not Chinese either.*

NUTS & BOLTS 1

WORD ORDER IN SIMPLE STATEMENTS

As you have seen, the word order of simple statements in Chinese is much the same as in English. This can be seen in the sentence **Wǒ shì lǎoshī** *(I am a teacher),* which has this structure:

Subject + *to be* (**shì**) + noun.

This word order can be used to link a noun or pronoun to another noun, as in these examples:

Tā shì lǜshī.

He/She is a lawyer.

Wáng xiǎojiě shì hùshi.

Miss Wang is a nurse.

Tā shì Zhōngguórén.

She is Chinese.

Keep in mind that in Chinese, the words for nationalities you've learned so far are nouns.

PRACTICE 1

Translate the following simple statements into English:

1. Wǒ shì yóukè.
2. Tā shì xuésheng.
3. Tā shì lǎoshī.
4. Wǒmen shì Měiguórén.
5. Tāmen shì Fǎguórén.
6. Wáng xiǎojiě shì yīshēng.
7. Wáng xiānsheng shì lǜshī.

SENTENCE LIST 2

Qǐngwèn nín guìxìng?	*May I ask your (fml.) last name?*
Wǒ xìng Huáng.	*My last name is Huang.*
Wǒ jiào Huáng Xìn.	*My name is Huang Xin.*
Wǒ hěn hǎo.	*I'm very well.*
Qǐngwèn ní jǐ suì?	*May I ask how old you are?*
Wǒ shí bā suì.	*I'm eighteen years old.*
Nín shì yīshēng ma?	*Are you (fml.) a doctor?*
Nǐmen shì yóukè ma?	*Are you (pl.) tourists?*

NOTES

Notice that Chinese has two verbs that can be used to give your name. The verb **xìng** is used to give last names, and the verb **jiào** is usually used to give full names. Remember that the order of full names in Chinese is last name followed by first name. The verb **jiào** can also be used to give first names when the conversation is between/among people who have a close relationship with each other.

NUTS & BOLTS 2
NUMBERS 11–20

Now let's add onto the numbers you know by looking at 11 through 20. As you can see in the table below, the teens are formed with **shí** *(ten)* plus a number from 1 through 9. The number 20 is formed by adding **shí** right after **èr** *(two)*:

shí yī	*eleven*
shí èr	*twelve*
shí sān	*thirteen*
shí sì	*fourteen*
shí wǔ	*fifteen*
shí liù	*sixteen*
shí qī	*seventeen*
shí bā	*eighteen*
shí jiǔ	*nineteen*
èrshí	*twenty*

PRACTICE 2
Translate the following numbers in Chinese:

1. 11
2. 15
3. 20

4. 18
5. 13

Tip!

So far, you've seen that Chinese grammar is very different from English grammar in a few ways. For example, there are no conjugated verb forms, so **shì** can mean *to be, is, am, are, was,* or *were.* There are no plural forms in Chinese either, so **xuésheng** can be translated as *student* or *students,* depending on the context. You've also learned that there are no articles in Chinese, so **xuésheng** can actually mean any of the following: *student, a student, the student,* and *students.* Chinese does have special words called measure words, which are used to quantify a noun, and which are used in some special circumstances that you'll learn later. But by now it should be clear that as a student of Chinese, you don't have to worry about irregular verb forms, genders, plurals, or many of the difficult grammatical structures that students of other languages have to master. Of course, Chinese is difficult in its own ways—tones, writing, and plenty of other constructions that you'll encounter as you progress. No language is <u>all</u> easy!

ANSWERS

PRACTICE 1: 1. I am a tourist. **2.** He/She is a student. **3.** He/She is a teacher. **4.** We are American. **5.** They are French. **6.** Miss Wang is a doctor. **7.** Mr. Wang is a lawyer.

PRACTICE 2: 1. shí yī; **2.** shí wǔ; **3.** èrshí; **4.** shí bā; **5.** shí sān

——————— Lesson 4 (conversations) ———————

CONVERSATION 1

The fourth lesson of each Unit covers conversations in the form of two different dialogues. In this dialogue, a man and a woman are talking outside a language school.

> **Mali:** Nín hǎo ma?
> **Hai:** Wǒ hěn hǎo. Xièxie.
> **Mali:** Nín shì lǎoshī ma?

Hai:	Wǒ bú shì lǎoshī. Wǒ shì xuésheng.
Mali:	Duìbuqǐ.
Hai:	Búyàojǐn. Nǐ yě shì xuésheng ma?
Mali:	Wǒ bú shì xuésheng, wǒ shì lǎoshī.
Hai:	Qǐngwèn nín guìxìng?
Mali:	Wǒ xìng Zhāng, Zhōngwén míngzi jiào Mǎlì. Nǐ ne?
Hai:	Wǒ xìng Wáng, jiào Wáng Hǎi.
Mali:	Zàijiàn.
Hai:	Zàijiàn.

Mary:	*How are you (fml.)?*
Hai:	*I'm very well. Thank you.*
Mary:	*Are you (fml.) a teacher?*
Hai:	*No, I'm not. I'm a student.*
Mary:	*Sorry.*
Hai:	*That's okay. (lit., It doesn't matter.) Are you a student too?*
Mary:	*I'm not a student. I'm a teacher.*
Hai:	*May I ask your (fml.) last name?*
Mary:	*My last name is Zhang. (My) Chinese first name is Mali. How about you?*
Hai:	*My last name is Wang. I'm called Wang Hai.*
Mary:	*Goodbye.*
Hai:	*Goodbye.*

NOTES

In the dialogue, you came across two so-called particles: **ma** and **ne**. Particles are little words that are added to words, phrases, or sentences for different reasons. **Ma,** for example, indicates that the sentence is a question. **Ne** does as well, but it can be translated more along the lines of *and how about . . . ?* We'll come back to those particles in this lesson, and you'll learn many more as you progress through this course.

NUTS & BOLTS 1

Yes/no question formation

As you saw in the dialogue, the question particle **ma** is used at the end of a sentence to signal that the sentence is a question rather than a statement. As an example, let's look at: **Nín shì lǎoshī ma?** *(Are you (fml.) a teacher?).* The structure of this simple question is:

Subject + *to be* **(shì)** + noun + question particle **(ma)**?

The word order of a simple yes/no question in Chinese is different from that in English, because there is no change in word order between the statement and the question. The only change is the use of the particle **ma** at the end of the sentence. Take a look at some more examples, as well as some responses:

Nǐmen shì yóukè ma?

Are you (pl.) tourists?

–Shì, wǒmen shì yóukè.

–Yes, we're tourists.

–Bù, wǒmen bú shì yóukè.

–No, we're not tourists.

Nín shì Měiguórén ma?

Are you (fml.) American?

–Shì, wǒ shì Měiguórén.

–Yes, I'm American.

–Bù, wǒ bú shì Měiguórén. Wǒ shì Fǎguórén.

–No, I'm not American. I'm French.

PRACTICE 1

Please translate the following sentences into Chinese:

1. Are you (fml.) Chinese?

2. Is she a student?

3. Is he a teacher?

4. Are you (plural) American?

5. Are they French?

6. Are you a teacher?

7. Are you a tourist?

8. Is she Chinese?

CONVERSATION 2

Mary runs into Hai at school one morning, but she's unfortunately forgotten who he is.

Hai: Zhāng lǎoshī, zǎo'ān.
Mali: Nín shì . . . ?
Hai: Wǒ shì Wáng Hǎi.
Mali: Duìbuqǐ, Wáng Hǎi.
Hai: Búyàojǐn. Zhāng lǎoshī, qǐngwèn nín shì
     nǎguórén?
Mali: Wǒ shì Měiguórén. Nǐ ne?
Hai: Wǒ shì Zhōngguórén.
Mali: Tāmen yě shì Zhōngguórén ma?
Hai: Bú shì. Tāmen shì Rìběnrén.
Mali: Nǐ jǐ suì?
Hai: Wǒ èrshí suì.

Hai: Good morning, teacher Zhang.
Mary: You (fml.) are . . . ?
Hai: I'm Wang Hai.
Mary: Sorry, Wang Hai.

Hai: No problem. Teacher Zhang, may I ask what
       nationality you (fml.) are?
Mary: I'm American. How about you?
Hai: I'm Chinese.
Mary: Are they also Chinese?
Hai: No. They're Japanese.
Mary: How old are you?
Hai: I'm twenty.

NOTES
Again, notice the use of the question particle **ma** in yes/no questions such as **Tāmen yě shì Zhōngguórén ma?** *(Are they also Chinese?)* But note that in questions that cannot be answered with yes
or no, such as **Nǐ jǐ suì?** *(How old are you?)*, **ma** is not used.

The use of the question particle **ne** is slightly different from that
of **ma**. As you know, it can be translated as *and how about . . . ?* or
and what about . . . ? So, if someone asks you a question and you'd
like to ask the same question back, you can just say **Nǐ/Nín ne?**
(And how about you?)

To express age, the word **suì** *(years old)* is placed after the appropriate number. For example, **suì** is combined with **èrshí** *(twenty)*
to form **èrshí suì,** which means *twenty years old*. Notice that there
is no form of **shì** *(to be)* in the answer. Ages and descriptive adjectives are not used with **shì**.

NUTS & BOLTS 2
NEGATION WITH BÙ
To negate a simple statement in Chinese, the word **bù** *(no, not)* is
placed before the verb. So, to negate **Wǒ shì lǎoshī** *(I'm a
teacher)*, you'd say **Wǒ bú shì lǎoshī** *(I'm not a teacher)*. The structure of that negative sentence is:

Subject + negative particle **(bù)** + *to be* **(shì)** + noun.

Wǒ bú shì Zhōngguórén.

I'm not Chinese.

Tāmen bú shì Rìběnrén.

They're not Japanese.

You've probably noticed that the tone of **bù** seems to be changing. When it's used before a one-syllable word of the fourth tone (such as **shì**), its tone changes from the fourth to the second: **bú shì.**

PRACTICE 2A

Answer the following simple questions in Chinese:

1. Nín shì Zhōngguórén ma? *(Answer: Yes)*

2. Tā shì xuésheng ma? *(Answer: No)*

3. Tā shì lǎoshī ma? *(Answer: Yes)*

4. Nǐmen shì Měiguórén ma? *(Answer: Yes)*

5. Tāmen shì Fǎguórén ma? *(Answer: No)*

PRACTICE 2B

Now fill in the blanks basing your answers on the second dialogue.

1. Mǎlì shì _____ (lǎoshī, xuésheng).

2. Hǎi shì _____ (lǎoshī, xuésheng).

3. Hǎi xìng _____.

4. Mǎlì xìng _____.

In Chinese, it is very common to address a person by adding a title before that person's last name. In the dialogue above, Hai calls Mali **Zhāng lǎoshī**, which literally means *teacher Zhang*. Please note that a person's title is the same for male or female. So, when addressing an office manager whose last name is **Hé**, you would use the title **jīnglǐ** (*manager*) and call that person **Hé jīnglǐ**, regardless of gender. However, you cannot call the student in the above dialogue **Wáng xuésheng** because, as in English, *student* is not considered a title in Chinese.

ANSWERS

PRACTICE 1: 1. Nín shì Zhōngguórén ma? **2.** Tā shì xuésheng ma? **3.** Tā shì lǎoshī ma? **4.** Nǐmen shì Měiguórén ma? **5.** Tāmen shì Fǎguórén ma? **6.** Nǐ shì lǎoshī ma? **7.** Nǐ shì yóukè ma? **8.** Tā shì Zhōngguórén ma?

PRACTICE 2A: 1. Wǒ shì Zhōngguórén. **2.** Tā bú shì xuésheng. **3.** Tā shì lǎoshī. **4.** Wǒmen shì Měiguórén. **5.** Tāmen bú shì Fǎguórén.

PRACTICE 2B: 1. lǎoshī; **2.** xuésheng; **3.** Wáng; **4.** Zhāng

UNIT 1 ESSENTIALS

At the end of each Unit you'll find a list of essential phrases. The grammar and vocabulary used should be familiar to you.

Nín hǎo ma?
How are you (fml.)?

Qǐngwèn nín guìxìng?
May I ask your (fml.) last name?

Wǒ xìng _____.
My last name is _____.

Duìbuqǐ.
Sorry./Excuse me.

Zàijiàn.
Goodbye.

Búyàojǐn.
It doesn't matter.

Wǒ jiào _____.
I'm called _____. (My name is _____.)

Qǐngwèn nǐ jǐ suì?
May I ask how old you are?

xuésheng
student

lǎoshī
teacher

Zǎo'ān.
Good morning.

Xièxie.
Thank you.

UNIT 2
Talking about family

In Unit 2, you'll learn a lot of vocabulary that will help you to talk about your family and describe where you live in Chinese. You'll also learn some more basics of Chinese grammar, including the useful verb **yǒu** *(to have)*.

——————— Lesson 5 (words) ———————

WORD LIST 1
Here's a list of words that refer to people and family members.

jiā	*family, home*
bàba	*father*
māma	*mother*
érzi	*son*
nǚ'ér	*daughter*
gēge	*older brother*
jiějie	*older sister*
dìdi	*younger brother*
mèimei	*younger sister*
xiōngdìjiěmèi	*sibling*
yéye	*grandfather (paternal side)*
nǎinai	*grandmother (paternal side)*
wàigōng	*grandfather (maternal side)*
wàipó	*grandmother (maternal side)*
péngyou	*friend*
línjū	*neighbor*
nánrén	*man*
nǚrén	*woman*

| nǚhái'ér/nǚhái | *girl* |
| nánhái'ér/nánhái | *boy* |

NUTS & BOLTS 1
FAMILY TERMS

There are two ways to refer to or address your grandparents in Chinese, depending on whether they are your mother's or father's parents. For example, your father's father must be addressed as **yéye**, and your mother's father is **wàigōng**. Since these words define separate genealogical relationships, they cannot be used interchangeably. Similarly, you probably noticed that there are also different words for *brother* and *sister*, depending on age.

If you look closely at the word for *sibling* in Chinese (**xiōngdìjiěmèi**), you'll see that it is composed of four syllables, which would be written in Chinese with four different characters. They are: **xiōng** *(older brother)*, **dì** *(younger brother)*, **jiě** *(older sister)*, and **mèi** *(younger sister)*. So, **xiōngdìjiěmèi** is a descriptive word that actually includes all possible relationships between brothers and sisters.

As you will see in the next Word list, there are many different family terms in Chinese and most of them are distinguished by gender as well as by age or by whether the person is on your mother's or father's side. Some terms specify all of these things. As with the different words for grandparents, other family terms must be used for the specific person they refer to and cannot be used interchangeably.

PRACTICE 1

How would you address the following people in your family in Chinese?

1. Your father
2. Your mother
3. Your older brother
4. Your younger sister
5. Your younger brother

WORD LIST 2

Here are some more words for relatives that you should know.

bóbo	*uncle (father's older brother)*
bómǔ	*aunt (father's older brother's wife)*
shūshu	*uncle (father's younger brother)*
shěnshen	*aunt (father's younger brother's wife)*
gūgu	*aunt (father's sister)*
gūzhàng	*uncle (father's sister's husband)*
jiùjiu	*uncle (mother's brother)*
jiùmǔ/jiùmā	*aunt (mother's brother's wife)*
yímǔ/yímā	*aunt (mother's sister)*
yízhàng	*uncle (mother's sister's husband)*
tánggē	*cousin (father's brother's son who is older than you)*
tángdì	*cousin (father's brother's son who is younger than you)*
tángjiě	*cousin (father's brother's daughter who is older than you)*
tángmèi	*cousin (father's brother's daughter who is younger than you)*
biǎogē	*cousin (mother's sibling's or father's sister's son who is older than you)*
biǎodì	*cousin (mother's sibling's or father's sister's son who is younger than you)*
biǎojiě	*cousin (mother's sibling's or father's sister's daughter who is older than you)*
biǎomèi	*cousin (mother's sibling's or father's sister's daughter who is younger than you)*

NOTES

All of those family terms probably seem very complicated. After all, there are eight words for *cousin*! But there is an easy way to remember which one to use. In general, you will notice that words used in Chinese for addressing family members all have two syllables. Just remember to use the prefix **táng** when addressing cousins who share the same last name as you, and use the prefix **biǎo** when their last name is different from yours. In all cases, the syllable that follows is dependent on the age and gender of the cousin you want to address. For example, if your father's brother's daughter, Nancy, is one year older than you, then you would use the suffix **jiě** and refer to her as your **tángjiě**. If your mother's brother's son, David, is younger than you, then you would use the suffix **dì** and address him as **biǎodì**.

NUTS & BOLTS 2
SIMPLE SENTENCES WITH ADJECTIVES

In English, if you want to link a noun and an adjective, you use a form of *to be: the girl is short, the mountains are tall*, etc. In Chinese, though, normally **shì** *(to be)* is not placed between a noun and an adjective when using that adjective to describe the noun. Instead, the adverb **hěn** *(very)* is used:

Tā hěn gāo.
He/She is tall.

Tāmen hěn cōngmíng.
They are intelligent.

Nà ge nánrén hěn qiángzhuàng.
That man is strong.

Zhè ge chéngshì hěn piàoliang.
This city is beautiful.

In colloquial Chinese, it's very common to add a degree adverb such as **hěn** *(very)* or **tǐng** *(quite, very)* before the adjective. This doesn't really add meaning to the sentence, but instead simply links a subject to the adjective that describes it. However, there are times when **hěn** and **tǐng** do add meaning. You will learn more about this later on in the lesson.

PRACTICE 2

Each of the following short sentences in Chinese tells you something about its subject, but not all of them are grammatically correct. Read each sentence, and determine whether it's correct or not. If it's incorrect, correct the error.

1. Biǎogē gāo.

2. Yéye shì gāo.

3. Tā shì dìdi.

4. Shūshu shì lǎoshī.

5. Tángjiě shì xuésheng.

Culture note

In China, it is important to know how to refer to or address a family member correctly. Depending on the age and generation, everyone in a family tree is addressed differently by different family members. For instance, you would call your paternal grandmother **nǎinai,** while your father's sister's children would call her **wàipó.** Using the correct terms for family members not only demonstrates your knowledge of family relationships but also shows respect and politeness toward the people addressed. Furthermore, according to Chinese tradition, you should not address your elders by referring to their names directly, but instead by using the appropriate family titles.

Traditionally, Chinese families have very close ties and as a result, correct words of address are used repeatedly in daily conversation. In fact, while relatives usually do not live together in modern Chinese cities, it is still common in the countryside for family members from the father's side to live together and for a married son and his family to live with his parents.

ANSWERS

PRACTICE 1: 1. bàba; **2.** māma; **3.** gēge; **4.** mèimei; **5.** dìdi

PRACTICE 2: 1. incorrect (change to biǎogē hěn gāo);
2. incorrect (change to yéye hěn gāo); **3.** correct; **4.** correct;
5. correct

――――――――――― Lesson 6 (phrases) ―――――――――――

PHRASE LIST 1

Learn the following phrases, which use measure words between a
number and the noun.

yí ge rén	*one/a person*
liǎng ge rén	*two people*
yì tiáo gǒu	*one/a dog*
sān tiáo gǒu	*three dogs*
yì zhī bǐ	*one/a pen*
sì zhī bǐ	*four pens*
yì zhāng zhǐ	*one/a sheet of paper*
yì běn shū	*one/a book*
yí ge jiějie	*one/an older sister*
yí ge gēge	*one/an older brother*
yì tiáo lù	*one/a road*
yì zhī bēizi	*one/a cup, one/a glass*
yì zhāng chuáng	*one/a bed*
yì běn zìdiǎn	*one/a (character) dictionary*

NOTES

Notice how **yī** *(one)* appears to change tones. Remember from
Unit 1 that **yī** changes to the second tone before a syllable in the
fourth tone and to the fourth tone before a syllable in the first,
second, or third tone.

yí ge rén
one/a person

yì tiáo gǒu
one/a dog

Ge is in the fourth tone (**gè**), but it is most often written without any tone at all.

NUTS & BOLTS 1
MEASURE WORDS

In Chinese, a measure word is needed when a noun is counted with a number, or when a demonstrative *(this* or *that)* is used. The measure word is placed between the demonstrative or number and the noun itself. There are different measure words for different types of nouns, so let's get started by learning a few of the most important ones.

Measure word	Used with	Examples
ge	people	**yí ge rén** *(one/a person)* **sān ge nǚrén** *(three women)*
tiáo	objects that are long and thin, also some animals	**yì tiáo xiàn** *(one/a string)* **wǔ tiáo yú** *(five fish)* **sì tiáo gǒu** *(four dogs)*
zhī	objects that are pointed and thin, utensils, and some animals	**yì zhī wǎn** *(one/a bowl)* **liǎng zhī jī** *(two chickens)* **liù zhī bǐ** *(six pens)*

Measure word	Used with	Examples
zhāng	objects that have a flat surface	**qī zhāng zhuōzi** *(seven tables)* **jiǔ zhāng zhǐ** *(nine pieces of paper)*
běn	books	**sān běn shū** *(three books)*

Notice in the above examples, and also in the Phrase list, expressions with **yī** *(one)* are translated as *one/a*. Don't forget that Chinese doesn't have articles, so a noun on its own can be translated with *the* or *a* depending on context. Use **yī** plus a measure word only when you want to emphasize that there is one of something. Don't use it everywhere you'd use an indefinite article in English.

You also may have noticed that in the Phrase list and the above examples, *two* is translated as **liǎng**, not **èr**. You will learn more about the uses of these two different translations of the word *two* in Unit 4.

PRACTICE 1
Translate each of the following nouns, and then find the right measure word. Form phrases with the number **wǔ** *(five)*.

1. *book*
2. *dog*
3. *pen*
4. *bed*

5. *people*
6. *string*
7. *cup*
8. *chicken*

PHRASE LIST 2
Here are some phrases that will help you to describe where you live.

zhè ge gōngyù	*this apartment*
zhè ge fángzi	*this house*

piàoliang de fángzi	*(a) beautiful house*
nà ge fángjiān	*that room*
nà ge dà fángjiān	*that big room*
nà ge wòfáng	*that bedroom*
nà ge xiǎo wòfáng	*that small bedroom*
zhè ge chúfáng	*this kitchen*
gānjìng de chúfáng	*a clean kitchen*
nà ge wèishēngjiān	*that bathroom*
hěn zāng de wèishēngjiān	*a very dirty bathroom*
zhè zhāng shāfā	*this sofa*
zhè zhāng zhuōzi	*this table*
zhè bǎ yǐzi	*this chair*
zhè zhāng chuáng	*this bed*
zhè zhāng zhàopiàn	*this photograph*
nà tái diànnǎo	*that computer*
zhè tái diànshì	*this television*

NUTS & BOLTS 2
DEMONSTRATIVES

Zhè *(this)* and **nà** *(that)* are demonstratives in Chinese. When they are followed by a noun, a measure word is needed in between **zhè/nà** and the noun.

zhè ge rén	*this person*
nà ge rén	*that person*
zhè tiáo gǒu	*this dog*
nà zhī bǐ	*that pen*

Nà ge rén hěn piàoliang.
That person is beautiful.

Nà tiáo gǒu hěn dà.
That dog is big.

Zhè ge wèishēngjiān hěn zāng!
This bathroom is dirty!

Zhè ge wòfáng hěn xiǎo!
This bedroom is small!

Note that these sentences contain the meaning of *very* only when **hěn** is stressed. Otherwise, **hěn** is used only for grammatical reasons. See Nuts & bolts 2 in Lesson 8.

For the plural forms of **zhè** and **nà**, a collective measure word **xiē** can be added after **zhè** or **nà**: **zhè xiē** *(these)* and **nà xiē** *(those)*. **Xiē** is invariable—it can be used with any noun. For example:

zhè xiē rén	*these people*
nà xiē bēizi	*those cups*

Zhè xiē nǚhái hěn kě'ài.
These girls are adorable.

Nà xiē chē hěn kuài.
Those cars are fast.

Nà xiē fángzi hěn dà.
Those houses are big.

PRACTICE 2
Translate the following sentences into Chinese.

1. *That dog is big.*
2. *This house is beautiful.*
3. *That sofa is new* (xīn).

4. *These photographs are beautiful.*

5. *This bed is small.*

6. *That chair is small.*

7. *This kitchen is big.*

Culture note

Another useful room name to know is **kètīng**, which literally means *guest room*. It is used the same way as a living room in the U.S. **Fàntīng** is a room where people eat. It literally means *rice room* and is commonly translated as *dining room* in English. Also note that **wèishēngjiān** can mean *restroom*, *toilet*, or *bathroom*.

ANSWERS

PRACTICE 1: 1. wǔ běn shū; **2.** wǔ tiáo gǒu; **3.** wǔ zhī bǐ; **4.** wǔ zhāng chuáng; **5.** wǔ ge rén; **6.** wǔ tiáo xiàn; **7.** wǔ ge bēizi; **8.** wǔ zhī jī

PRACTICE 2: 1. Nà tiáo gǒu hěn dà. **2.** Zhè ge fángzi hěn piàoliang. **3.** Zhè zhāng shāfā hěn xīn. **4.** Zhè xiē zhàopiàn hěn piàoliang. **5.** Zhè zhāng chuáng hěn xiǎo. **6.** Nà bǎ yǐzi hěn xiǎo. **7.** Zhè ge chúfáng hěn dà.

Lesson 7 (sentences)

SENTENCE LIST 1

Wǒ yǒu sān ge dìdi.	*I have three younger brothers.*
Wǒ yǒu yì zhī bǐ.	*I have one pen.*
Tā yǒu yí ge fángzi.	*He has a house.*
Tā yǒu yí ge dà fángzi.	*He has a big house.*
Nín yǒu zhuōzi ma?	*Do you have a table/desk?*
Nǐ yǒu gēge ma?	*Do you have an older brother?*
Zhè ge fángzi yǒu sān ge wòfáng.	*This house has three bedrooms.*

Nà ge fángzi yǒu yí ge hěn dà de chúfáng.	*That house has a very big kitchen.*

NUTS & BOLTS 1
YǑU *(TO HAVE)*

Yǒu is a special verb in Chinese. It has a few different usages, but one of its most common functions is to indicate possession, like the English verb *to have*. Typically, **yǒu** is placed immediately after the subject of a sentence, and it's followed by an object, along with its measure word if necessary.

Wǒ yǒu fángzi.
I have a house.

Tāmen yǒu liǎng ge fángzi.
They have two houses.

Wǒmen yǒu sān ge mèimei.
We have three younger sisters.

To ask a question with **yǒu**, you can use the question particle **ma** at the end of the sentence.

Nǐ yǒu fángzi ma?
Do you have a house?

PRACTICE 1
Translate the following sentences into English:

1. Wǒ yǒu zhuōzi.

2. Nǐ yǒu fángzi ma?

3. Měiguórén yǒu gǒu.

4. Tā yǒu gēge ma?

5. Nǐmen yǒu shū ma?

6. Nǐ yǒu tàitai ma?

7. Tā yǒu sān ge lǎoshī.

SENTENCE LIST 2

Wǒ yǒu bǐ hé zhǐ.	*I have a pen and paper.*
Wǒ yǒu yì zhī māo hé yì tiáo gǒu.	*I have one cat and one dog.*
Wǒ yǒu diànshì hé diànnǎo.	*I have a TV and computer.*
Nǐ yǒu shōuyīnjī hé diànnǎo ma?	*Do you have a radio and computer?*
Wǒmen yǒu qìshuǐ hé jiǔ.	*We have soda and wine.*
Wǒ hé tā shì Zhōngguórén.	*She and I are Chinese.*
Nǐ yǒu zhè piàn xīn de jīguāng chàngpiàn ma?	*Do you have the new CD?*
Tā yǒu yí liàng piàoliang de chē.	*He has a beautiful car.*
Tāmen yǒu hěn hǎo de píjiǔ.	*They have very good beer.*

NUTS & BOLTS 2

THE CONNECTION WORD HÉ *(AND)*

Hé *(and)* can be used to connect two nouns or two phrases. For example, *an apple and an orange* can be expressed as **píngguǒ hé júzi.** But note that not every *and* in English can be translated as **hé.** Sometimes the English *and* has a sense of *then,* as in: *please sign and return this document.* For now, however, we'll just focus on **hé,** which is the *and* that simply combines two things.

Wǒmen yǒu shū hé zìdiǎn.
We have a book and dictionary.

Nà shì yí ge nánrén hé yí ge nǚrén.
That is a man and a woman.

If two pronouns are connected by **hé** and one of them is **wǒ** *(I),* the order of the pronouns can be **wǒ hé** plus the second pronoun. This is the opposite of what people are taught to do in English, where *I* or *me* is supposed to come last.

Wǒ hé tā zài zhèlǐ.
He/She and I are here.

Wǒ hé tā shì Měiguórén.
He/She and I are American.

PRACTICE 2
Translate the following sentences into English:

1. Nǐ hé tā shì péngyou.

2. Wǒ hé Wáng xiānsheng shì línjū.

3. Wáng xiānsheng hé Wáng xiǎojiě yǒu bǐ.

4. Nǐ hé Wáng tàitai shì péngyou ma?

5. Wǒ yǒu zhuōzi hé shū.

6. Wǒmen yǒu yì zhī māo hé sì tiáo gǒu.

7. Nǐ yǒu lùshī ma?

8. Lǎoshī yǒu fángzi ma?

ANSWERS
PRACTICE 1: 1. I have a table. 2. Do you have a house?
3. Americans have dogs. 4. Does he/she have an older brother?
5. Do you (pl.) have a book? 6. Do you have a wife? 7. He/She
has three teachers.

PRACTICE 2: 1. You and he/she are friends. 2. Mr. Wang and I
are neighbors. 3. Mr. Wang and Miss Wang have a pen. 4. Are
you and Mrs. Wang friends? 5. I have a table and a book. 6. We
have a cat and four dogs. 7. Do you have a lawyer? 8. Does the
teacher have a house?

CONVERSATION 1

Wang Hai and his classmate Jess are talking about their families.

Hai: Jié Xī, zǎo'ān!

Jess: Wáng Hǎi, zǎo'ān!

Hai: Jié Xī, nǐ yǒu xiōngdìjiěmèi ma?

Jess: Méiyǒu, wǒde jiā zhǐyǒu sān kǒu rén. Wǒ, bàba hé māma. Wáng Hǎi, nǐ jiā yǒu jǐ kǒu rén?

Hai: Wǒ jiā yǒu wǔ kǒu rén. Bàba, māma, jiějie, dìdi hé wǒ.

Jess: Ā, nǐde jiā zhēn rènao.

Hai: Wǒmen háiyǒu yì tiáo xiǎogǒu hé liǎng zhī māo.

Jess: Wǒ jiā méiyǒu gǒu, yě méiyǒu māo, zhǐyǒu sān tiáo yú.

Hai: *Good morning, Jess!*

Jess: *Good morning, Wang Hai!*

Hai: *Jess, do you have any siblings?*

Jess: *No. My family has only three people: (my) father, (my) mother, and myself. Wang Hai, how many people are there in your family?*

Hai: *My family has five people: (my) father, (my) mother, (my) older sister, (my) younger brother and myself.*

Jess: *Oh, your home is really bustling.*

Hai: *We also have a puppy and two cats.*

Jess: *My family doesn't have a dog or cat. We only have three fish.*

NOTES

When you talk about a number of family members, the measure word **kǒu** *(lit., mouth)* is used instead of **ge**.

Also note how the adverb **yě** *(also)* is used in this example from the dialogue: **wǒ jiā méiyǒu gǒu, yě méiyǒu māo.** This sentence was translated as *my family doesn't have a dog or cat.* However, the translation is literally *my family doesn't have a dog, also not a cat.* The adverb **yě** *(also)* is placed before the verb, as in these other examples:

Tā shì shí bā suì, wǒ yě shì shí bā suì.
He is eighteen years old. I'm also eighteen years old.

Wǒ shì lǎoshī, tāmen yě shì lǎoshī.
I am a teacher. They're teachers too.

In the sentence translated as *we also have a puppy and two cats,* the Chinese uses **háiyǒu,** but not **yě. Háiyǒu** means *in addition* here.

Finally, notice the punctuation and translation of those last two examples. In Chinese, it's perfectly grammatical to join two full sentences and separate them only with a comma. This would be a run-on sentence in English, so translations of this and similar sentences often separate the two sentences or add *and* in between the two.

NUTS & BOLTS 1
POSSESSIVES
This dialogue gives a good example of how possessives are formed and used in Chinese. The possessive particle **de** is added to a pronoun to form the possessive, as shown in the following chart:

wǒde	*my/mine*
nǐde	*your/yours*
nínde *(fml.)*	*your/yours*
tāde	*his, her, its/his, hers, its*

wǒmende	our/ours
nǐmende *(pl.)*	your/yours
tāmende	their/theirs

Wǒmende lǎoshī shì Měiguórén.

Our teacher is American.

Tāmende fángzi hěn piàoliang.

Their house is beautiful.

Tāde gǒu dà, wǒde gǒu xiǎo.

Her dog is big, and my dog is small.

Note that English has possessive adjectives *(my house, your car)* and possessive pronouns *(mine, yours)*. In Chinese, the same forms are used for both types of possessives.

Zhè shì wǒde bǐ.

This is my pen.

Zhè zhī bǐ shì wǒde.

This pen is mine.

The particle **de** is also used with nouns and names to indicate possession. Here are a few examples:

Zhè shì lǎoshī de bǐ.

This is the teacher's pen.

Zhè shì Jié Xī de bǐ.

This is Jess's pen.

Xiàng de bízi hěn cháng.

The elephant's trunk is long.

Sometimes, the possessive particle can be omitted when it indicates a close personal relationship. For example, the expression **wǒde māma** *(my mother)* can be also expressed as **wǒ māma**.

PRACTICE 1
Please indicate whether the following statements are *true* **(shì)** or *false* **(fēi)** in Chinese:

1. Jess yǒu yí ge gēge.

2. Hai yǒu yí ge mèimei.

3. Hai de jiā yǒu sì kǒu rén.

4. Jess de māma yǒu yí ge dìdi.

5. Hai méiyǒu bàba, yě méiyǒu māma.

6. Jess de jiā yǒu sān tiáo yú.

7. Jess de jiā yǒu sān kǒu rén.

8. Hai yǒu yì tiáo xiǎogǒu.

CONVERSATION 2
Wang Hai has invited Jess to his home.

> Hai: Qǐng zuò!
> Jess: Wáng Hǎi, nǐde jiā hěn piàoliang! Yǒu jǐ ge wòfáng?
> Hai: Wǒmende gōngyù tài xiǎo le, zhǐyǒu sān ge wòfáng hé yí ge yùshì. Wǒ hé dìdi yòng yí ge fángjiān.
> Jess: Nà shì nǐmende zhàopiàn ma?
> Hai: Shì, nà shì wǒmende zhàopiàn.
> Jess: Zhè shì nǐde jiějie ma?
> Hai: Búshì, zhè shì wǒ māma.
> Jess: Duìbuqǐ.
> Hai: Búyàojǐn. Wǒ māma shì lǎoshī.
> Jess: Tā hěn niánqīng.

Hai: Please sit down.

Jess: Wang Hai, your home is very pretty! How many bedrooms do you have?

Hai: Our apartment is too small. We only have three bedrooms and one bathroom. (My) younger brother and I share (lit., use) a room.

Jess: Is that your (family's) photo?

Hai: Yes, that's our photo.

Jess: Is this your older sister?

Hai: No. This is my mother.

Jess: Sorry.

Hai: That's alright. My mother is a teacher.

Jess: She looks very young.

NOTES

Notice that when Hai asked Jess to please sit down, he said: **Qǐng zuò!** As in English, when you ask someone to do something in Chinese, the word **qǐng** *(please)* is used to preface your request for the sake of politeness.

Qǐng hē chá.

Please have some tea. (lit., Please drink tea.)

Qǐng jìnlái.

Please come in.

NUTS & BOLTS 2

ADVERBS: HĚN *(VERY)* AND TÀI *(TOO)*

Adverbs are words or phrases that indicate how or how often something is done. They modify adjectives and verbs, but not nouns.

In Chinese, adjectives do not change form when they are used as adverbs. In other words, there's no ending *-ly*. So, **kuài** can be translated as an adjective *(fast, quick)* or as an adverb *(fast, quickly)*, and so can **màn** *(slow, slowly)*. The difference is how these words are used, to modify nouns (as adjectives) or verbs (as adverbs).

Nà bù chē hěn kuài.

That car is fast.

Tā kāichē kāi de hěn kuài.

He drives very fast.

Note the use of the particle **de** between the verb and the adverb in the last example. You will learn more about this adverbial construction in Unit 8.

Also note the use of the adverb **hěn** *(very)* between the noun **chē** *(car)* and the adjective **kuài** *(fast)* in the first example. As you know, it is common in Chinese to add a degree adverb like **hěn** or **tài** *(too, exceedingly)* before an adjective to help link that adjective with the subject. In this case, the adverb does not add any meaning: **nà bù chē hěn kuài** *(that car is fast)*. Another example would be **tā hěn gāo** *(he is tall)*.

However, if stress is placed on **hěn,** then it does mean *very*. In other words, **tā hěn gāo** would mean *he is very tall* and **nà bù chē hěn kuài** would mean *that car is very fast* if **hěn** is stressed.

Wáng xiǎojiě <u>hěn</u> piàoliang.

Miss Wang is very pretty.

Měiguórén <u>hěn</u> gāo.

Americans are very tall.

Zhè zhī bǐ <u>tài</u> guì.

This pen is too expensive.

Nín <u>tài</u> kèqì.

You're too polite.

PRACTICE 2

Insert **tài** or **hěn** into the following sentences, using the English cues. Then translate each sentence.

1. Zhè ge kètīng dà. *(very)*
2. Nǐde dìdi niánqīng. *(too)*
3. Wáng xiānsheng de fángzi xiǎo. *(very)*
4. Tāde línjū de chē guì. *(very)*
5. Nà tiáo gǒu hǎo. *(very)*
6. Wǒde fángzi dà. *(very)*
7. Zhè zhī māo xiǎo. *(too)*

ANSWERS

PRACTICE 1: 1. fēi (false); **2.** fēi (false); **3.** fēi (false); **4.** fēi (false); **5.** fēi (false); **6.** shì (true); **7.** shì (true); **8.** shì (true)

PRACTICE 2: 1. Zhè ge kètīng hěn dà. (This living room/guest room is very big.) **2.** Nǐde dìdi tài niánqīng. (Your younger brother is too young.) **3.** Wáng xiānsheng de fángzi hěn xiǎo. (Mr. Wang's house is very small.) **4.** Tāde línjū de chē hěn guì. (His neighbor's car is very expensive.) **5.** Nà tiáo gǒu hěn hǎo. (That dog is very good.) **6.** Wǒde fángzi hěn dà. (My house is very big.) **7.** Zhè zhī māo tài xiǎo. (This cat is too small.)

UNIT 2 ESSENTIALS

bàba
father

māma
mother

xiōngdìjiěmèi
sibling

nánrén
man

nǚrén
woman

Nǐ jiā yǒu jǐ kǒu rén?
How many people are there in your family?

Tā hěn gāo.
He is (very) tall.

yí ge rén
one/a person

liǎng ge rén
two people

zhè ge fángzi
this house

zhè xiē rén
these people

Wǒ yǒu fángzi.
I have a house.

Wǒ hé tā shì Měiguórén.
He/She and I are American.

Tāde gǒu dà, wǒde gǒu xiǎo.
Her dog is big, and my dog is small.

Zhè zhī bǐ shì wǒde.
This pen is mine.

Qǐng jìnlái.
Please come in.

Nín tài kèqì.
You're too polite.

UNIT 3
Everyday life and likes/dislikes

In this Unit, you'll learn lots of new basic vocabulary, including the days of the week and the months of the year. You'll also learn a lot of common verbs, and you'll find out how to express whether you like or dislike something.

—————————— Lesson 9 (words) ——————————

WORD LIST 1
Here are the days of the week in Chinese and some other useful vocabulary for talking about the week.

lǐbài yī/xīngqī yī	*Monday*
lǐbài èr/xīngqī èr	*Tuesday*
lǐbài sān/xīngqī sān	*Wednesday*
lǐbài sì/xīngqī sì	*Thursday*
lǐbài wǔ/xīngqī wǔ	*Friday*
lǐbài liù/xīngqī liù	*Saturday*
lǐbài tiān/xīngqī tiān	*Sunday*
jīntiān	*today*
zhōumò	*weekend*
gōngzuòrì	*weekday (lit., workday)*
zǎoshang	*morning*
xiàwǔ	*afternoon*
bàngwǎn/wǎnshang	*evening*
wǎnshang	*night*

NUTS & BOLTS 1
DAYS OF THE WEEK

As you can see in the Word list, there are two ways to express the days of the week in Chinese. You have a choice of combining either the word **lǐbài** or **xīngqī** (both of which mean *week)* with a number from **yī** *(one)* to **liù** *(six)* to indicate one of the first six days of a week. Both of these forms are correct, but **xīngqī** is more formal and is often used in written language and/or formal occasions. In each case, note that the number used to indicate the day of the week is placed immediately after **lǐbài** or **xīngqī**.

Given this pattern, you might think that **lǐbài qī** or **xīngqī qī** would be the logical way of saying *Sunday*. However, these two forms don't exist in Chinese. Instead, the word **tiān** (which literally means *day*) is placed after **lǐbài** or **xīngqī** to express the seventh day of the week.

Jīntiān shì lǐbài jǐ?
What day is today?

–Jīntiān shì lǐbài èr.
–Today is Tuesday.

PRACTICE 1
Multiple choice: Choose the correct translation in Chinese.

1. *Monday*
   a. xīngqī yī
   b. xīngqī tiān
   c. xīngqī sān

2. *Sunday*
   a. xīngqī yī
   b. xīngqī qī
   c. xīngqī tiān

3. *Wednesday*
   a. xīngqī liù
   b. xīngqī qī
   c. xīngqī sān

4. *Tuesday*
    a. lǐbài wǔ
    b. xīngqī èr
    c. xīngqī liù

5. *Friday*
    a. lǐbài wǔ
    b. xīngqī liù
    c. xīngqī yī

6. *Saturday*
    a. lǐbài wǔ
    b. lǐbài sān
    c. xīngqī liù

7. *Thursday*
    a. lǐbài yī
    b. lǐbài sān
    c. lǐbài sì

8. *weekend*
    a. gōngzuòrì
    b. xīngqī tiān
    c. zhōumò

WORD LIST 2

Here are some useful words related to the months and seasons.

nián	*year*
yī yuè	*January*
èr yuè	*February*
sān yuè	*March*
sì yuè	*April*
wǔ yuè	*May*
liù yuè	*June*
qī yuè	*July*
bā yuè	*August*
jiǔ yuè	*September*
shí yuè	*October*
shí yī yuè	*November*
shí èr yuè	*December*

jìjié	*season*
chūntiān	*spring*
xiàtiān	*summer*
qiūtiān	*autumn, fall*
dōngtiān	*winter*

NUTS & BOLTS 2
EXPRESSING MONTHS AND DATES

As you can see, it's very easy to learn the months of the year in Chinese. All you need to do is place the word **yuè** *(month)* immediately after a number from **yī** *(one)* to **shí èr** *(twelve)*. For instance, October is the tenth month of the year, so it would be **shí** *(ten)* + **yuè** *(month)* = **shí yuè** *(October)*.

It's also very easy to express dates in Chinese. All you need to do is put a number from **yī** *(one)* to **sānshí yī** *(thirty-one)*—you've only learned up through 20 so far, but we'll come back to the others—right before the word **hào** (which literally means *number*). So, the first day of the month is **yī hào** *(lit., number one)* while the thirty-first day of the month is **sānshí yī hào** *(lit., number thirty-one)*.

To give a specific day and month, say the name of the month first and then the day. For example, July 4th would be expressed as **qī yuè sì hào**, where **qī yuè** is the seventh month of the year (July), and **sì hào** is the 4th day of the month.

Jīntiān shì jǐ yuè jǐ hào?
What is the date today?

–**Jīntiān shì sān yuè èrshí hào.**
–*Today is March 20th.*

–**Jīntiān shì bā yuè sān hào.**
–*Today is August 3rd.*

PRACTICE 2
Multiple choice: Choose the correct translation in Chinese.

1. *November*
   a. shí yuè
   b. shí yī yuè
   c. sān yuè

2. *March*
   a. shí yuè
   b. shí èr yuè
   c. sān yuè

3. *July*
   a. qī yuè
   b. shí yuè
   c. sì yuè

4. *December*
   a. shí yuè
   b. shí èr yuè
   c. sān yuè

5. *August*
   a. shí yuè
   b. bā yuè
   c. yī yuè

6. *January*
   a. yī yuè
   b. shí èr yuè
   c. sān yuè

7. *May*
   a. yī yuè
   b. shí yuè
   c. wǔ yuè

8. *June*
   a. liù yuè
   b. shí èr yuè
   c. sān yuè

9. *September*
   a. yī yuè
   b. shí èr yuè
   c. jiǔ yuè

10. *the fourth day of the month*
   a. shí hào
   b. sì hào
   c. yī hào

Culture note

In the past, the Chinese used a lunar calendar called the **nónglì**, which literally means *agriculture calendar*. The first month of the lunar calendar is known as **yī yuè** or **zhēngyuè** *(lit., exact)*. The first ten days of each lunar month are expressed using the prefix **chū** followed by a number from one to ten: **chūyī** *(1st day)*, **chūèr** *(2nd day)*, **chūsān** *(3rd day)*, **chūsì** *(4th day)*, **chūwǔ** *(5th day)*, **chūliù** *(6th day)*, **chūqī** *(7th day)*, **chūbā** *(8th day)*, **chūjiǔ** *(9th day)*, and **chūshí** *(10th day)*.

Nowadays, the lunar calendar is still used to mark important Chinese festivals, such as the Lunar New Year, which is the first day of the first month in the lunar calendar. This date falls sometime between January and February, and the exact date varies each year according to the Western calendar. This is because the lunar calendar and the Western calendar mark time in substantially different ways. While the Western calendar divides the year up neatly into twelve months regardless of the lunar cycle, the lunar calendar divides the year into twelve months based on the phases of the moon, with an additional 13th month added to the year in a Leap Year.

ANSWERS
PRACTICE 1: 1. a; 2. c; 3. c; 4. b; 5. a; 6. c; 7. c; 8. c

PRACTICE 2: 1. b; 2. c; 3. a; 4. b; 5. b; 6. a; 7. c; 8. a; 9. c; 10. b

———————— Lesson 10 (phrases) ————————

PHRASE LIST 1

wǒ chīfàn	*I eat (a meal)*
tā yóuyǒng	*she swims*
nǐ kāichē	*you drive (a car)*
tāmen tiàowǔ	*they dance (a dance)*
tā chànggē	*he sings (a song)*
tā zuòfàn	*she cooks (a meal)*

shàngxué	*to go to school*
shàngbān	*to go to work*
kàn shū	*to read a book*
wǒ shuìjiào	*I sleep/I go to bed*
lái	*to come*
lái Měiguó	*to come to the U.S.*
qù	*to go*
qù yínháng	*to go to the bank*
hē shuǐ	*to drink water*

NUTS & BOLTS 1
VERBS

Let's review what you've learned about Chinese verbs. You've learned two verbs so far: **shì** *(to be)* and **yǒu** *(to have)*. You know that Chinese verbs don't conjugate, meaning that they don't change forms depending on when the action takes place or to agree with their subject. So depending on the context, **shì** *(to be)* can be translated as *am, is, are, was,* or *were,* and **yǒu** *(to have)* can be translated as *have, has,* or *had.*

Now let's move on to other verbs. If you look at the verbs listed in the Phrase list above, you will see some "simple" verbs like **lái** *(to come)* and **qù** *(to go),* which are made up of only one syllable. Since every character in Chinese is one syllable, such verbs are only written with one character. Some other examples of one-syllable verbs include **jiàn** *(to see),* **zǒu** *(to leave/to walk),* **jiào** *(to call),* and **xìng** *(to be called a last name).*

Wǒ xué Zhōngwén.
I study Chinese.

Wǒ jiào Jié Xī.
I'm called Jess./My (first) name is Jess.

Wǒde péngyou lái Měiguó.
My friend is coming to America.

There are also a lot of verbs in Chinese that are made up of two characters, and therefore two syllables, although they fall into a few different categories. Two of these categories are regular two-syllable verbs and verb-object verbs. These types of verbs look alike—they both have two syllables—but they behave slightly differently.

Let's start with verb-object verbs. Verb-object verbs are two-syllable verbs that combine a verb with an object in order to help clarify the nature or purpose of an action. The verb **chīfàn**, for example, is made of the verb **chī** *(to eat)* and the object **fàn** *(meal, cooked rice)*, which helps to qualify the act of eating by leaving no ambiguity as to what's being eaten.

Note that, as in the case of other verb-object verbs listed above, such as **kāichē** *(to drive)*, **tiàowǔ** *(to dance)*, **chànggē** *(to sing)*, and **zuòfàn** *(to cook)*, the object (such as **chē**-*car;* **wǔ**-*a dance;* **gē**-*song;* **fàn**-*meal, cooked rice* in the above examples) always takes the position of the second syllable. You should also keep in mind that the object contained within these verbs is usually not translated literally into English, although its meaning is usually implicit in the translation.

Wáng tàitai xǐhuan tiàowǔ hé chànggē.
Mrs. Wang likes dancing and singing.

Wǒ zuòfàn.
I cook.

Tā kāichē qù Niǔ Yuē.
He drives to New York.

Two-syllable verbs are just that—verbs made up of two syllables, like **rènshi** *(to know, to meet)*, **míngbai** *(to understand)* or **jiǎnchá** *(to examine, to check)*. The difference in use between regular two-syllable verbs and verb-object verbs is that when a suffix or adverb is used, a verb-object verb can be split into two parts (the verb and the object), while a two-syllable verb cannot. For example:

Wǒ tiàole liǎng nián de wǔ. OR **Wǒ tiàowǔ tiàole liǎng nián.**
I have danced for two years.

Wǒ jiǎnchále.
I examined.

The particle **le** is a suffix that indicates a completed action and is often used to express the past. You will learn more about it in Unit 5.

As you know, to negate a verb in Chinese, whether it's a one-syllable verb or a two-syllable compound verb phrase, the negative particle **bù** is added before the verb.

Wǒ bú qù nà jiā cānguǎn.
I don't go to that restaurant.

Tā bù kāichē qù Niǔ Yuē.
He doesn't (won't) drive to New York.

Wǒ bú zuòfàn.
I don't cook.

Wǒ bú rènshi tā.
I don't know him.

PRACTICE 1
Multiple choice: Fill in the blank with the right verb.

1. Wǒ _____ (sleep).
    a. zuòfàn
    b. shuìjiào
    c. tiàowǔ

2. Wǒmen _____ *(eat).*

    a. zuòfàn
    b. shuìjiào
    c. chīfàn

3. Nǐ _____ *(go to work).*

    a. shàngbān
    b. shuìjiào
    c. chīfàn

4. Tā _____ *(dance).*

    a. shàngbān
    b. tiàowǔ
    c. chīfàn

5. Wáng xiānsheng hé Wáng tàitai _____ *(sing).*

    a. chànggē
    b. shuìjiào
    c. chīfàn

6. Wǒde línjū _____ *(cook).*

    a. zuòfàn
    b. tiàowǔ
    c. chīfàn

7. Xuésheng _____ *(go to school).*

    a. chànggē
    b. shuìjiào
    c. shàngxué

8. Wǒ bù _____ *(drive).*

    a. shàngxué
    b. kāichē
    c. chànggē

PHRASE LIST 2

měitiān	*every day*
měitiān zǎoshang	*every morning*
měitiān xiàwǔ	*every afternoon*
měitiān bàngwǎn/wǎnshang	*every evening*
měitiān wǎnshang	*every night*
měinián	*every year*
měi ge lǐbài/xīngqī	*every week*
měi ge yuè	*every month*
měi ge zhōumò	*every weekend*
měi ge lǐbài/xīngqī sān	*every Wednesday*

měinián sì yuè	*every April*
měinián xiàtiān	*every summer*
měi ge xiǎoshí/zhōngtóu	*every hour*
měi ge rén	*everyone*
měi tái diànnǎo	*every computer*
měi zhāng zhuōzi	*every table*
yíqiè	*everything*

NUTS & BOLTS 2
Měi *(EVERY/EACH)*

When **měi** *(every/each)* is combined with a noun, a measure word is often inserted between **měi** and the noun. This is shown above by such expressions as **měi ge yuè** *(every month)* and **měi zhāng zhuōzi** *(every table)*, where **gè (ge)** and **zhāng** are the appropriate measure words for **yuè** and **zhuōzi** respectively. However, you will also see that there are some exceptions to this rule: **měitiān** *(every day)*, **měinián** *(every year)*, **měifēn** *(every minute)*, and **měimiǎo** *(every second)*. In the above cases, **měi** is linked directly to the noun. This is because **tiān** *(day)*, **nián** *(year)*, **fēn** *(minute)*, and **miǎo** *(second)* function grammatically as both nouns and measure words in these expressions.

Wǒ měitiān shàngbān.
I go to work every day.

Wǒmen měinián xiàtiān dōu shàng shān.
We go to the mountains every summer.

Tā měitiān zǎoshang dōu zài zhèlǐ chī zǎocān.
She eats breakfast here every morning.

Tāmen měi ge lǐbài wǔ wǎnshang dōu qù tiàowǔ.
They go to dance every Friday night.

Tāmen měi ge zhōumò qù kàn diànyǐng.
They go to a movie every weekend.

Please note that an adverb **dōu** *(all)* is added in some of the above examples. In colloquial Chinese, **dōu** is added to indicate that an action repeatedly happens at a certain time and/or at a certain place.

PRACTICE 2
Multiple choice: Fill in the blanks.

1. Wǒ měi _____ yuè dōu qù Zhōngguó. *(I go to China every month.)*
   a. ge
   b. tiáo
   c. *none*

2. Tā měi _____ nián bā yuè dōu lái Měiguó. *(He comes to the U.S. in August every year.)*
   a. ge
   b. tiáo
   c. *none*

3. Měi _____ rén dōu yǒu fángzi. *(Everyone has a house.)*
   a. ge
   b. tiáo
   c. bù

4. Měi _____ fángzi dōu hěn piàoliang. *(Every house is very pretty.)*
   a. ge
   b. tiáo
   c. *none*

5. Měi _____ lǎoshī dōu shì Zhōngguórén. *(Every teacher is Chinese.)*
   a. ge
   b. tiáo
   c. *none*

6. Měi _____ lù dōu hěn cháng. *(Every road is very long.)*
   a. ge
   b. tiáo
   c. *none*

7. Wǒ měi _____ xīngqī dōu tiàowǔ. *(I dance every week.)*
   a. ge
   b. tiáo
   c. *none*

8. Wǒ měi _____ tiān zuòfàn. *(I cook every day.)*
   a. ge
   b. tiáo
   c. *none*

ANSWERS

PRACTICE 1: **1.** b; **2.** c; **3.** a; **4.** b; **5.** a; **6.** a; **7.** c; **8.** b

PRACTICE 2: **1.** a; **2.** c; **3.** a; **4.** a; **5.** a; **6.** b; **7.** a; **8.** c

————————— Lesson 11 (sentences) —————————

SENTENCE LIST 1

Wǒ xǐhuan chūntiān.	*I like spring.*
Wǒ bù xǐhuan xiàtiān.	*I don't like summer.*
Wǒ xǐhuan měitiān tiàowǔ.	*I like dancing/to dance every day.*
Wǒ měi ge zhōumò yóuyǒng.	*I swim every weekend.*
Wáng tàitai hé Wáng xiānsheng xǐhuan chànggē.	*Mrs. Wang and Mr. Wang like singing.*
Wǒde lǎoshī xǐhuan zuòfàn.	*My teacher likes cooking.*
Tāmen xǐhuan Zhōngguó.	*They like China.*
Nǐ xǐhuan tā ma?	*Do you like him?*
Wǒmen xǐhuan lǐbài yī tiàowǔ.	*We like to dance on Monday.*

NOTES

Remember that verb forms in Chinese do not change as much as in English. So *tiàowǔ* can be translated as *dance, dances, to dance, danced,* or *dancing,* depending on the subject and the grammatical context. For instance, in the sentence **Wǒ xǐhuan měitiān tiàowǔ,** the subject **wǒ** *(I)* is followed by the verb **xǐhuan** *(to like),* so the sentence could be translated as *I like dancing every day* or *I like to dance every day.*

NUTS & BOLTS 1

XǏHUAN/BÙ XǏHUAN *(TO LIKE/NOT LIKE)*

The verb **xǐhuan** means *to like* in Chinese. It can be followed by a noun or a verb, just as in English.

Wǒ xǐhuan píngguǒ.
I like apples.

Wǒ xǐhuan zuòfàn.
I like to cook.

In order to express a dislike, simply add the negative particle **bù** *(not)* before **xǐhuan** to form **bù xǐhuan** *(do/does/did not like)*.

Tā bù xǐhuan huā.
He doesn't like flowers.

Wǒ bù xǐhuan měitiān shàngbān.
I don't like to go to work every day.

Tā yǐqián bù xǐhuan huā.
She didn't like flowers in the past.

PRACTICE 1
Translate the following sentences into English.

1. Wáng tàitai měitiān zuòfàn.

2. Nǐmen xǐhuan chànggē ma?

3. Tāde dìdi xǐhuan měi ge zhōumò tiàowǔ.

4. Wǒ měinián qù Zhōngguó.

5. Tāmen bù xǐhuan yīshēng ma?

6. Gǒu bù xǐhuan māo.

7. Wǒde māma xǐhuan wǒde bàba.

SENTENCE LIST 2

Wǒ zài kàn diànshì.	*I'm watching television.*
Tāmen zài chīfàn.	*They are eating (a meal).*
Wáng xiānsheng hé Wáng tàitai zài tiàowǔ.	*Mr. Wang and Mrs. Wang are dancing.*

Nǐ zài tīng ma?	*Are you listening?*
Tā zuò zhe.	*She is sitting.*
Zhāng lǎoshī ná zhe yì běn shū.	*Teacher Zhang is holding a book.*
Tāde jiějie kàn zhe wǒ.	*Her older sister is looking at me.*
Tā ná zhe yì běn shū chànggē.	*She is holding a book to sing.*
Tā zhàn zhe ma?	*Is he standing?*

NUTS & BOLTS 2
USE OF ZÀI AND ZHE

In Chinese, the word **zài** or **zhe** can be combined with a verb to indicate an ongoing action (**zài**) or state of being (**zhe**), much in the same way as *-ing* does in English. As the examples above show, **zhe** is placed after the verb, and **zài** comes before the verb.

Wǒ zài hē kāfēi.

I am drinking coffee.

Tā zài zuò gōngkè.

He is doing his homework.

Tā tǎng zhe bú dòng.

He is lying motionless.

Dàmén chǎng zhe.

The door is open. (lit., The door is opening.)

The difference between **zài** and **zhe** is subtle. Remember that **zài** refers to an ongoing and continuous action while **zhe** usually refers to an ongoing state of being. Here are a few examples to illustrate this difference.

Tāde jiějie zài chuān hóng xiézi.

Her older sister is putting on red shoes. (action)

Tāde jiějie chuān zhe hóng xiézi.

Her older sister is wearing red shoes. (state)

Tā zài guān mén.

He is closing the door.

Qiánmén guān zhe.

The front door is closed. (lit., The front door is closing.)

Note that **zài** is not only used to indicate an ongoing or continuous action in the present tense. It can also indicate a past action, in which case it would be translated as *was/were . . . -ing* in English:

Tā zuótiān zài kāichē.

He was driving yesterday.

Notice in the example above that the verb **kāichē** doesn't change form to show past tense, as it would in English. Instead, it is only the presence of the adverb **zuótiān** *(yesterday)* that indicates tense. We'll come back to expressing tense in Chinese later, but for now keep in mind that adverbs of time often play the role of tense endings like *-ed* in English.

PRACTICE 2
Fill in the blanks in the following sentences using **zhe** or **zài**. The translations are given to help you.

1. Wǒ _____ kàn shū. *(I am reading.)*

2. Lǐ xiānsheng _____ chī shuǐguǒ. *(Mr. Li is eating fruit.)*

3. Nǐ hé mèimei _____ tiàowǔ. *(You and your younger sister are dancing.)*

4. Tā zhàn _____. *(He is standing.)*

5. Tāmen _____ tīng yīnyuè. *(They are listening to music.)*

6. Tāde gǒu _____ shuìjiào. *(Her dog is sleeping.)*

7. Wǒ kàn _____ wǒde línjū de huā. *(I am looking at my neighbor's flowers.)*

8. Wáng tàitai _____ zuòfàn. *(Mrs. Wang is cooking.)*

Culture note

It's not common in Chinese to use the word **ài** *(to love)* colloquially to say that you care about someone. Instead, the verb **xǐhuan** *(to like)* is more often used to express such feelings.

Wǒ xǐhuan nǐ.
I like you./I love you.

Wǒ hěn xǐhuan nǐ.
I like you very much./I love you very much.

ANSWERS

PRACTICE 1: 1. Mrs. Wang cooks every day. **2.** Do you (pl.) like to sing (singing)? **3.** His younger brother likes to dance (dancing) every weekend. **4.** I go to China every year. **5.** Don't they like doctors? **6.** Dogs don't like cats. **7.** My mother likes my father.

PRACTICE 2: 1. zài; **2.** zài; **3.** zài; **4.** zhe; **5.** zài; **6.** zài; **7.** zhe; **8.** zài

---

————————— Lesson 12 (conversations) —————————

CONVERSATION 1

Wang Hai and Jess are practicing Chinese.

Hai: Jié Xī, nǐ zài zuò shénme?
Jess: Wǒ zài liànxí Zhōngwén.
Hai: Hǎo, ràng wǒ kǎo kǎo nǐ.
Jess: Hǎo ba.
Hai: Yì nián yǒu jǐ ge yuè?
Jess: Shí èr ge yuè.

Hai: Yí ge lǐbài yǒu jǐ tiān?
Jess: Qī tiān.
Hai: Jīntiān shì jǐ hào, lǐbài jǐ?
Jess: Jīntiān shì shí èr yuè sì hào, lǐbài yī.
Hai: Nǎ ge yuè zuì lěng?
Jess: Èr yuè.

Hai: *Jess, what are you doing?*
Jess: *I'm practicing (my) Chinese.*
Hai: *Okay. Let me test you.*
Jess: *Alright.*
Hai: *How many months are there in a year?*
Jess: *Twelve months.*
Hai: *How many days are there in a week?*
Jess: *Seven days.*
Hai: *What's today's date and what day of the week is it?*
Jess: *Today is Monday, December 4th.*
Hai: *Which month is the coldest?*
Jess: *February.*

NOTES

Ràng wǒ means *let me*. It is always followed by another verb, in this case the verb **kǎo** *(to give a test)*.

Notice that the veb **kǎo** is doubled: **ràng wǒ kǎo kǎo nǐ.** This is called verb reduplication, and it's used in Chinese to signify that something is being done a little bit, or to a lesser degree than might be expected. Here, it means *let me give you a little quiz* rather than a long, formal examination. Here are some other examples of verb reduplication:

Wǒmen tántan.
We're having a little chat.

Wǒ qīnglǐ qīnglǐ fángzi.
I'm tidying up the house a bit.

The expression **hǎo ba** literally means *fine.* You can translate it as *okay, alright* or *go ahead,* depending on the context.

The question word **jǐ** *(how many)* requires the use of a measure word when combined with a noun, as in the case of **jǐ ge yuè** *(how many months)*. Another question word meaning *how many* in Chinese is **duōshǎo,** which is often used in everyday conversation to ask how much something costs **(duōshǎo qián?)**. You will learn more about these question words in Unit 4.

Nǎ is a demonstrative question pronoun. When combined with a noun and its measure word, it means *which* as can be seen in the phrase **nǎ ge yuè** *(which month)*.

NUTS & BOLTS 1
SUPERLATIVE WITH ZUÌ
Zuì means *the most* and is placed before an adjective to indicate the superlative, or the *-est* form in English. Here are some examples:

Tā zuì piàoliang.
She is the prettiest.

Měiguó chē zuì guì.
American cars are the most expensive.

Notice the word order in the last example. The adjective **Měiguó** *(American)*, which describes **chē** *(cars)*, comes right before the noun, just as in English. The phrase **zuì guì** *(most expensive)* comes at the end of the sentence, also just as in English. The major difference of course is that there is no verb *is* in Chinese in adjective sentences such as this.

PRACTICE 1A
Answer the following questions in English.

1. Jīntiān shì jǐ hào?

2. Yì nián yǒu jǐ ge yuè?

3. Yí ge lǐbài yǒu jǐ tiān?

4. Shí èr yuè yǒu jǐ tiān?

PRACTICE 1B
Insert the word **zuì** into the following sentences to make a superlative statement.

1. Wǒ gāo.

2. Tāde chē kuài.

3. Nà xiē fángzi dà.

4. Nà bǎ yǐzi xiǎo.

CONVERSATION 2
Hai and Jess are talking about Jess's birthday.

Hai: Jié Xī, nǐde shēngrì shì nǎ tiān?
Jess: Shí èr yuè shí wǔ hào.
Hai: Jīntiān shì jǐ hào?
Jess: Shí èr yuè shí wǔ hào.
Hai: Shēngrì kuàilè!
Jess: Xièxie!
Hai: Nǐ xǐhuan shénme shēngrì dàngāo?
Jess: Wǒ xǐhuan qiǎokèlì. Nǐ ne?
Hai: Wǒ bù xǐhuan qiǎokèlì. Wǒ xǐhuan xiāngcǎo.

Hai: *Jess, what day is your birthday?*
Jess: *December 15th.*
Hai: *What's today's date?*
Jess: *December 15th.*
Hai: *Happy birthday!*
Jess: *Thank you!*
Hai: *What (kind of) birthday cake do you like?*
Jess: *I like chocolate. How about you?*
Hai: *I don't like chocolate. I like vanilla.*

NOTES

Happy birthday is expressed in Chinese as **shēngrì kuàilè.** The word order here is the exact opposite of English since **shēngrì kuàilè** literally translates as *birthday happy.*

Notice the word order of Chinese questions with question words:

Nǐde shēngrì shì nǎ tiān?
lit., Your birthday is what day?

Nǐ xǐhuan shénme shēngrì dàngāo?
lit., You like what (kind of) birthday cake?

In English, question words typically come at the beginning of the questions, but not in Chinese. We'll take a closer look at this in the Nuts & bolts section.

NUTS & BOLTS 2
QUESTION WORD SHÉNME *(WHAT)*

Let's take a look at the very important and useful question word **shénme** *(what).* As you saw in the dialogue, question words in Chinese are not placed at the beginning of questions. Taken literally, questions in Chinese sound like English "echo" questions: *You ate what? They did what?*

In other words, **shénme**, along with most other question words in Chinese, doesn't "move." It is in the same position in the question as it is in the answer. **Nǐ xǐhuan <u>shénme</u> shēngrì dàngāo? Wǒ xǐhuan <u>qiǎokèlì</u>.** *(What kind of birthday cake do you like? I like chocolate.)* So, to ask about something in Chinese, use **shénme** in place of the thing or person you are asking about.

Nà shì shénme?
What is that?

Nǐ chī shénme?
What do you eat?

Nǐmen zài zuò shénme?
What are you doing?

Tā xǐhuan kàn shénme shū?
What does she like to read?

Note that **shénme** can also be translated as *what kind of:*

Nǐ xǐhuan shénme shuǐguǒ?
What kind of fruit do you like?

Tā xǐhuan shénme diànyǐng?
What kind of movies does he like?

PRACTICE 2
Translate the following sentences into English.

1. Nǐ xǐhuan chī shénme?
2. Tāde dìdi zài zuò shénme?
3. Zhè shì shénme?
4. Tā bù xǐhuan shénme?
5. Nǐ hē shénme?
6. Tā kàn shénme shū?

ANSWERS
PRACTICE 1A: 1. (it depends on today's date); **2.** twelve;
3. seven; **4.** thirty-one

PRACTICE 1B: 1. Wǒ zuì gāo. **2.** Tāde chē zuì kuài. **3.** Nà xiē
fángzi zuì dà. **4.** Nà bǎ yǐzi zuì xiǎo.

PRACTICE 2: 1. What do you like to eat? **2.** What is his/her
younger brother doing? **3.** What is this? **4.** What does he/she
not like? **5.** What do you drink? **6.** What book does he/she
read?

UNIT 3 ESSENTIALS
Jīntiān shì lǐbài jǐ?
What day is today?

Jīntiān shì lǐbài èr.
Today is Tuesday.

Jīntiān shì jǐ yuè jǐ hào?
What is the date today?

Jīntiān shì sān yuè èrshí hào.
Today is March 20th.

Wǒ chīfàn.
I eat (a meal).

Wǒ měitiān shàngbān.
I go to work every day.

Wǒ bù xǐhuan měitiān shàngbān.
I don't like to go to work every day.

Tā zài guān mén.
He is closing the door.

Qiánmén guān zhe.
The front door is closed. (lit., The door is closing.)

Wǒ xǐhuan nǐ.
I like you./I love you.

Tā zuì piàoliang.
She is the prettiest.

Nà shì shénme?
What is that?

Shēngrì Kuàilè.
Happy Birthday.

UNIT 4
Going shopping

In Unit 4, you'll learn how to talk about colors, clothing, and money. You'll also learn some essential expressions for shopping and more about numbers and negation.

Let's get started!

———————————— Lesson 13 (words) ————————————

WORD LIST 1

yīfu	*clothes, clothing*
mǎi	*to buy*
chuān	*to wear*
T-xùshān/tīxùshān	*T-shirt*
chènshān	*shirt*
kùzi	*pants*
liányīqún	*dress*
qúnzi	*skirt*
qúnkù	*culottes*
wàitào	*coat*
jiákè	*jacket*
yǔyī	*raincoat*
qípáo	*traditional Chinese dress*
wàzi	*socks*
xiézi	*shoes*
xuēzi	*boots*
yùndòngxié	*sneakers*
màozi	*hat*
pídài	*belt*

nèikù	*underpants*
shǒubiǎo	*watch*
jièzhi	*ring*

NUTS & BOLTS 1
MEASURE WORDS FOR CLOTHING AND ACCESSORIES

As you know, a measure word needs to be placed before a noun if it is preceded by a number or demonstrative. In the previous Units, you learned some important measure words and how measure words work with some time expressions and other phrases. Now, let's see how measure words are used when you talk about clothing.

Generally, two measure words are used when describing articles of clothing in Chinese: **jiàn** and **tiáo**. **Jiàn** is used for garments worn over the upper part or full length of the body, and **tiáo** is used for garments worn over the lower half of the body:

yí jiàn chènshān	*one/a shirt*
zhè jiàn wàitào	*this overcoat*
sì tiáo qúnzi	*four skirts*
yì tiáo kùzi	*one/a pair of pants*

When talking about shoes and footwear, however, the measure word **shuāng** *(pair)* is normally used. If you want to specify a particular number of shoes, socks, or boots other than a pair, use the measure word **zhī**:

yì shuāng xiézi	*one/a pair of shoes*
yì zhī xiézi	*one shoe*

Here are some more examples of measure words used with clothing:

Wǒ yǒu yí jiàn T-xùshān.
I have a T-shirt.

Wǒ chuān zhe yí jiàn yǔyī.
I'm wearing a raincoat.

Wǒ yǒu yì tiáo kùzi.
I have a pair of pants.

Wǒ yǒu qī shuāng wàzi.
I have seven pairs of socks.

Wǒ yǒu yì zhī xuēzi.
I have one boot.

Note that **yì tiáo** is translated as *a pair of* with certain articles of clothing, such as pants. Keep in mind that it's not the same *a pair of* that's used with footwear, which is **yì shuāng**.

There are different measure words used for accessories and other types of clothing. Here are the most common ones:

yí ge shǒubiǎo	*a watch*
yí duì ěrhuán	*a pair of earrings*
yì tiáo xiàngliàn	*a necklace*
yì zhī zhúozi	*a bracelet*
yì méi jièzhi	*a ring*
yì dǐng màozi	*a hat*

PRACTICE 1
Complete the following phrases with the appropriate measure word, and then translate.

1. Yì _____ qúnzi. (ge/jiàn/tiáo)
2. Yí _____ chènshān. (ge/jiàn/tiáo)
3. Yí _____ jiákè. (ge/jiàn/tiáo)
4. Yì _____ xiézi. (shuāng/jiàn/tiáo)
5. Yì _____ kùzi. (shuāng/jiàn/tiáo)
6. Yí _____ ěrhuán. (duì/jiàn/tiáo)
7. Yí _____ shǒubiǎo. (ge/jiàn/tiáo)
8. Yì _____ xiàngliàn. (ge/jiàn/tiáo)

WORD LIST 2
Here are the Chinese words for some important colors.

hóngsè	*red*
júhóngsè	*orange*
huángsè	*yellow*
lǜsè	*green*
lánsè	*blue*
zǐsè	*purple*
fěnhóngsè	*pink*
zōngsè	*brown*
hēisè	*black*
báisè	*white*
huīsè	*gray*
yínsè	*silver*
jīnsè	*golden*
shēn	*dark*
shēn lánsè	*dark blue*
qiǎn	*light*
qiǎn hóngsè	*light red*

NUTS & BOLTS 2
COLORS

Colors are expressed in Chinese as a combination of one or two syllables that identify a specific hue, along with the additional syllable **sè**, which generically means *color*. The use of **sè** is usually necessary.

Zhè běn shū shì hóngsè de.

This book is red.

Nà xiē kùzi shì lánsè de.

Those pants are blue.

The syllable **de** is also necessary when a color is used as a descriptive adjective right before a noun:

Wǒ yǒu yì běn hóngsè de shū.

I have a red book.

Tā chuān zhe yì tiáo lánsè de kùzi.

She's wearing blue pants.

Note that **hóngsè** and **lánsè** are both composed of two syllables. In general, if an adjective with two syllables directly precedes a noun, or if **hěn** *(very)* is used, then **de** usually has to be placed in between the adjective and the noun. If, however, the adjective only has one syllable, and isn't preceded by **hěn**, then **de** is frequently omitted. For example: **dà bízi** *(big nose)*.

The particle **de** is also usually omitted when the adjective is the name of a country, a language, or a place of origin, even if the adjective has two syllables.

In addition, note that both **sè** and **de** are normally omitted when adjectives describing color are used in combination with certain monosyllabic nouns where the color is an intrinsic property of the noun.

yì duǒ hóng huā	*a red flower*
lǜcǎo	*green grass*
lántiān	*blue sky*
báiyún	*white cloud*

PRACTICE 2

Match the Chinese colors on the left with their English translations on the right.

1. báisè	a. *pink*
2. lǜsè	b. *blue*
3. lánsè	c. *white*
4. fěnhóngsè	d. *gray*
5. hóngsè	e. *red*
6. huángsè	f. *green*
7. hēisè	g. *yellow*
8. huīsè	h. *black*

Culture note

Colors can have very different meanings in different traditions. For example, to the Chinese, red symbolizes luck, happiness and prosperity, and is therefore commonly used for celebrations such as birthdays, New Year festivities, and weddings. By contrast, white and black are the traditional colors of funerals in China, so they're not considered appropriate for celebrating a marriage, as they are in Western tradition. However, with the growing popularity of Western culture in China, many young couples have challenged the tradition by opting for a white bridal gown and black tuxedo at their wedding.

ANSWERS
PRACTICE 1: 1. tiáo (one/a skirt); **2.** jiàn (one/a shirt); **3.** jiàn (one/a jacket); **4.** shuāng (one/a pair of shoes); **5.** tiáo (one/a pair of pants); **6.** duì (one/a pair of earrings); **7.** ge (one/a watch); **8.** tiáo (one/a necklace)

PRACTICE 2: 1. c; **2.** f; **3.** b; **4.** a; **5.** e; **6.** g; **7.** h; **8.** d

——————————— Lesson 14 (phrases) ———————————

PHRASE LIST 1

Duōshǎo qián?	*How much (money)?*
Duōshǎo?	*How much?/How many?*
. . . yǒu méiyǒu . . . ?	*Do (you) have . . . ?*
méiyǒu	*don't/doesn't have*
láojià	*excuse me (asking for a favor)*
búcuò	*(pretty) good, not bad*
bù hǎoyìsi	*to find it embarrassing (to do something)*
. . . hǎo bù hǎo?	*. . . is it alright?*
Méiyǒu wèntí.	*No problem.*
dǎ zhé	*to give a discount*

NUTS & BOLTS 1
NEGATION WITH MÉIYǑU
You've already learned that you can make a verb negative by placing the particle **bù** in front of it:

Wǒ bú qù yīyuàn.
I don't go to the hospital.

However, you can't negate **yǒu** *(to have)* with **bù**. Instead you have to use the form **méiyǒu** *(doesn't/don't/didn't have)*.

Wǒ méiyǒu chē.
I don't have a car.

Wáng tàitai méiyǒu Yīngwén shū.
Mrs. Wang doesn't have an English book.

Tāde gēge méiyǒu lǎoshī.
His older brother doesn't have a teacher.

Tā jīntiān zǎoshang méiyǒu kè.
She didn't have class this morning.

PRACTICE 1

Make the following sentences negative. Then try to give the English translations of your answers.

1. Tāde xuésheng yǒu bǐ.

2. Wǒ yǒu yì zhī gǒu.

3. Jīntiān shì lǐbài èr.

4. Chén xiānsheng yǒu tàitai.

5. Tā chànggē.

6. Měiguórén xué Zhōngwén.

7. Tā kāichē qù Niǔ Yuē *(New York)*.

8. Tā rènshi wǒde lǎoshī.

PHRASE LIST 2

Here are some useful words that will come in handy when you go grocery shopping.

yì hé màipiàn	*one/a box of cereal*
yì hé niúnǎi	*one/a carton of milk*

yí guàn tāng	*one/a can of soup*
yì bāo táng	*one/a bag of sugar*
yí ge píngguǒ	*one/an apple*
yí ge júzi	*one/an orange*
yì tiáo xiāngjiāo	*one/a banana*
yí chuàn pútáo	*one/a bunch of grapes*
yí bàng báicài	*one/a pound of bok choy*
yí bàng fānqié/xīhóngshì	*one/a pound of tomatoes*
yí bàng mǎlíngshǔ	*one/a pound of potatoes*
yí bàng yángcōng	*one/a pound of onions*
yí bàng suàntóu	*one/a pound of garlic*
yí bàng hóngluóbo	*one/a pound of carrots*

NOTES

The measure word **gè** is used for most fruits. For instance, **yí ge lízi** *(a pear)*, **yí ge lǐzi** *(a plum)*, **yí ge shìzi** *(a persimmon)*, and **yí ge xīguā** *(a watermelon)*. This is because most fruits are large and round in shape, which is what the measure word **gè** denotes (as you know, although **gè** is in the fourth tone, it is often spoken and written without any tone: **ge**). Not surprisingly, grapes and bananas therefore use different measure words which apply more accurately to objects that are small and round **(chuàn)** or long and narrow **(tiáo)**.

The measure words used for vegetables are based on units of weight rather than on size or shape, such as **bàng** *(pound)* or **gōngjīn** *(kilogram)*. However, you can also use the measure word **kē** for vegetables (or for plants in general) when speaking of them piecemeal or as a general category: **yì kē báicài** *(a head of bok choy)* or **yì kē shù** *(a tree)*. Note that, although they sound the same, when written in character form, the **kē** 颗 for small items like bok choy and the **kē** 棵 for plants are different characters.

NUTS & BOLTS 2
ASKING *HOW MUCH* AND *HOW MANY*

In Chinese, the word **jǐ** *(how many)* is used with countable nouns to ask about the number of people or objects. **Jǐ** is always followed by a measure word, and these two words come before the countable noun.

Jǐ is only used when there are fewer than ten of something. For example:

Nǐ yǒu jǐ tiáo qúnzi?
How many skirts do you have?

–Wǒ yǒu sān tiáo qúnzi.
–I have three skirts.

Here are some other questions with **jǐ**:

Tā yǒu jǐ tiáo hóngsè de qúnzi?
How many red skirts does she have?

Jīntiān nǐ mǎile jǐ běn shū?
How many books did you buy today?

Nǐ chīle jǐ ge píngguǒ?
How many apples did you eat?

Nǐ mǎile jǐ bàng báicài?
How many pounds of bok choy did you buy?

Nǐ yǒu jǐ ge péngyou xǐhuan chī Zhōngguó cài?
How many of your friends like Chinese food?

For countable nouns of any or unlimited number, the word **duōshǎo** *(how many)* is used. It is placed right before the countable noun without a measure word. So, in other words, for countable nouns with quantities below ten, you use either **jǐ** (plus a measure word) or **duōshǎo** (on its own), and for quantities above ten, you may only use **duōshǎo**.

Nǐ zhǔle jǐ ge xīhóngshì? OR Nǐ zhǔle duōshǎo xīhóngshì?
How many tomatoes did you cook?

–Wǒ zhǔle liù ge.
–I cooked six (of them).

Nà ge nóngmín zhòngle duōshǎo xīhóngshì?
How many tomatoes did that farmer grow?

–Nà ge nóngmín zhòngle yíwàn zhū xīhóngshì.
–That farmer grew ten thousand bushels of tomatoes.

To ask about uncountable things, like **miànbāo** *(bread)*, **kōngqì** *(air)*, **shuǐ** *(water)*, **yóu** *(oil)*, and so on, use **duōshao**. In this case, it is translated as *how much* and it goes right before the noun, without any measure word:

Nǐ kěyǐ chī duōshǎo miànbāo?
How much bread can you eat?

–Wǒ kěyǐ chī wǔ piàn.
–I can eat five pieces.

Nǐ yào duōshǎo shuǐ?
How much water do you need?

–Wǒ yào yì píng.
–I need one bottle (of water).

Here are some more examples of **duōshǎo** used with both countable and uncountable nouns:

Nǐ hē duōshǎo kāfēi?
How much coffee do you drink?

Zuótiān xiàle duōshǎo yǔ?

How much rain fell yesterday?

Nǐ mǎile duōshǎo yóu?

How much oil did you buy?

Tā shàng cì mǎile duōshǎo shuāng hóngsè de xuēzi?

How many red boots did she buy last time?

Note, however, that **duōshǎo** is probably most frequently used in Chinese when asking for the price of something. In this case, **duōshǎo** is used along with **qián** *(money)* to form the phrase **duōshǎo qián** *(how much money)*:

Nǐ yǒu duōshǎo qián?

How much (money) do you have?

Zhè xiē píngguǒ duōshǎo qián?

How much are these apples?

Nà tiáo hóngsè de qúnzi duōshǎo qián?

How much is that red skirt?

PRACTICE 2

Match the Chinese sentences in the column on the left with the English translations on the right.

1. Tā yǒu jǐ shuāng báisè de xuēzi?	a. *How much is your house?*
2. Nǐ yào duōshǎo shuǐ?	b. *How many pairs of white boots does he/she have?*
3. Nǐmende xuéxiào yǒu duōshǎo xuésheng?	c. *How many apples can he/she eat?*
4. Nǐde fángzi duōshǎo qián?	d. *How many students are there in your school?*

5. Niǔ Yuē yǒu duōshǎo rén?	e. *How many books did you buy yesterday?*
6. Nǐ yǒu duōshǎo qián?	f. *How much water do you need?*
7. Tā kěyǐ chī jǐ ge píngguǒ?	g. *How much (money) do you have?*
8. Zuótiān nǐ mǎile jǐ běn shū?	h. *How many people are there in New York?*

ANSWERS

PRACTICE 1: 1. Tāde xuésheng méiyǒu bǐ. (His/Her students don't have pens.) **2.** Wǒ méiyǒu yì zhī gǒu. (I don't have a/one dog.) **3.** Jīntiān bú shì lǐbài èr. (Today is not Tuesday.) **4.** Chén xiānsheng méiyǒu tàitai. (Mr. Chen doesn't have a wife.) **5.** Tā bú chànggē. (He/She doesn't sing.) **6.** Měiguórén bù xué Zhōngwén. (Americans don't study Chinese.) **7.** Tā bù kāichē qù Niǔ Yuē. (He/She doesn't drive to New York.) **8.** Tā bú rènshi wǒde lǎoshī. (He/She doesn't know my teacher.)

PRACTICE 2: 1. b; **2.** f; **3.** d; **4.** a; **5.** h; **6.** g; **7.** c; **8.** e

─────────── Lesson 15 (sentences) ───────────

SENTENCE LIST 1

Nǐmen yǒu shénme yánsè de qúnzi?	*What color skirts do you have?*
Wǒ yǒu yì tiáo hóngsè de qúnzi.	*I have a red skirt.*
Nǐmen yǒu zǐsè de màozi ma?	*Do you have purple hats?*
Wǒ xǐhuan hóng huā.	*I like red flowers.*
Tā xǐhuan zhè tiáo yínsè de xiàngliàn.	*She likes the silver (colored) necklace.*

Wǒde māma chàng "Yínsè de yuèguāng."	*My mother sings "Silver moonlight."*
Wáng xiǎojiě hé Chén xiǎojiě xǐhuan jīnsè de zhuózi.	*Miss Wang and Miss Chen like golden (colored) bracelets.*
Nà jiàn huángsè de chènshān shì tāde.	*That yellow shirt is his.*
Zhè tiáo hēisè de kùzi shì wǒde.	*This pair of black pants is mine.*
Méigui yǒu duōshǎo zhǒng yánsè?	*How many colors of roses are there?*
Cǎihóng yǒu jǐ zhǒng yánsè?	*How many colors are there in a rainbow?*
Cǎihóng yǒu qī zhǒng yánsè.	*A rainbow has seven colors.*
Wǒ kěyǐ kànkàn qítā yánsè de qúnzi ma?	*Can I take a look at a skirt in a different color?*
Wǒ bù xǐhuan zhè ge yánsè.	*I don't like this color.*
Wǒ gěi nín dǎ zhé.	*I'm giving you a discount.*

NOTES

You learned earlier that colors in Chinese usually contain the syllable sè, as in hēisè *(black)* or hóngsè *(red)*. Note that the word yánsè is used to mean *color* when no specific hue is indicated, as in Cǎihóng yǒu jǐ zhǒng yánsè? *(How many colors are there in a rainbow?)* Also note that the measure word zhǒng *(kind)* is used when yánsè refers to multiple colors.

NUTS & BOLTS 1

THIS ONE AND THAT ONE

As you know, the demonstratives in Chinese are zhè *(this)* and nà *(that)*. They are always followed by a meaure word. In other words, *this book* and *that book* are expressed as zhè běn shū and nà běn shū in Chinese.

Remember also that the plural forms are **zhè xiē** *(these)* and **nà xiē** *(those)* and since **xiē** serves as the measure word for both, no additional measure word is needed: **Wǒ xǐhuan nà xiē shū** *(I like those books)*.

So far, we have only talked about demonstratives that directly precede a noun: *this person, that pen*. In English, these are known as demonstrative adjectives. Demonstratives that stand on their own—*this is mine, I want these, I like this one*—are known as demonstrative pronouns. In English, the word *one* is sometimes added after the demonstrative to help indicate that it is a demonstrative pronoun: *this one, that one, those ones*.

As in English, Chinese demonstratives can be used as both adjectives and pronouns. In other words, you can use the same words for both. Here are some examples:

Zhè ge duōshǎo qián?
How much is this?

Zhè ge yí kuài qián.
This one is one yuan.

Gěi wǒ nà xiē.
Give me those.

Wǒ mǎi wùlǐ kèběn. Zhè běn duōshǎo qián?
I'm buying a physics textbook. How much is this one?

Note that there is no context in the first two examples, so **ge** is used as a general measure word. However, in the last sentence, it is clear the speaker is referring to a textbook, so the measure word **běn** is used.

Also note that although the word *one* is added onto the demonstrative in a few of the above sentences in English, no additional word is needed in Chinese.

PRACTICE 1

Match the Chinese sentences in the right column with the English translations on the left.

1. *Give me these.*	a. Gěi wǒ nà ge.
2. *My mother likes this pair of earrings.*	b. Zhè xiē báisè de xuēzi shì wǒde.
3. *That woman is my teacher.*	c. Zhè ge.
4. *I'm buying this one.*	d. Wǒde māma xǐhuan zhè duì ěrhuán.
5. *How much are those skirts?*	e. Nà xiē qúnzi duōshǎo qián?
6. *Give me that one.*	f. Nà ge nǚrén shì wǒ de lǎoshī.
7. *These white boots are mine.*	g. Wǒ mǎi zhè ge.
8. *This one.*	h. Gěi wǒ zhè xiē.

SENTENCE LIST 2

Zhè ge duōshǎo qián?	*How much is this?*
Xīguā yí ge duōshǎo qián?	*How much does a watermelon cost?*
Júzi yí bàng duōshǎo qián?	*How much is a pound of oranges?*
Zhè ge yí kuài qián.	*This one is/costs one yuan.*
Xīguā yí ge qī kuài wǔ máo.	*Watermelons are/cost 7.50 RMB each (lit., for one).*
Júzi yí bàng jiǔ máo jiǔ fēn.	*Oranges are/cost 0.99 RMB a pound.*
Kùzi yì tiáo bāshísì kuài líng yī.	*One pair of pants is/costs 84.01 RMB.*
Tài guì le!	*That's too expensive!*
Hěn piányi!	*That's cheap! (lit., Very cheap!)*
Tài duō le.	*That's too much. (lit., Too much.)*

Jiàqián dī yìdiǎn ba.	*Can you lower your price a little bit? (lit., Price lower a little bit.)*
Wǒ yǒu yì máo.	*I have 0.10 RMB.*
Wǒ méiyǒu sān máo wǔ.	*I don't have 0.35 RMB.*
Zhèlǐ shì shí kuài.	*Here is 10 RMB.*
Zhǎo nín sān kuài yì máo sān.	*Here's your 3.13 RMB in change.*
Wǒ kěyǐ shuākǎ ma?	*Can I pay by credit card?*
Bù kěyǐ. Wǒmen zhǐ shōu xiànjīn.	*You can't. We only accept cash.*
Yínháng zài nǎli?	*Where is a bank?*
Tíkuǎnjī zài nǎli?	*Where is an ATM machine?*

NUTS & BOLTS 2
CURRENCY OF CHINA: MONEY EXPRESSIONS

Rénmínbì (RMB), which literally means *people's currency*, is the official currency in China. The basic unit is the **yuán**, which is usually known as **kuài** in colloquial Chinese. One **yuán** is divided into ten **jiǎo**, which is also referred to colloquially as **máo**. One **jiǎo** is further divided into ten **fēn**. Comparing these monetary units to American currency, the **yuán** is equivalent to the dollar, the **jiǎo** to the dime, and the **fēn** to the penny.

When mentioning Chinese currency in everyday conversation, **yuán** and **kuài** are equally used, as are **jiǎo** and **máo,** although in different areas people have different preferences.

Note that it is optional to place **fēn** and **qián** *(money)* at the end in conversation. For example, 8.57 RMB could be spoken as **bā kuài wǔ máo qī fēn qián** or just **bā kuài wǔ máo qī.**

Here are some other useful constructions involving money:

fù xiànjīn	*to pay in cash*
yòng zhīpiào fùqián	*to pay by check*
shuākǎ	*to pay by credit card*
Wǒmen bù zhǎo líng qián.	*We need exact change/the exact amount. (lit., We can't make change.)*
měi ge wǔ kuài	*each one costs 5 RMB (5 yuan)*
wǔ kuài shí ge	*they are ten for 5 RMB (5 yuan)*
èrshí kuài	*the price is 20 RMB (20 yuan)*

PRACTICE 2

Translate the following expressions into English based on the example below.

Ex. Shí jiǔ kuài

19 RMB

1. Jiǔ kuài
2. Sì máo
3. Qī yuán wǔ jiǎo
4. Bā kuài wǔ máo

5. Sān kuài líng sān fēn
6. Liù kuài bā máo
7. Yí kuài bā máo wǔ
8. Shí èr kuài

Culture note

To see pictures of Chinese currency, go to: http://www.chinatoday .com/fin/mon/ or http://www.chinatour.com/currency/currency.htm.

Until recently, people in China paid for all their daily purchases in cash. That's why you may hear that Chinese people like to carry a lot of cash with them when they go shopping. Nowadays, paying by bank card is acceptable in the stores in cities. However, credit cards are still not very popular and paying by check is a new concept that has only recently been introduced to China.

Major banks in China are owned and run by the government. The most popular national bank is called **Zhōngguó Jiànshè Yínghág** (*China Construction Bank*), which has branches in every province throughout the country.

ANSWERS
PRACTICE 1: 1. h; **2.** d; **3.** f; **4.** g; **5.** e; **6.** a; **7.** b; **8.** c

PRACTICE 2: 1. 9 RMB; **2.** 0.40 RMB; **3.** 7.50 RMB; **4.** 8.50 RMB; **5.** 3.03 RMB; **6.** 6.80 RMB; **7.** 1.85 RMB; **8.** 12.00 RMB

——————— Lesson 16 (conversations) ———————

CONVERSATION 1
Jess wants to buy a purple dress, but her size is out of stock. The shopkeeper asks her to come back the next week.

Diànzhǔ: Xiǎojiě, nín yào shénme dōngxi?
Jess: Nǐmen yǒu qúnzi ma?
Diànzhǔ: Yǒu. Qǐng guòlái. Zhè shì zuì xīn de kuǎnshì, yánsè búcuò, jiàqián yě bú guì.
Jess: Hěn piàoliang. Zhè tiáo qúnzi duōshǎo qián?
Diànzhǔ: Liǎng bǎi wǔshí kuài. Wǒ gěi nǐ dǎ zhé, yì bǎi bāshíbā.
Jess: Wǒ xǐhuan zǐsè. Nǐmen yǒu zǐsè de qúnzi ma?
Diànzhǔ: Ràng wǒ kànkan. Zǐsè zhǐyǒu zhōnghào, nín chuān jǐhào?
Jess: Wǒ chuān dàhào.

Diànzhǔ:	Bù hǎoyìsi. Wǒmen xiànzài méiyǒu dàhào, nǐ xià ge xīngqī zài guòlái hǎo bù hǎo?
Jess:	Hǎo ba. Qǐng nǐ bǎ qúnzi liú gěi wǒ, wǒ xià ge xīngqī zài guòlái.
Diànzhǔ:	Méiyǒu wèntí. Zàijiàn.
Jess:	Zàijiàn.

Shopkeeper:	Miss, can I help you? (lit., what do you need)
Jess:	Do you have any skirts?
Shopkeeper:	Yes. Please come over here. This is the latest style. The color is good and the price isn't high (lit., not expensive).
Jess:	Very pretty. How much is this skirt?
Shopkeeper:	250 RMB. I'll give you a discount. (You can have it for) 188 RMB.
Jess:	I like purple. Do you have the skirt in purple?
Shopkeeper:	Let me check. I only have purple in medium. What size do you wear?
Jess:	I wear large.
Shopkeeper:	I'm sorry. We don't have large now. Could you come back next week?
Jess:	Okay. Please keep the skirt for me. I'll come again next week.
Shopkeeper:	No problem. Goodbye.
Jess:	Goodbye.

NOTES

Note that, in Chinese, the word for size *large* is **dàhào,** *medium* is **zhōnghào,** and *small* is **xiǎohào.**

Here are some more adjectives that you can use to describe clothing: **piàoliang** *(pretty, beautiful),* **xīn** *(new),* **jiù** *(old),* **shímáo** *(fashionable, in style),* **guòshí** *(out of style),* **jǐn** *(tight),* **tài xiǎo** *(too small),* **tài dà** *(too large).*

NUTS & BOLTS 1

NUMBERS 21–1,000

You've already learned how to express numbers from *one* to *twenty*. Now, let's see how to form numbers from *twenty-one* to *a thousand* in Chinese. For *twenty, thirty, forty,* and so on, simply add -shí after a number from two to nine. For example, èr *(two)* + shí *(ten)* = èrshí *(twenty)*. To add a number in the ones place after the tens place, as in 2<u>1</u> or 9<u>9</u>, just say that number after -shí:

21 èrshí yī	60 liùshí
25 èrshí wǔ	70 qīshí
30 sānshí	80 bāshí
40 sìshí	90 jiǔshí
50 wǔshí	99 jiǔshí jiǔ

In Chinese, 100 and 1,000 are called yìbǎi and yìqiān respectively. Therefore, to say 200, 300, etc., just add bǎi after a number from one through nine. For 2,000, 3,000, etc., add qiān after the appropriate number.

For the numbers from 101 to 109, 201 to 209, 301 to 309, and so on, use the word líng *(zero)* before the number in the ones place. For other numbers, simply add the number without saying hé *(and)*.

100 yìbǎi	150 yìbǎi wǔshí
101 yìbǎi líng yī	159 yìbǎi wǔshí jiǔ
109 yìbǎi líng jiǔ	200 èrbǎi

110 yìbǎi yī shí	300 sānbǎi
111 yìbǎi yī shí yī	900 jiǔbǎi
115 yìbǎi yī shí wǔ	999 jiǔbǎi jiǔshí jiǔ
120 yìbǎi èrshí	1,000 yìqiān
123 yìbǎi èrshí sān	

PRACTICE 1
Translate the following numbers into English.

1. yìbǎi bāshí sān
2. sìbǎi líng èr
3. wǔbǎi wǔshí wǔ
4. liùbǎi

5. yìqiān
6. bābǎi liùshí
7. yìbǎi yì shí sān
8. sānbǎi èrshí

CONVERSATION 2
Now listen as Jess buys groceries.

Diànyuán: Nín mǎi shénme dōngxi?
Jess: Mǎlíngshǔ yí bàng duōshǎo qián?
Diànyuán: Wǔ máo qián yí bàng.
Jess: Gěi wǒ liǎng bàng. Nǐmen yǒu báicài ma?
Diànyuán: Yǒu. Jīntiān de báicài hěn xīnxiān. Nín yào duōshǎo?
Jess: Gěi wǒ sān bàng.
Diànyuán: Yí kuài wǔ máo yí bàng. Sān bàng yào sì kuài wǔ máo. Hái yào shénme ma?
Jess: Gěi wǒ sān ge fānqié.
Diànyuán: Sān ge fānqié wǔ máo. Yígòng liù kuài.
Jess: Zhèlǐ shí kuài.
Diànyuán: Hǎo, zhǎo nín sì kuài. Xièxie.

Salesman:	What can I do for you? (lit., What do you want to buy?)
Jess:	How much is one/a pound of potatoes?
Salesman:	0.5 RMB a pound.
Jess:	Give me two pounds. Do you have bok choy?
Salesman:	Yes. The bok choy is very fresh today. How much do you want?
Jess:	Give me three pounds.
Salesman:	It's 1.50 RMB a pound. That would be 4.50 RMB for three pounds. What else do you want?
Jess:	Give me three tomatoes.
Salesman:	It's 0.50 RMB for three tomatoes. The total is 6 RMB.
Jess:	Here's 10.00 RMB.
Salesman:	Okay, here's 4.00 RMB in change. Thank you.

NUTS & BOLTS 2

QUANTITY EXPRESSIONS AND THE NUMBER *TWO* (ÈR AND LIǍNG)

As you know, there are two ways of saying *two* in Chinese: **èr** and **liǎng**. These two expressions serve different functions.

Èr is used for counting when the number *two* stands alone. For example, when you say: yī, èr, sān . . . (*one, two, three . . .*). **Èr** is also used when it is combined with most cardinal numbers:

èrshí	twenty
èrshí èr	twenty-two
èrbǎi	two hundred
yìbǎi wǔshí èr	one hundred and fifty-two

Liǎng is used with a measure word when it quantifies a noun. In other words, **liǎng** is used when you say that there are two of something.

| liǎng ge píngguǒ | two apples |
| liǎng běn shū | two books |

However, keep in mind that you would say **shí èr ge píngguǒ** (*twelve apples*), not **shí liǎng ge píngguǒ**.

Also note that the number 2 is usually **liǎng** when used with the money units **yuán/kuài** and **jiǎo/máo**.

Here are some more quantity-related expressions in Chinese.

yì dá jīdàn	one dozen eggs
dàgài shí ge rén	about ten people
wǔshí liàng chē zuǒyòu	around fifty cars
bú gòu yìbǎi bàng	fewer than 100 pounds

PRACTICE 2
Fill in the missing Chinese word in the following sentences, using the translations as cues.

1. Wǒ yǒu _____ ge píngguǒ. (*I have two apples.*)

2. Tā _____ shí suì. (*He is twenty years old.*)

3. Yī jiā _____ děngyú sān. (*One plus two equals three.*)

4. Wáng tàitai méiyǒu _____ ge gēge. (*Mrs. Wang doesn't have two older brothers.*)

5. Wǒ hé Zhāng lǎoshī qù guò _____ ge dìfang. (*Teacher Zhang and I went to two places.*)

6. Wǒde biǎojiě yǒu _____ tiáo gǒu. (*My cousin has two dogs.*)

7. Zhè shì yì bǎi líng _____ hào. *(This is number 102.)*

8. Māma měitiān chī _____ ge júzi. *(My mother eats two oranges every day.)*

ANSWERS

PRACTICE 1: 1. 183; **2.** 402; **3.** 555; **4.** 600; **5.** 1,000; **6.** 860; **7.** 113; **8.** 320

PRACTICE 2: 1. liǎng; **2.** èr; **3.** èr; **4.** liǎng; **5.** liǎng; **6.** liǎng; **7.** èr; **8.** liǎng

UNIT 4 ESSENTIALS

Wǒ yǒu yì tiáo kùzi.
I have a pair of pants.

Wǒ yǒu yì shuāng xiézi.
I have a pair of shoes.

Wǒ méiyǒu yì běn hóngsè de shū.
I don't have a red book.

Nǐ zhǔle jǐ ge xīhóngshì? OR Nǐ zhǔle duōshǎo xīhóngshì?
How many tomatoes did you cook?

Nín yào shénme dōngxi?
Can I help you? (lit., what do you need)

Duōshǎo qián?
How much (money)?

Wǒ gěi nín dǎ zhé.
I'm giving you a discount.

Zhè ge duōshǎo qián?
How much is this?

Zhè ge yí kuài qián.
This one is (costs) one yuan.

Wǒ kěyǐ shuākǎ ma?
Can I pay by credit card?

Wǒmen zhǐ shōu xiànjīn.
We only accept cash.

Gěi wǒ liǎng bàng.
Give me two pounds.

Méiyǒu wèntí.
No problem.

UNIT 5
Doctors and health

In this Unit, you'll learn how to talk about your health and lots of useful vocabulary related to the body. You'll also learn more about negation, how to express commands, and how to ask *how* and *how long*. Plus, you will learn how to express completed actions in Chinese. Let's get started!

——————— Lesson 17 (words) ———————

WORD LIST 1

yǎnjing	*eye*
ěrduo	*ear*
zuǐba	*mouth*
zuǐchún	*lips*
liǎn	*face*
bízi	*nose*
bózi	*neck*
étóu	*forehead*
sǎngzi	*throat*
liǎnjiá	*cheek*
yáchǐ	*tooth*
shétou	*tongue*

NUTS & BOLTS 1
NEGATION WITH BÙ AND BÚSHÌ BEFORE ADJECTIVES AND ADVERBS

You already know that you can negate most verbs by placing the negative particle **bù** before the verb. You can also use **bù** before an adjective, with a similar negative meaning.

Zhè ge nǚháizi měi.

This girl is pretty.

Nà ge nǚháizi bù měi.

That girl is not pretty.

Note, however, that when an adjective is modified by an adverb expressing quantity or degree, such as **hěn** *(very)*, **bù** can no longer be used to form the negative. Instead, the word **búshì** is placed before the modifying adverb in order to negate the sentence.

Wǒde jiějie hěn měi.

My older sister is very pretty.

Wǒde jiějie búshì hěn měi.

My older sister is not very pretty.

Měiguó hěn dà.

America is very big.

Měiguó búshì hěn dà.

America is not very big.

Rìběn chē tài guì.

Japanese cars are too expensive.

Rìběn chē búshì tài guì.

Japanese cars are not too expensive.

PRACTICE 1
Negate the following sentences by adding **búshì** or **bù**.

1. Dìguódàshà hěn gāo. *(The Empire State Building is very tall.)*

2. Nà jiàn wàitaò tài guì. *(That coat is too expensive.)*

3. Tā cōngmíng. *(She is intelligent.)*

4. Zhè ge fángzi tài guì. *(This house is too expensive.)*

5. Nà liàng chē hěn kuài. *(That car is fast.)*

6. Zhè xiē píngguǒ hěn xiāng. *(These apples are very aromatic.)*

7. Tāde gǒu xiǎo. *(Her dog is small.)*

WORD LIST 2

shǒu	*hand*
shǒuzhǐ	*finger*
tuǐ	*leg*
xiǎotuǐ	*calf*
jiǎo	*foot*
zhǐjia	*fingernail*
zhǒu	*elbow*
shǒuwàn	*wrist*
dàtuǐ	*thigh*
zúgēn	*heel*
dùzi	*belly*
bèijǐ/bèibù	*back*
jiānbǎng	*shoulder*
xiōngbù	*chest*

NUTS & BOLTS 2
COMMANDS

The imperative, or command form, in Chinese is very easy. Just use the basic verb form without any subject. **Qǐng** *(please)* can be used to make the command more polite.

Qǐng zài shuō yí cì.
Please repeat that. (lit., Please say it once again.)

Qǐng zhāngkài zuǐba.
Please open your mouth.

To form a negative command, the negative particle **bié** *(don't)* is placed in front of the verb. **Bié** and the verb are usually placed at the head of the sentence.

Bié kàn tài duō diànshì.
Don't watch too much TV.

Bié chī lěng de dōngxi.
Don't eat cold food.

Bié qù.
Don't go.

You can also use the word **búyào** in Chinese to make negative commands. Like **bié**, **búyào** is placed in front of the verb at the beginning of the sentence. **Bié** and **búyào** are interchangeable:

Búyào pèng nà tiáo gǒu.
Don't touch that dog.

Bié pèng nà tiáo gǒu.
Don't touch that dog.

PRACTICE 2
Choose the appropriate negative particle (**bié** or **bù**) in the following sentences.

1. Nàli tài wēixiǎn. Nǐ _____ qù. *(It's too dangerous there. Don't go.)*

2. Wǒmen _____ chī ròu. *(We don't eat meat.)*

3. Zhè ge fángzi tài guì. Wǒ _____ mǎi. *(This house is too expensive. I'm not buying it.)*

4. Tiānqì tài lěng. Tā _____ qù shàngxué. *(The weather is too cold. He is not going to school.)*

5. Nǐ _____ shūfu. _____ hē jiǔ. *(You don't feel well. Don't drink wine.)*

6. Tāde huā _____ guì. *(His flowers are not expensive.)*

7. Lǎoshī láile. _____ shuìjiào. *(The teacher is coming. Don't sleep.)*

ANSWERS

PRACTICE 1: 1. Dìguódàshà búshì hěn gāo. **2.** Nà jiàn wàitaò búshì tài guì. **3.** Tā bù cōngmíng. **4.** Zhè ge fángzi búshì tài guì. **5.** Nà liàng chē búshì hěn kuài. **6.** Zhè xiē píngguǒ búshì hěn xiāng. **7.** Tāde gǒu bù xiǎo.

PRACTICE 2: 1. bié; **2.** bù; **3.** bù; **4.** bù; **5.** bù, bié; **6.** bù; **7.** bié

——————————— Lesson 18 (phrases) ———————————

PHRASE LIST 1

bù shūfu	*do/does/did not feel well*
zháoliáng	*to catch a cold*
fāshāo	*to have a fever*
lā dùzi	*to have diarrhea*
wèi tòng/dùzi tòng	*to have a stomachache/abdominal pain*
tóuyūn	*to feel dizzy*
tóu tòng	*to have a headache*
yǒu yìdiǎnr késòu	*to have a slight cough*
tùle hěn duō cì	*to vomit many times*
xiǎng tù	*to feel nauseous*
sǎngzi tòng	*to have a sore throat*
xiōngbù tòng	*to have chest pain*
chū zhěn	*to make a medical house call (a doctor)*
fādǒu	*to shiver*
liúxiě	*to bleed*
fāyán	*inflammation*
qù yīyuàn	*to go to the hospital*
qù zhěnsuǒ	*to go to a clinic*
zěnme yàng?	*how . . . ?*

NUTS & BOLTS 1
EXPRESSING A COMPLETED ACTION WITH LE

A common way to express the simple past *(-ed)* or the present perfect tense *(have + verb)* in Chinese is to add the particle **le** immediately after the verb. This particle indicates that an action has been completed.

Tā chīle yào.
He took (lit., ate) the medicine.

Wǒ qùle Zhōngguó.
I went to China.

Tāmen chàngle sān shǒu Yīngwén gē.
They have sung three English songs.

But be careful. **Le** doesn't always refer to the past. It stresses completion of an action, so it can also refer to an action that will be completed in the future.

Lǐbài sān wǒ yǐjīng fēidào le Zhōngguó.
I will already have flown to China by Wednesday.

Tā jīntiān wǎnshang bā diǎn yǐjīng shuìle.
She'll already have slept by 8 pm tonight.

Le can also be used to indicate that a current situation or condition is different from the way things were in the immediate past. It's typically used in Chinese to indicate a change in time, weather, or season.

Dōngtiān láile.
It's winter. (lit., Winter has come.)

Wǔ diǎn le.
It's five o'clock.

Xiàyǔle.

It's raining.

Wǒ méiyǒu qián le.

I don't have money now.

Of course, it is also possible to simply say **wǒ méiyǒu qián** *(I don't have money)*. The difference in meaning between that phrase and **wǒ méiyǒu qián le** is that the addition of **le** stresses that the current situation is different. So, **wǒ méiyǒu qián le** implies that the person recently had money but doesn't now.

When **le** is added after an adjective, however, it implies *has become* + adjective. When **le** is added after **shì** *(to be)*, it means *to be . . . now*. For example:

Tā pàng le.

He has become fat. (He was not fat before.)

Wǒde dìdi gāo le.

My younger brother has become tall. (He was not tall before.)

Tā shì xuésheng le.

He is a student now. (He was not before.)

PRACTICE 1
Translate the following sentences into English, paying careful attention to the meaning expressed by **le**.

1. Tā lái Měiguó wǔ nián le.

2. Wáng tàitai qùle yīyuàn.

3. Zhāng lǎoshī mǎile liǎng běn shū.

4. Xīngqī sān le.

5. Dìdi chīle yào.

6. Nà ge rén mǎile sān tiáo qúnzi.

7. Wǒ míngbaile.
8. Tāde péngyou qùle zhěnsuǒ.

PHRASE LIST 2

bìngle	to be sick
dǎ zhēn	to give/get an injection
liáng tǐwēn	to take (someone's) temperature
bǎmài	to check (someone's) pulse
chī yào	to take medicine
bāozā shāngkǒu	to bind up a wound, to apply a bandage (to a wound)
dǎ shígāo	to have a plaster cast/to be placed in a cast
féngxiàn	to stitch up (a cut)
zuò xīndiàntú	to take a cardiogram
duōjiǔ	how long
fàn qián fú	(medication) to be taken before a meal
fàn hòu fú	(medication) to be taken after a meal

NUTS & BOLTS 2

ASKING *HOW LONG?*

Use the phrase **duōjiǔ**, which literally means *how long*, to ask about the duration of something. Notice that you can ask about both a completed action and an uncompleted action by using **le**.

Nǐ bìngle duōjiǔ?
How long have you been sick?

Nǐ kéle duōjiǔ?
How long have you been coughing?

Wǒ yào děng duōjiǔ?
How long do I need to wait?

Nǐ děngle duōjiǔ?
How long have you been waiting?

Nǐ xuéle Zhōngwén duōjiǔ?

How long have you been studying Chinese?

PRACTICE 2

Pick sentences from the column on the right that best answer each question in the column on the left.

1. Nǐ bàba yǒu chē ma?	a. Wǒ qùle liǎng nián.
2. Nǐ qùle Zhōngguó duōjiǔ?	b. Liǎng tiān.
3. Nǐ chīle fàn méiyǒu?	c. Wǒ míngbai.
4. Tā bìngle duōjiǔ?	d. Tā chàngle wǔ ge zhōngtóu.
5. Nǐ xuéle Zhōngwén duōjiǔ?	e. Tā yǒu.
6. Zhè ge duōshǎo qián?	f. Shí kuài.
7. Nǐ míngbai ma?	g. Wǒ xuéle sān ge yuè.
8. Tā gēge chàngle duōjiǔ?	h. Wǒ chīle.

Tip!

In Unit 3, we studied how verb-object verbs are two-syllable words that consist of a verb followed by an object that clarifies the purpose of an action. **Chīfàn** *(to eat)* and **chànggē** *(to sing)* are two examples of verb-object verbs. The nouns **fàn** *(meal, cooked rice)* and **gē** *(song)* are used as objects to clarify and emphasize what is being eaten **(chī)** and what is being sung **(chàng)**.

Remember that these object syllables can be attached to the verb, or separated from it, without affecting meaning at all. This is particularly evident when the particle **le** is added to indicate a completed action.

Wǒ chīle fàn.
I ate the/a meal.

As you know, there's another category of two-syllable verbs in Chinese that do not show this flexibility, so they're grammatically distinct from verb-object verbs. Examples of inseparable two-syllable verbs include **míngbai** *(to understand)* and **rènshi** *(to know someone).*

Tā míngbai wǒde Zhōngwén.
He understands my Chinese.

Tā míngbaile wǒde huà.
He understood what I said.

Wǒ rènshi Wáng tàitai.
I know Mrs. Wang.

Tāmen rènshile sān nián.
They have known (each other) for three years.

Notice that the particle **le** (or anything else) can never separate **bai** from **míng** or **shi** from **rèn**.

ANSWERS

PRACTICE 1: 1. He/She has been in the U.S. for five years. **2.** Mrs. Wang went to the hospital. **3.** Teacher Zhang bought two books. **4.** It's Wednesday. **5.** My younger brother took the medicine. **6.** That person bought three skirts. **7.** I understand now. **8.** His/Her friend went to the clinic.

PRACTICE 2: 1. e; **2.** a; **3.** h; **4.** b; **5.** g; **6.** f; **7.** c; **8.** d

SENTENCE LIST 1

Nǐ nǎli bù shūfu?	*What's troubling you? (lit., Where don't you feel well?)*
Wǒ fāshāo.	*I have a fever.*
Wǒ tóu tòng hé dùzi tòng.	*I have a headache and abdominal pain.*
Nǐ tòngle duōjiǔ?	*How long have you been in pain?*
Tòngle liǎngtiān.	*I've been in pain for two days.*
Nǐ xiànzài juéde zěnme yàng?	*How do you feel now?*
Wǒ yǒudiǎnr bù shūfu.	*I don't feel very well.*
Wǒ xiǎng tù.	*I'm nauseous./I'm sick to my stomach.*
Wǒ hěn lèi.	*I'm very tired.*
Nǐde màibó yǒudiǎnr kuài.	*Your pulse is a little fast.*
Nǐ zuìjìn zěnme yàng?	*How have you been doing recently?*
Wǒ hěn máng.	*I'm very busy.*

NUTS & BOLTS 1

ASKING *HOW?*

The phrase **zěnme yàng?** (sometimes shortened to **zěnyàng**) is used to ask the question *how?* It can be put in front of a verb to ask how something is done, or after a noun to ask how someone is doing.

Nǐmen zěnyàng qù kàn yīshēng?

How do you go to (see) the doctor?

–Wǒmen zuò gōngchē qù kàn yīshēng.

– We take a bus to go to (see) the doctor.

Nǐde bàba xiànzài zěnme yàng?

How is your father doing now?

PRACTICE 1

Pick sentences from the column on the right that best answer each question in the column on the left. Translate the answer that you choose.

1. Tā méiyǒu qián. Tā zěnyàng qù Niǔ Yuē?	a. Tā měitiān zuò gōngchē.
2. Nín zuìjìn zěnme yàng?	b. Tài guì.
3. Nà ge xuésheng měitiān zěnme yàng shàngxué?	c. Tā bú zuòfàn. Tā qù péngyou de jiā chīfàn.
4. Zhè ge fángzi zěnme yàng?	d. Wǒ měitiān kàn Zhōngwén shū.
5. Nǐ xiànzài juéde zěnme yàng?	e. Tā màile *(sold)* tāde chē qù Niǔ Yuē.
6. Tā zěnme yàng zuòfàn?	f. Wǒ xiǎng tù.
7. Nǐ zěnyàng xué Zhōngwén?	g. Wǒ hěn hǎo. Xièxie.

SENTENCE LIST 2

Tā chīle yào.	*He took the medicine.*
Tā méiyǒu chī yào.	*He didn't take the medicine.*
Tā hái méiyǒu chī yào.	*He hasn't taken the medicine yet.*
Wǒde bàba mǎile yí liàng xīn chē.	*My father bought a new car.*
Wǒde bàba méiyǒu mǎi xīn chē.	*My father didn't buy a new car.*
Wǒde bàba hái méiyǒu mǎi xīn chē.	*My father hasn't bought a new car yet.*
Zhāng lǎoshī bìngle.	*Teacher Zhang was sick.*
Zhāng lǎoshī méiyǒu bìng.	*Teacher Zhang was not sick.*

NUTS & BOLTS 2
NEGATING COMPLETED ACTIONS: MÉIYŎU

You learned that **le** is used in Chinese to show that an action has been completed. To express negation of completed actions, the negative phrase **méiyŏu** is used. This typically expresses that someone failed to accomplish something, or never undertook it in the first place. Notice that **le** is not used in the negative constructions.

Zhāng lǎoshī méiyŏu kàn diànshì.
Teacher Zhang didn't watch TV.

Tā méiyŏu qù.
He didn't go.

Don't forget the other use of **méiyŏu,** which is the negative form of the verb **yŏu** *(to have).* In those constructions, **méiyŏu** is followed by a noun. But in the constructions discussed here, **méiyŏu** is followed by a verb and is usually translated as *did not.*

You can add the word **hái** *(still)* before **méiyŏu,** forming the phrase **hái méiyŏu** *(not yet).* Notice that this construction is usually translated into the English present perfect tense *(has/have done).*

Wŏde māma hái méiyŏu chīfàn.
My mother hasn't eaten yet.

Tā hái méiyŏu qù.
He hasn't gone yet.

PRACTICE 2
Use **bù** or **méiyŏu** to negate the following sentences, and then translate your answers.

1. Wŏ qùle Zhōngguó.
2. Tā xǐhuan dǎ zhēn.

3. Nà ge yīshēng chīle yào.

4. Zhè ge Měiguórén mǎile sì běn Yīngwén shū.

5. Chén lǎoshī shàngxué.

6. Wáng tàitai láile.

7. Wǒde māma bìngle.

8. Zhāng tàitai qù kàn yīshēng.

ANSWERS

PRACTICE 1: 1. e (He/She sold his/her car to go to New York.); **2.** g (I'm very well. Thank you.); **3.** a (He/She takes the bus every day.); **4.** b (Too expensive.); **5.** f (I am feeling nauseous.); **6.** c. (He/She doesn't cook. He/She goes to his/her friend's home to eat.); **7.** d (I read Chinese books every day.)

PRACTICE 2: 1. Wǒ méiyǒu qù Zhōngguó. (I didn't go to China.) **2.** Tā bù xǐhuan dǎ zhēn. (She doesn't like getting injections.) **3.** Nà ge yīshēng méiyǒu chī yào. (That doctor didn't take the medicine.) **4.** Zhè ge Měiguórén méiyǒu mǎi sì běn Yīngwén shū. (This American didn't buy four English books.) **5.** Chén lǎoshī bú shàngxué. (Teacher Chen doesn't go to school.) **6.** Wáng tàitai méiyǒu lái. (Mrs. Wang didn't come.) **7.** Wǒde māma méiyǒu bìng. (My mother was not sick.) **8.** Zhāng tàitai bú qù kàn yīshēng. (Mrs. Zhang isn't going to see a doctor.)

──────── Lesson 20 (conversations) ────────

CONVERSATION 1

Jess doesn't feel well, so she goes to the doctor's office.

Yīshēng: **Nín nǎli bù shūfu?**
Jess: **Wǒ jīntiān yǒu diǎnr tóu tòng, quánshēn dōu tòng.**
Yīshēng: **Nínde tǐwēn shì sānshí jiǔ dù, yǒu diǎnr fāshāo. Qǐng zhāngkāi zuǐba, ràng wǒ kàn yí kàn.**

Jess:	Yīshēng, wǒ shì shénme bìng?
Yīshēng:	Sǎngzi yǒu diǎnr fāyán. Nín jīntiān yǒu méiyǒu késòu?
Jess:	Yǒu yìdiǎnr. Sǎngzi yě yǒu diǎnr tòng.
Yīshēng:	Shì gǎnmào.
Jess:	Yào dǎzhēn ma? Wǒ zuì pà dǎ zhēn.
Yīshēng:	Búyòng dǎzhēn. Bié hē lěng de dōngxi, chī diǎnr yào, xiūxi yì liǎng tiān jiù kěyǐ le.

Doctor:	*What seems to be troubling you?*
Jess:	*I feel a little dizzy and I have a headache. My whole body is aching.*
Doctor:	*Your temperature is 39 (degrees Celsius). You have a mild fever. Please open your mouth and let me take a look.*
Jess:	*Doctor, what's wrong with me?*
Doctor:	*Your throat is inflamed. Are you coughing?*
Jess:	*A little. My throat also hurts a bit.*
Doctor:	*You have a cold.*
Jess:	*Do I need a shot? I'm very (lit., most) afraid of getting injections.*
Doctor:	*It's not necessary to get an injection. Just don't drink anything cold, take the medication (I'm going to prescribe for you), give your body a good rest for one or two days, and you'll be fine.*

NOTES

Wǒ shì shénme bìng?, which can be translated as *What's wrong with me?*, literally means *What illness am I?* Another way of saying this is **Wǒ yǒu shénme bìng?** *(lit., What illness do I have?).*

Yì liǎng tiān can be translated as *one to two days* or *one or two days.* In order to express an approximate number of days, people, objects, etc., two consecutive numbers are joined together and then followed by the noun that they're quantifying: **wǔ liù tiān** *(five to/or six days)*, **wǔ liù ge rén** *(five to/or six people)*, **sān sì ge yuè** *(three to/or four months).* But don't forget to use a measure word after the last number. As you learned in Unit 3, the word **tiān** itself can function as a measure word, so you don't need an additional measure word. But with **yuè** and **rén**, you need the measure word **ge**.

NUTS & BOLTS 1
ASKING *WHERE?*

You've already learned some useful question words such as **shénme** *(what)* and **duōshǎo** *(how much)*. Now let's look at **nǎli**, which is used to ask the question *where?* in Chinese. **Nǎli** is actually a combination of the question word **nǎ** *(which)*, which you learned about in Unit 3, and **lǐ** *(place)*. So literally, **nǎli** means *which place?* One thing to keep in mind is that if you're asking for a location, the preposition **zài** *(in, at, on)* needs to precede the word **nǎli**. The answer would then include the same preposition.

Nǐ nǎli tòng?

Where does it hurt? (lit., Where do you feel pain?)

Nǐ zài nǎli?

Where are you?

Zhāng xiānsheng zài nǎli shàngbān?

Where does Mr. Zhang work?

Wáng tàitai zhù zài nǎli?

Where does Mrs. Wang live?

–Wáng tàitai zhù zài Fǎguó.

–Mrs. Wang lives in France.

Don't forget that **zài** is also used as a particle to indicate continuous or ongoing actions, as you learned in Lesson 11. In that construction, it's combined with a verb. When it's combined with **nǎli** or with a place, it expresses location.

Tāmen zài chànggē.

They are singing.

Wǒ zhù zài Niǔ Yuē.
I live in New York.

PRACTICE 1

Pick sentences from the column on the right that best answer each question in the column on the left. Then translate the answer that you've chosen.

1. Tāmen qù nǎli kàn yīshēng?	a. Wǒde bízi hěn tòng.
2. Nǐde lǎoshī zài nǎli jiāo *(teach)* Yīngwén?	b. Wǒde lǎoshī zài Zhōngguó jiāo Yīngwén.
3. Nǐmen zài nǎli shuìjiào?	c. Wǒmen lǐbài tiān zài xuéxiào chīfàn.
4. Tā qùle nǎli?	d. Niǔ Yuē Dà Xué. *(New York University.)*
5. Nǐ nǎli bù shūfu?	e. Wǒmen zài wòfáng shuìjiào.
6. Wǒmen lǐbài tiān zài nǎli chīfàn?	f. Tāmen qù yīyuàn kàn yīshēng.
7. Nǐ zài nǎli xué Zhōngwén?	g. Tā qùle Zhōngguó.

CONVERSATION 2

Now listen to the following dialogue where Hai asks Jess about her health.

Hai: Jié Xī, zuótiān nǐ yǒu méiyǒu shàng hànyǔ kè?
Jess: Wǒ méiyǒu shàngkè. Wǒ bìngle.
Hai: Nǐ shì shénme bìng? Nǐ kànle yīshēng méiyǒu?
Jess: Wǒ kànle yīshēng. Yīshēng shuō zhǐshì gǎnmào.

Hai: Nǐ chīle yào méiyǒu?
Jess: Wǒ wàngle. Xièxie nǐ tíxǐng wǒ.
Hai: Búyòng kèqì. Hǎohao xiūxi, bié zài zháoliáng le.
Jess: Xièxie!

Hai: *Jess, did you attend Chinese class yesterday?*
Jess: *No, I didn't. I was sick yesterday.*
Hai: *What was wrong with you? Did you see a doctor?*
Jess: *I did. The doctor said it was only a cold.*
Hai: *Have you taken any medicine?*
Jess: *I forgot to. Thank you for reminding me.*
Hai: *You're welcome. Get a good rest and don't catch a cold again.*
Jess: *Thanks!*

NOTES

The verb **wàng** means *to forget,* and it's usually used in combination with the particle **le.** This is similar to the English expression *I forgot* or *I've forgotten.*

Tíxǐng means *to remind.* In the set phrase **Xièxie nǐ tíxǐng wǒ** *(Thank you for reminding me),* there is no equivalent in Chinese for the English preposition *for* and the *-ing* form of *to remind.*

Notice that **zài** means *again* in **bié zài zháoliáng le** *(don't catch a cold again).* Even though this adverb **zài** is pronounced (and spelled in **pīnyīn**) the same way as the particle/preposition **zài,** it's not the same word in written Chinese. When **zài** is used as a particle or a preposition, its written character is 在. But when **zài** is used as an adverb meaning *again,* the written character is 再. There are words like this in English as well; words that have the same pronunciation but different meanings and spellings. For instance, *bear/bare, here/hear,* and *for/four.*

NUTS & BOLTS 2
ASKING QUESTIONS ABOUT COMPLETED ACTIONS WITH YǑU MÉIYǑU

You've already learned that you can change a statement into a yes/no question (simple question) by adding the particle **ma** at the end of the statement. This construction is used in everyday Chinese regardless of verb tense, and it applies to ongoing as well as completed actions. Here are a few examples that show how you can ask whether something happened in the past using the particle **ma**:

Tā qùle Niǔ Yuē.
He went to New York.

Tā qùle Niǔ Yuē ma?
Did he go to New York?

Wǒde tóngxué kànle yīshēng.
My classmate saw a doctor.

Nǐde tóngxué kànle yīshēng ma?
Did your classmate see a doctor?

Another way of asking whether an action has been completed is to add the phrase **yǒu méiyǒu** before the verb. This construction is used interchangeably with the **ma** construction.

Nǐ yǒu méiyǒu chī yào?
Did you take (your) medicine?

Tā yǒu méiyǒu qù yīyuàn?
Did he go to the hospital?

Nǐ bàba yǒu méiyǒu lā dùzi?
Did your father have diarrhea?

Nǐ bàba yǒu méiyǒu kàn yīshēng?
Did your father see a doctor?

Note that when **yǒu méiyǒu** is used to formulate a question about a past action, the particle **le** is not needed, since **yǒu méiyǒu** itself implies the past tense. However, if the **yǒu** is dropped and **méiyǒu** alone is used at the end of a question, the particle **le** is necessary to indicate a past action. The structure is: verb + **le** + **méiyǒu**, and the question can be translated into the present perfect tense *(have/has done)*.

Nǐ chīle yào méiyǒu?
Have you (already) taken your medicine?

Nǐ bàba kànle yīshēng méiyou?
Has your father seen a doctor?

To summarize, there are three distinct ways of asking questions about past actions in Chinese. The first two **(ma** and **yǒu méiyǒu)** are used interchangeably to inquire about a completed action. The third (verb + **le** + **méiyǒu)** is used when you want to question whether something has already happened.

1) **Tā qùle ma?**	*Did he go?*
2) **Tā yǒu méiyǒu qù?**	*Did he go?*
3) **Tā qùle méiyǒu?**	*Has he gone already?*

Note that when answering this last question in the negative, you must add the adverb **hái** *(still)* before **méiyǒu** + verb in your answer:

Tā hái méiyǒu qù.
He hasn't gone yet./He still hasn't gone.

PRACTICE 2

Pick the question from the column on the right that best fits an answer in the column on the left. Translate the question that you've chosen.

1. Wǒ méiyǒu shuìjiào.	a. Lǐbài sān tā yǒu méiyǒu qù yīyuàn?
2. Tāde péngyou méiyǒu lā dùzi.	b. Zhāng xiānsheng de línjū yǒu méiyǒu qù kàn yīshēng?
3. Wǒ hái méiyǒu mǎi xiézi.	c. Nǐmen yǒu méiyǒu hē jiǔ?
4. Zhāng xiānsheng de línjū méiyǒu qù kàn yīshēng.	d. Nǐ yǒu méiyǒu shuìjiào?
5. Chén tàitai méiyǒu chī yào.	e. Tāde péngyou yǒu méiyǒu lā dùzi?
6. Lǐbài sān tā méiyǒu qù yīyuàn.	f. Nǐ mǎile xiézi méiyǒu?
7. Tā jīntiān méiyǒu chīfàn.	g. Chén tàitai yǒu méiyǒu chī yào?
8. Wǒmen méiyǒu hē jiǔ.	h. Tā jīntiān yǒu méiyǒu chīfàn?

Culture note

In China, especially in rural areas where there has traditionally been a concern about having enough to eat, it is very common to hear people greet each other by asking **Nǐ chīfàn le ma?** *(Have you eaten yet?)* In reply to this question, people either answer **Chīle** *(Yes, I've eaten)* or **Hái méi chī** *(No, I haven't eaten yet).* However, this dialogue doesn't literally refer to the act of eating. It is instead a way of opening conversation when you meet a friend or relative.

Nǐ hǎo ma? and **Nǐ xiànzài zěnme yàng?** are two other popular ways of saying *Hello* in Chinese and are akin to the English expressions *How are you?* and *How are you doing?* respectively. While both of these greetings might seem to ask for information about someone's health, they are in fact inquiries into a person's overall mood or state of being. As in English, an equally general reply is expected. Consequently, in response to the phrase **Nǐ hǎo ma,** you would usually say **hǎo** *(fine/ok/great)*. You could also say **bú tài hǎo** *(not very good),* but this is not often heard when people meet for the first time. Likewise, you might typically reply to the greeting **Nǐ xiànzài zěnme yàng** by saying **bú cuò** *(pretty good).*

In fact, Chinese people generally don't mention personal health issues unless they are quite familiar with each other. This is especially true when it comes to sex-related health issues, which are still taboo in Chinese culture and are therefore rarely discussed in public. Most Chinese people are even highly uncomfortable talking to their doctors about these issues.

At the same time, the Chinese also pay a good deal of attention to traditional medicine and its treatments, which include **zhēnjiǔ** *(acupuncture),* **xuéwèi ànmó** *(acupressure),* and **bá huǒguàn** *(cupping).*

ANSWERS
PRACTICE 1: 1. f, Tāmen qù yīyuàn kàn yīshēng. (They go to the hospital to see a doctor.) **2.** b, Wǒde lǎoshī zài Zhōngguó jiāo Yīngwén. (My teacher teaches English in China.) **3.** e, Wǒmen zài wòfáng shuìjiào. (We sleep in the bedroom.) **4.** g, Tā qùle Zhōngguó. (He/She went to China.) **5.** a, Wǒde bízi hěn tòng. (My nose hurts.) **6.** c, Wǒmen lǐbài tiān zài xuéxiào chīfàn. (We eat at school on Sunday.) **7.** d, Niǔ Yuē Dà Xué. (New York University.)

PRACTICE 2: **1.** d, Nǐ yǒu méiyǒu shuìjiào? (Did you sleep?) **2.** e, Tāde péngyou yǒu méiyǒu lā dùzi? (Did his/her friend have diarrhea?) **3.** f, Nǐ mǎile xiézi méiyǒu? (Did you buy shoes?) **4.** b, Zhāng xiānsheng de línjū yǒu méiyǒu qù kàn yīshēng? (Did Mr. Zhang's neighbor go to see a doctor?) **5.** g, Chén tàitai yǒu méiyǒu chī yào? (Did Mrs. Chen take the medicine?) **6.** a, Lǐbài sān tā yǒu méiyǒu qù yīyuàn? (Did he/she go to the hospital on Wednesday?) **7.** h, Tā jīntiān yǒu méiyǒu chīfàn? (Did he/she eat today?) **8.** c, Nǐmen yǒu méiyǒu hē jiǔ? (Did you (pl.) drink wine?)

UNIT 5 ESSENTIALS

Qǐng zài shuō yí cì.

Please repeat that. (lit., Please say it once again.)

bù shūfu

do/does/did not feel well

zháoliáng

to catch a cold

fāshāo

to have a fever

Nǐde bàba xiànzài zěnme yàng?

How is your father doing now?

Bié qù.

Don't go.

Nǐ xuéle Zhōngwén duōjiǔ?

How long have you been studying Chinese?

Wǒ hěn lèi.

I'm very tired.

Wǒ hěn máng.

I'm very busy.

Wǒde bàba méiyǒu mǎi xīn chē.
My father didn't buy a new car.

Wǒde bàba hái méiyǒu mǎi xīn chē.
My father hasn't bought a new car yet.

Nǐ zài nǎli?
Where are you?

Nǐ chīfàn le ma?
Have you eaten yet?

Nǐ hǎo ma?
How are you?

Búyòng kèqì.
You're welcome.

UNIT 6
On the phone and making appointments

In this Unit, you'll learn how to tell time and how to make an appointment on the phone. You'll also learn key grammar, such as time expressions, the use of **shéi** (*who*), and the important verbs **qù** (*go*) and **lái** (*come*).

——————— Lesson 21 (words) ———————

WORD LIST 1
Here are some important words you will need to know to tell time in Chinese.

shízhōng	*clock*
shǒubiǎo	*watch*
zhōngtóu	*hour(s)*
fēnzhōng	*minute(s)*
fēn	*minute(s)*
miǎo	*second(s)*
diǎn	*o'clock*
kè	*quarter*
bàn	*half*
xiànzài	*now*
děng	*to wait*
dàyuē	*about*
zuǒyòu	*around*
chà (chà shí fēn yī diǎn)	*to, before (ten minutes to/before one o'clock)*

NUTS & BOLTS 1
TELLING TIME

To ask what time it is, use the expression **xiànzài jǐdiǎn?** *(what time is it now?)* By itself, **jǐdiǎn** simply means *what time?* or *when?*

To answer with a full hour, use the word **diǎn** right after the number. Don't forget that **liǎng** is used in place of **èr** to mean *two* when a noun is being counted or measured.

Xiànzài yī diǎn.
It's 1:00 now.

Xiànzài liǎng diǎn.
It's 2:00 now.

To answer with a half hour, use **bàn** *(half)* or **sānshí fēn** *(thirty minutes).*

si diǎn bàn	4:30
wǔ diǎn sānshí fēn	5:30

To answer with a quarter hour, use **yí kè** *(a quarter)* or **shí wǔ fēn** *(fifteen minutes).*

liǎng diǎn yí kè	2:15
wǔ diǎn shí wǔ fēn	5:15

To say that it's a quarter to or before a certain hour, use **sān kè** *(three quarters)* or **sìshí wǔ fēn** *(forty-five minutes).*

| yī diǎn sān kè | *1:45* |
| wǔ diǎn sìshí wǔ fēn | *5:45* |

To say that it's a certain number of minutes past the hour, just give that number. You can also use the word **fēn** *(minutes).*

| wǔ diǎn èrshí wǔ fēn | *5:25* |
| qī diǎn shí yī fēn | *7:11* |

If the number of minutes after the hour is less than ten, then you generally add the word **líng** *(zero)* before a single digit. For example:

| liù diǎn líng wǔ fēn | *6:05* |
| bā diǎn líng sān fēn | *8:03* |

If the number of minutes before the hour is ten or less, you can use the word **chà** *(to, before)* before the number of minutes. Notice that the entire **chà** phrase can come before or after the whole hour.

| qī diǎn chà jiǔ fēn | *6:51* |
| chà jiǔ fēn qī diǎn | *6:51* |

As you noticed in the Word list, there are two different words in Chinese that mean *minute(s).* The first, **fēnzhōng,** is used to talk about an amount of time (in minutes) that has passed. The second, **fēn,** is used to tell the time. **Fēn** and **fēnzhōng** are not interchangeable.

sān diǎn èrshí fēn	*3:20*
Wǒ dúle èrshí fēnzhōng.	*I've read for twenty minutes.*

Note that a measure word does not need to be placed between **fēnzhōng** and the quantifying number that precedes it.

As in English, *hours* and *o'clock* are also expressed in Chinese by two different words: **zhōngtóu** and **diǎn. Zhōngtóu** is used to talk about an amount of time (in hours) that has passed, and **diǎn** is used for telling time:

yī diǎn	*1:00*
Tā qùle yí ge zhōngtóu.	*She went for an hour.*

Note that in colloquial Chinese the measure word **ge** must be placed between **zhōngtóu** and the quantifying number that precedes it.

PRACTICE 1
Match the Chinese word in the column on the right to the English word in the column on the left.

1. *clock*	a. kè
2. *quarter*	b. shízhōng
3. *half*	c. děng
4. *o'clock*	d. zhōngtóu

5. *now*	e. bàn
6. *to wait*	f. diǎn
7. *hour*	g. chà
8. *to, before*	h. xiànzài

Now match the time to the correct expression in Chinese.

9. 1:30	a. liǎng diǎn líng yī fēn
10. 8:00	b. chà shí fēn liù diǎn
11. 4:15	c. liù diǎn shí fēn
12. 2:01	d. shí yī diǎn sìshí sì fēn
13. 7:45	e. bā diǎn
14. 6:10	f. sì diǎn yí kè
15. 5:50	g. yī diǎn bàn
16. 11:44	h. chà yí kè bā diǎn

WORD LIST 2
Here are more useful time expressions. You should already be familiar with some of them.

jīntiān	*today*
míngtiān	*tomorrow*
zuótiān	*yesterday*
qiántiān	*the day before yesterday*
hòutiān	*the day after tomorrow*
zhōngwǔ	*noon*

bànyè	*midnight*
yǐqián	*ago*
zhīqián	*before*
zhīhòu	*after*
jīntiān zǎoshang	*this morning*
jīntiān xiàwǔ	*this afternoon*
jīntiān wǎnshang	*tonight, this evening*
zǒngshì	*always*
cónglái méiyǒu	*never*
tōngcháng	*usually*
jīngcháng	*often, frequently*

NUTS & BOLTS 2
USE OF TIME EXPRESSIONS AND HUÌ

In English, time expressions are typically positioned after the verb, as in *I went to school yesterday*. In Chinese, though, time expressions such as **jīntiān** *(today)* and **zuótiān** *(yesterday)* come before the verb:

Wǒ jīntiān shàngxué.
I'm going to school today.

Wáng tàitai zuótiān qùle Měiguó.
Mrs. Wang went to the U.S. yesterday.

Zhāng lǎoshī hé xuésheng míngtiān zhōngwǔ chīfàn.
Teacher Zhang and (his) students will eat together at noon tomorrow.

Wǒmen jīngcháng qù kàn diànyǐng.
We often go to a movie.

It's also possible to place the time expressions at the beginning of the sentence, before the subject:

Jīntiān wǒ shàngxué.
Today I'm going to school.

Zuótiān Wáng tàitai qùle Měiguó.

Yesterday Mrs. Wang went to the U.S.

Míngtiān zhōngwǔ Zhāng lǎoshī hé xuésheng chīfàn.

Tomorrow at noon Teacher Zhang and (his) students will eat (lunch) together.

Where you place the time expression depends on what you want to emphasize. If you want to emphasize time, then you can put the time expression first, before the subject. If not, then the time word is generally placed after the subject, but before the verb.

The three examples above also show you something about time expressions and verb tense in Chinese. In English, verbs are inflected to show tense: *walks, walking, walked,* etc. As you know, however, Chinese verbs do not change form based on tense, or when the action is taking place. Instead, this job is done with particles, such as **le,** which you learned in Lesson 18, and time expressions. So for example, **chīfàn,** which means *to eat,* can be translated as *will eat* when it's used with a time expression like **míngtiān** *(tomorrow).*

Chinese does also have a kind of auxiliary verb like *will* to express the future: **huì.** Ordinarily, **huì** is used before the main verb to indicate the future tense when no other future time expression is used. But it's not necessary to add **huì** to a sentence when a time word such as **míngtiān** *(tomorrow)* or **hòutiān** *(the day after tomorrow)* is used:

Zhāng lǎoshī hé xuésheng huì zài jiā lǐ chīfàn.

Teacher Zhang and (his) students will eat at home.

Zhāng lǎoshī hé xuésheng hòutiān zài jiā lǐ chīfàn.

Teacher Zhang and (his) students will eat at home the day after tomorrow.

Zhīqián *(before)* and **zhīhòu** *(after)* are time expressions whose placement might be confusing to English speakers. Both of these words come after the time that they qualify (1:00 after) rather than before it (after 1:00), as is the order in English:

Tā míngtiān yī diǎn zhīqián huìlái.

He will come before one o'clock tomorrow.

Wǒ bànyè yī diǎn zhīhòu shuìjiào.

I go to bed after one o'clock in the morning (lit., one o'clock after midnight).

Yǐqián *(ago)* is a time expression that is used to specify events that took place in the (relatively) distant past. As in the case of **zhīqián** and **zhīhòu,** it is placed immediately after the period of time to which it refers:

Hěn jiǔ yǐqián tā mǎile zhè ge fángzi.

He bought this house a long time ago.

Wǒmen sān ge zhōngtóu yǐqián chīle fàn.

We ate three hours ago.

PRACTICE 2

Fill in the blanks by translating the words and phrases in parentheses. Then translate the complete sentences.

1. Wǒmen _____ *(yesterday)* qù kàn diànyǐng.

2. Nǐ _____ *(the day before yesterday)* yǒu méiyǒu shàngxué?

3. Wáng xiānsheng _____ *(tomorrow)* qù Zhōngguó.

4. _____ *(This morning)* wǒ méiyǒu chī.

5. Nà ge rén _____ *(tonight)* lái tiàowǔ.

6. Tā hé lǎoshī _____ *(tomorrow afternoon)* yóuyǒng.

7. Tāde línjū bā diǎn _____ *(after)* bú kàn diànshì.

8. Wǒmende xiǎogǒu liǎng diǎn _____ *(before)* xǐhuan chī xiāngjiāo.

Culture note

It's not appropriate to give a clock to a Chinese person on his or her birthday, especially if the person is elderly. This is because the expression *to give a clock as a gift* translates as **sòng zhōng** in Chinese, which sounds exactly the same as another expression that means *to bid farewell to someone at a funeral*. These expressions are of course written differently in Chinese, but the pronunciation is identical. You can imagine how the recipient might feel if he or she received such a gift!

ANSWERS

PRACTICE 1: 1. b; **2.** a; **3.** e; **4.** f; **5.** h; **6.** c; **7.** d; **8.** g; **9.** g; **10.** e; **11.** f; **12.** a; **13.** h; **14.** c; **15.** b; **16.** d

PRACTICE 2: 1. Wǒmen zuótiān qù kàn diànyǐng. (We went to a movie yesterday.) **2.** Nǐ qiántiān yǒu méiyǒu shàngxué? (Did you go to school the day before yesterday?) **3.** Wáng xiānshēng míngtiān qù Zhōngguó. (Mr. Wang will go to China tomorrow.) **4.** Jīntiān zǎoshang wǒ méiyǒu chī. (This morning I didn't eat.) **5.** Nà ge rén jīntiān wǎnshang lái tiàowǔ. (That person will come and dance tonight). **6.** Tā hé lǎoshī míngtiān xiàwǔ yóuyǒng. (He/She and his/her teacher will go swimming tomorrow afternoon.) **7.** Tāde línjū bā diǎn zhīhòu bú kàn diànshì. (His/Her neighbor doesn't watch TV after eight o'clock.) **8.** Wǒmende xiǎogǒu liǎng diǎn zhīqián xǐhuan chī xiāngjiāo. (Our puppy likes eating bananas before two o'clock.)

--------- Lesson 22 (phrases) ---------

PHRASE LIST 1

zhè ge xīngqī/lǐbài	*this week*
shàng ge xīngqī/lǐbài	*last week*
xià ge xīngqī/lǐbài	*next week*
zhè ge yuè	*this month*
shàng ge yuè	*last month*

xià ge yuè	*next month*
jīnnián	*this year*
qùnián	*last year*
míngnián	*next year*
qiánnián	*the year before last*
hòunián	*the year after next*
èr líng yī líng nián	*(year) 2010*
yī jiǔ jiǔ sān nián	*(year) 1993*

NUTS & BOLTS 1
MORE ON TIME EXPRESSIONS

Note that **nián** *(year)* and **tiān** *(day)* do not require an additional measure word when combined with **jīn**, **qù**, or **míng**. As was mentioned in Unit 3, this is because **nián** and **tiān** are themselves measure words. However, it is necessary to add a measure word when placing **zhè**, **shàng**, or **xià** before **xīngqī/lǐbài** *(week)* or **yuè** *(month)* because neither of these are measure words and therefore they require the addition of **ge**.

Please also note that *this, last,* and *next* are each translated into different Chinese words, depending on whether you are qualifying **nián** and **tiān** or **lǐbài** and **yuè**.

Wǒmen xià ge xīngqī zǒu.
We're leaving next week.

Míngnián wǒ qù Zhōngguó.
Next year I'll go to China.

Tāmen shàng ge yuè kànle nà ge diànyǐng.
They saw that movie last month.

PRACTICE 1

Choose the correct time expressions and then translate the complete sentences.

1. Wǒmen _____ (year before last) láile Zhōngguó.
   - a. qiánnián
   - b. qiántiān
   - c. hòuniàn

2. Tāde māo _____ (next month) qù yīyuàn.
   - a. shàng ge yuè
   - b. xià ge yuè
   - c. wǔ ge yuè

3. Zhāng tàitai _____ (this week) bú zuòfàn.
   - a. nà ge lǐbài
   - b. nǎ ge lǐbài
   - c. zhè ge lǐbài

4. Wǒde línjū de xiānsheng _____ (last year) mǎile yí liàng xīn chē.
   - a. míngnián
   - b. qùnián
   - c. qiánnián

5. Tā _____ (last week) bìngle, méiyǒu shàngxué.
   - a. xià ge lǐbài
   - b. shàng ge lǐbài
   - c. zhè ge lǐbài

6. Nǐde péngyou _____ (next year) qù Zhōngguó xué Zhōngwén.
   - a. míngnián
   - b. qùnián
   - c. qiánnián

7. Nǐmen _____ (last month) qùle nǎli?
   - a. jǐ ge yuè
   - b. shàng ge yuè
   - c. xià ge yuè

PHRASE LIST 2

yí huìr	*a while*
liǎng diǎn	*two o'clock*
sān diǎn bàn	*half past three*
wǔ diǎn yí kè	*a quarter past five*
wǔ diǎn shí wǔ fēn	*five fifteen*

liù diǎn sān kè	*a quarter to seven (lit., three quarters past six)*
liù diǎn sìshí wǔ fēn	*six forty-five*
chà yí kè qī diǎn	*a quarter to seven*
liǎng ge zhōngtóu	*two hours*
sān fēnzhōng	*three minutes*
Xià cì jiàn!	*See you next time!*
Děng huìr jiàn!	*See you later!*
Huítóu jiàn!	*See you soon!*
zhǔnshí	*on time*
shéi	*who*

NUTS & BOLTS 2
USE OF SHÉI (WHO)

By now, you've learned the question words **shénme** *(what)*, **jǐ** *(how many)*, **duōshao** *(how many/how much)*, **zěnme yàng** *(how)*, **nǎ** *(which)*, **duōjiǔ** *(how long)*, and **nǎli** *(where)*.

Now let's look at **shéi** *(who)*:

Nǐ shì shéi?

Who are you?

Nà ge rén shì shéi?

Who is that person?

Shéi shàng ge lǐbài qùle Měiguó?

Who went to the U.S. last week?

Shéi yǒu yí kuài qián?

Who has one yuan?

Don't forget that question words in Chinese don't "move." So, in Chinese, *who are you?* literally means *you are who?*

PRACTICE 2

Match each question from the column on the left to the best answer in the column on the right. Then translate the answers.

1. Qǐngwèn nǐ shì shéi?	a. Wǒ shí bā suì.
2. Nà ge rén shì shéi?	b. Shí kuài qián.
3. Nǐ jǐ suì?	c. Bú cuò. Nǐ ne?
4. Nǐ yǒu mèimei ma?	d. Nà ge rén shì wǒde gēge.
5. Nǐ zhù zài nǎli?	e. Wǒ zuì xǐhuan wǒde māma.
6. Zhè ge duōshǎo qián?	f. Wǒ shì Wáng Yǒu.
7. Nǐ zuì xǐhuan shéi?	g. Wǒ yǒu sān ge mèimei.
8. Nǐ zuìjìn zěnme yàng?	h. Wǒ zhù zài Shànghǎi.

ANSWERS

PRACTICE 1: 1. a, Wǒmen qiánnián láile Zhōngguó. (We came to China the year before last.) **2.** b, Tāde māo xià ge yuè qù yīyuàn. (His/Her cat will go to the hospital next month.) **3.** c, Zhāng tàitai zhè ge lǐbǎi bú zuòfàn. (Mrs. Zhang is not going to cook this week.) **4.** b, Wǒde línjū de xiānsheng qùnián mǎile yí liàng xīn chē. (My neighbor's husband bought a new car last year.) **5.** b, Tā shàng ge lǐbài bìngle, méiyǒu shàngxué. (He/She was sick last week and didn't go to school.) **6.** a, Nǐde péngyou míngnián qù Zhōngguó xué Zhōngwén. (Your friend will go to China to study Chinese next year.) **7.** b, Nǐmen shàng ge yuè qùle nǎli? (Where did you (pl.) go last month?)

PRACTICE 2: **1.** f, Wǒ shì Wáng Yǒu. (I'm Wang You.) **2.** d, Nà ge rén shì wǒde gēge. (That person is my elder brother.) **3.** a, Wǒ shí bā suì. (I'm 18 years old.) **4.** g, Wǒ yǒu sān ge mèimei. (I have three younger sisters.) **5.** h, Wǒ zhù zài Shànghǎi. (I live in Shanghai.) **6.** b, Shí kuài qián. ([It's] 10 yuan.) **7.** e, Wǒ zuì xǐhuan wǒde māma. (I like my mother the most.) **8.** c, Bú cuò. Nǐ ne? (Very well. How about you?)

─────────── **Lesson 23 (sentences)** ───────────

SENTENCE LIST 1

Let's look at some more time expressions having to do with the clock.

Xiànzài jǐdiǎn?	*What time is it now?*
Xiàwǔ yī diǎn.	*It's 1:00 pm.*
Xiàwǔ sì diǎn bàn.	*It's 4:30 pm.*
Wǎnshang liù diǎn sìshí wǔ fēn.	*It's 6:45 pm.*
Chà wǔ fēn qī diǎn.	*It's five to seven.*
Zǎoshang qī diǎn shí wǔ fēn.	*It's 7:15 am.*
Qī diǎn yí kè.	*It's a quarter past seven.*
Wǎnshang liùdiǎn.	*It's 6:00 pm.*
Zhōngwǔ shí èr diǎn.	*It's 12:00 pm.*
Zǎoshang jiǔ diǎn sānshí.	*It's 9:30 am.*
Shàngwǔ shí diǎn wǔshí wǔ fēn.	*It's 10:55 am.*
Wǎnshang liù diǎn líng sì fēn.	*It's 6:04 pm.*
Qī diǎn zhěng.	*It's 7 o'clock sharp.*
Chàbuduō bā diǎn.	*It's about 8:00.*

NUTS & BOLTS 1
More on telling time

Don't forget that you can ask the time with the question **xiànzài jǐdiǎn?** Literally, that phrase means *how many hours is it now?* In the answer, you don't need any kind of pronoun like *it*.

Yī diǎn.
(It's) 1:00.

Wǔ diǎn.
(It's) 5:00.

You can also use these types of expressions as adverbs to tell what time something happens. In English, you need the preposition *at* before the time expression, but in Chinese, simply use the time expression right before the verb:

Tā shí diǎn shuìjiào.
He sleeps at 10:00.

Wǒ shí yī diǎn sānshí fēn shuìjiào.
I sleep at 11:30.

Wǒ xiàwǔ sān diǎn yí kè qùle yīyuàn.
I went to the hospital at 3:15 pm.

Wǒ sān diǎn líng yī fēn zuò fēijī qù Shànghǎi.
I will take the plane to Shanghai at 3:01.

PRACTICE 1

Answer the following questions in Chinese:

1. Wáng xiānsheng jǐdiǎn shuìjiào? (10:30)

2. Tāmen jǐdiǎn shàngxué? (8:05)

3. Nǐmen jǐdiǎn chīfàn? (12:00)

4. Lǎoshī jǐdiǎn lái? (2:15)

5. Nǐde péngyou jǐdiǎn qù gōngzuò *(work)*? (9:00)

6. Māma jǐdiǎn qùle yīyuàn? (7:45)

SENTENCE LIST 2

Nǐ jǐdiǎn qù xuéxiào?	*What time are you going to school?*
Wǒ sān diǎn qù xuéxiào.	*I'm going to school at 3:00.*
Nǐmen shénme shíhou qù Zhōngguó?	*When are you going to China?*
Wǒmen míngtiān zǎoshang zuò fēijī qù Zhōngguó.	*We're taking a plane (to go) to China tomorrow morning.*
Tāde lǎoshī shénme shíhou bānle fángzi?	*When did his teacher move?*
Tāde lǎoshī qùnián bānle fángzi.	*His teacher moved last year.*
Nà ge rén shénme shíhou lái?	*When is that person coming?*
Tā dàyuē xià ge lǐbài lái.	*She is coming approximately next week.*

NUTS & BOLTS 2

SHÉNME SHÍHOU (WHEN)

The phrase **shénme shíhou** (*when*) is used in Chinese to ask when something will happen or when someone will do something. It is placed after the subject and before the main verb in a sentence.

Nǐmen shénme shíhou lái Niǔ Yuē?

When will you come to New York?

Nǐ shénme shíhou shàngxué?

When do you go to school? OR *When will you go to school?*

Tā shénme shíhou xiàkè?

When will she finish the class?

Tāmen shénme shíhou chī wǎn fàn?

When will they eat dinner?

PRACTICE 2
Translate the following sentences into Chinese.

1. *When will you go to China?*
2. *When/What time do you sleep?*
3. *When/What time do you go to school?*
4. *When did he buy the house?*
5. *When did they eat (a meal)?*
6. *When will you come?*
7. *When will your teacher come to New York?*

Tip!

Be careful when you translate *am* or *pm* into Chinese. While Westerners classify the hours between midnight and 11:59 in the morning as *am* and the hours between 12 noon and midnight as *pm*, the Chinese use a more extensive and varied set of time "zones" to break down a 24-hour period.

The hours that immediately follow 12 midnight, for example, are regarded as midnight or nighttime hours in China; whereas they are considered to be morning hours in the West. So, 1:00 am is therefore translated as **bànyè yī diǎn** *(1:00 after midnight)*. Here is the full set of words that are used in Chinese to specify a time period.

bànyè	*after midnight, midnight (lit., the middle of the night)*
zǎoshang	*before 10 am*
shàngwǔ	*after 10 am*
zhōngwǔ	*12 pm (noon)*
xiàwǔ	*before 6 pm*
wǎnshang	*after 6 pm*

ANSWERS

PRACTICE 1: 1. Wáng xiānsheng shí diǎn bàn shuìjiào. (Mr. Wang sleeps at 10:30.) **2.** Tāmen bā diǎn líng wǔ fēn shàngxué. (They go to school at 8:05.) **3.** Wǒmen shí èr diǎn chīfàn. (We eat at 12:00.) **4.** Lǎoshī liǎng diǎn shí wǔ fēn lái. (The teacher will come at 2:15.) **5.** Wǒde péngyou jiǔ diǎn qù gōngzuò. (My friend goes to work at 9:00.) **6.** Māma qī diǎn sān kè qùle yīyuàn. (My mother went to the hospital at 7:45.)

PRACTICE 2: 1. Nǐ shénme shíhou qù Zhōngguó? **2.** Nǐ shénme shíhou shuìjiào?/Nǐ jǐdiǎn shuìjiào? **3.** Nǐ shénme shíhou shàngxué?/Nǐ jǐdiǎn shàngxué? **4.** Tā shénme shíhòu mǎile fángzi? **5.** Tāmen shénme shíhòu chīle fàn? **6.** Nǐ shénme shíhòu lái? **7.** Nǐde lǎoshī shénme shíhòu lái Niǔ Yuē?

——————— Lesson 24 (conversations) ———————

CONVERSATION 1

Jess is calling Wang Hai on the phone. Wang Hai isn't at home, so Jess talks to his father instead.

Jess: Wèi, nín hǎo. Qǐngwèn Wáng Hǎi zài ma?

Hai de bàba: Nǐ hǎo. Tā gāng chūqùle. Wǒ shì tāde bàba. Nǐ shì nǎ yí wèi?

Jess: Wáng xiānsheng, nín hǎo. Wǒ shì tāde tóngxué Jié Xī.

Hai de bàba: Nǐ hǎo. Wǒ tīng guò nǐde míngzi. Tā shuō tā yǒu yí ge wàiguó tóngxué. Nǐ shì nǎguórén?

Jess: Wǒ shì Měiguórén.

Hai de bàba: Nǐde Zhōngwén búcuò. Xuéle duōjiǔ?

Jess: Wǒ zài Měiguó xuéle sì nián. Qùnián cái lái Zhōngguó. Wáng Hǎi jīngcháng bāng wǒ liànxí Zhōngwén.

Hai de bàba: Tā zuì ài bāngzhù biérén.

Jess: Qǐngwèn tā shénme shíhou huílái?

Hai de bàba: Tā gēn línjū qù dǎ qiú. Dàgài wǎnshang liù diǎn huílái chīfàn.

Jess: Máfan nín. Tā huílái de shíhou, qǐng tā gěi wǒ dǎ diànhuà.

Hai de bàba: Méi wèntí. Yǒukòng lái wǒmen jiā zuò zuo.

Jess: Hǎo. Xièxie. Zàijiàn.

Hai de bàba: Zàijiàn.

Jess: Hello. Can you please tell me if Wang Hai is at home?

Hai's father: Hello. He just went out. I'm his father. Who's calling?

Jess: How are you, Mr. Wang? I'm his classmate Jess.

Hai's father: How are you? I've heard your name before. Wang Hai told me he has a foreign classmate. Which country are you from?

Jess: I'm American.

Hai's father: Your Chinese is good. How long have you been studying?

Jess: I have studied Chinese for four years in the U.S. and came to China last year. Wang Hai often helps me practice my Chinese.

Hai's father: The thing he likes (lit., loves) most is to help people.

Jess: May I ask when he'll be back?

Hai's father: He went to play ball with some neighbors. He'll probably come back at six for dinner.

Jess: Could you please ask him to return my call when he comes back?

Hai's father: No problem. Please come visit us when you have free time.

Jess: Sure. Thanks. Goodbye.

Hai's father: Goodbye.

NOTES

Wèi means *hello* and is used when you pick up the telephone. It cannot be used to mean *hello* outside of a phone conversation, however.

Gāng is an adverb that means to have *just* done something. It's placed in front of the verb that it modifies:

Tā gāng zǒule.
He just left./He has just left.

Nǎ yí wèi is a polite form of *who (lit., which person)*. It's typically used in place of **shéi** *(who)* in telephone conversations where the person receiving the phone call does not know the caller.

Zhǎo means *to look for something or someone.*

Cái means *not until*, and it forms a link between a condition and a consequence. In the following example, **tā lái** *(he comes)* is the condition, and **wǒ qù** *(I go)* is the consequence. Notice that the conditional action comes before the consequence in Chinese, while in English the order is usually the reverse. Also notice that **cái** is placed before the verb in the consequence.

Tā lái wǒ cái qù.
I won't go until he comes.

Cái can also be used after conditions that are not full sentences, as in:

Nà ge xuésheng míngtiān cái lái shàngkè.
That student won't come to attend the class until tomorrow.

Another way to link two clauses is to use the expression **de shíhou** *(when/while)*. Note that while *when/while* is placed before the adverbial clause indicating time in English, in Chinese **de shíhou** is placed after the adverbial clause.

Wǒmen dǎ qiú de shíhou, tā jìnlái hē shuǐ.
While we were playing ball, he came in to drink some water.

Gēn means *and* in the sense of *along with someone*. It's often used in conjunction with **yìqǐ** *(together)* when two people perform the same action:

Wǒde māma gēn tāde māma yìqǐ qù mǎi dōngxi.

My mother and his mother are going together to buy things.

Yǒukòng means to *have free time*. It's a compound word that is made up of two parts: the verb **yǒu** *(to have)* and the noun **kòng** *(free time)*. **Kòng** literally means *empty* but in this context refers to **kòngxián shíjiān** *(free time)*. To say that someone is busy, you can use the negative form of **yǒukòng**, which is **méiyǒu kòng** or **méi kòng** *(do not have free time)*.

NUTS & BOLTS 1
USE OF GUÒ

You've already seen how the particle **le** is used in Chinese to indicate that an action has been completed, usually in the past. When used for this purpose, **le** is placed immediately after the main verb in a sentence.

Tā qùle Zhōngguó.

He went to China.

The word **guò** can also be used to show that an action has been completed. However, unlike **le** (which specifies a finite point in time when something ended), **guò** refers to the past in broader terms and indicates a past experience rather than a past event. It implies an unspecified time frame that stretches from the distant past up until the present, and is therefore usually translated into the present perfect tense in English.

Here are some examples that show the difference between **le** and **guò**:

Wǒ xuéle Zhōngwén liǎng nián.

I studied Chinese for two years.

Wǒ xué guò Zhōngwén.

I've studied Chinese before.

Tāde línjū qùle Zhōngguó.

His neighbor went to China.

Tāde línjū qù guò Zhōngguó.

His neighbor has been to China before.

Nǐ xiěle zì ma?

Did you write the characters?

–Wǒ xiěle.

–I did.

–Wǒ méiyǒu xiě.

–I didn't.

Nǐ xiě guò shūfǎ ma?

Have you ever written Chinese calligraphy before?

–Wǒ xiě guò.

–Yes, I have (written it before).

–Wǒ cónglái méiyǒu xiě guò.

–No, I've never written it before. OR *No, I haven't (ever written it before).*

Nǐmen kànle tāde shū méiyǒu?

Did you read his book?

–Wǒmen kànle.

–Yes, we did.

–Wǒmen hái méiyǒu kàn.

–No, we didn't read it yet.

Nǐmen kàn guò tāde shū méiyǒu?

Have you (ever) read his book before?

–Wǒmen kàn guò.

–Yes, we've read it already.

–**Wǒmen méiyǒu kàn guò.**

–*No, we haven't read it yet.*

Grammatically, **le** and **guò** share the same structural role when forming statements and questions. As you can see from the examples above, both appear next to the verb. However, in negation with **méiyǒu**, **le** is dropped, while **guò** is not.

PRACTICE 1

Complete each sentence by determining whether the blank should be replaced with (a) **guò**, (b) **le**, or (c) *nothing at all*. Then translate the full sentences.

1. Wǒmen méiyǒu qù _____ Zhōngguó.

2. Tāde tàitai zuótiān qù _____ Zhōngguó.

3. Nǐ qù _____ Zhōngguó méiyǒu?

4. Wǒ jīntiān méiyǒu _____ shàngxué.

5. Duìbuqǐ, tā gāng zǒu _____.

6. Nà zhī māo chī _____ sān tiáo yú.

7. Wáng xiānsheng qùnián mǎi _____ fángzi.

8. Wǒde shēngrì shì _____ sān yuè sān hào.

CONVERSATION 2

Wang Hai calls back and Jess asks him if he wants to go to a movie.

Jess: **Wèi, nín hǎo!**

Hai: **Wèi, Jié Xī, shì wǒ a, Wáng Hǎi. Wǒ bàba shuō nǐ gāngcái dǎ diànhuà lái. Yǒu shénme shì?**

Jess: **Nǐ míngtiān wǎnshang yǒukòng ma? Wǒ yǒu liǎng zhāng diànyǐng chóukuǎn de piào, shì Lǐ Ān de diànyǐng. Nǐ yǒu xìngqù ma?**

Hai: Wǒ kàn guò tā qítāde diànyǐng. Wǒ hěn
xǐhuan tāde diànyǐng.
Jess: Nà tài hǎo le. Wǒmen kěyǐ xiān chīfàn, ránhòu
qù kàn diànyǐng, zěnme yàng?
Hai: Hǎo. Dànshì wǒ míngtiān de kè hěn wǎn.
Diànyǐng jǐdiǎn kāishǐ?
Jess: Liù diǎn bàn kāishǐ. Zài xuésheng dàlóu
fàngyìng.
Hai: Wǒ liù diǎn cái xiàkè. Xiàkè zhīhòu, wǒ pǎo
guòlái zhǎo nǐ ba.
Jess: Zhēn bùhǎo yìsi. Ràng nǐ gǎn guòlái. Wǒmen
kàn wán diànyǐng zhīhòu cái chīfàn, zěnme
yàng?
Hai: Hǎo. Nà wǒmen míngtiān liù diǎn bàn jiàn.
Jess: Míngtiān jiàn.

Jess: Hello, how are you?
*Hai: Hi, Jess. It's me, Wang Hai. My father said that you
called. What's up?*
*Jess: Are you free tomorrow night? I have two fundraising
tickets to Ang Lee's movie. Are you interested in going?*
Hai: I've watched his other movies before. I like them a lot.
*Jess: That's great! We can eat first and then go to the movie.
What do you think?*
*Hai: Okay. But my class ends very late tomorrow. What
time does the movie start?*
Jess: 6:30. It's being shown in the student center.
*Hai: I won't finish class until 6:00. After class is over, I'll
run over to find you.*
*Jess: I'm really sorry to make you rush. After the movie,
we'll get something to eat. How's that?*
Hai: Okay. See you tomorrow at 6:30.
Jess: See you tomorrow.

NOTES

Notice that when Jess answers the telephone, she uses the polite
form of *you*, **nín,** even though Wang Hai is her friend. This is be-

cause she doesn't know yet who the caller is and therefore uses the formal **nín hǎo** rather than **nǐ hǎo,** which is used between people who are familiar with each other.

NUTS & BOLTS 2
LÁI *(TO COME)* AND QÙ *(TO GO)*
Lái *(to come)* and **qù** *(to go)* are two common verbs that can be used on their own, just as in English.

Wǒmen qù kàn diànyǐng.
We're going to a movie.

Wǒ zhè ge zhōumò qùle bówùguǎn.
I went to a museum this weekend.

Tāmen cóng Tái Wān lái.
They came from Taiwan.

Nǐ kěyǐ lái wǒ jiā wán ma?
Can you come and play at my home?

Both of these verbs can also be added as directional particles after another verb to indicate the direction that an action takes with regard to the physical location of the speaker. When the verb precedes **lái,** the action is shown to be toward the speaker. When the verb precedes **qù,** the action is away from the speaker.

Tā zǎoshang pǎo lái zhèlǐ, xiàwǔ pǎo qù nàli.
He runs here in the morning and runs there in the afternoon.

Tāmen kāichē lái wǒde jiā.
They are driving to my home.

Wǒmen kāichē qù tāde jiā.
We are driving to his home.

PRACTICE 2

Look over the second dialogue again and then determine whether the following sentences are *true* (**shì**) or *false* (**fēi**):

1. Wang Hai méiyǒu gěi Jess dǎ diànhuà.
2. Wang Hai méiyǒu kòng kàn diànyǐng.
3. Wang Hai méiyǒu kàn guò Lǐ Ān de diànyǐng.
4. Wang Hai hěn xǐhuan Lǐ Ān de diànyǐng.
5. Jess hé Wang Hai zài xuéxiào kàn diànyǐng.
6. Wang Hai míngtiān xiàwǔ sì diǎn xiàkè.

ANSWERS

PRACTICE 1: 1. a, Wǒmen méiyǒu qù guò Zhōngguó. (We haven't been to China before.) **2.** b, Tāde tàitai zuótiān qùle Zhōngguó. (His wife went to China yesterday.) **3.** a, Nǐ qù guò Zhōngguó méiyǒu? (Have you ever been to China before?) **4.** c, Wǒ jīntiān méiyǒu shàngxué. (I didn't go to school today.) **5.** b, Duìbuqǐ, tā gāng zǒule. (Sorry, he just left.) **6.** b, Nà zhī māo chīle sān tiáo yú. (That cat ate three fish.) **7.** b, Wáng xiānsheng qùnián mǎile fángzi. (Mr. Wang bought a house last year.) **8.** c, Wǒde shēngrì shì sān yuè sān hào. (My birthday is March 3.)

PRACTICE 2: 1. fēi (Wang Hai didn't call Jess back.); **2.** fēi (Wang Hai is not free to go to the movie.); **3.** fēi (Wang Hai hasn't watched Ang Lee's movies before.); **4.** shì (Wang Hai likes Ang Lee's movies a lot.); **5.** shì (Jess and Wang Hai will watch a movie at school.); **6.** fēi (Wang Hai will finish class at 4 pm.)

UNIT 6 ESSENTIALS

diǎn

o'clock

zhōngtóu

hour(s)

fēnzhōng
minute(s) (used to talk about the amount of time, in minutes, that has passed)

fēn
minute(s) (used to tell time)

miǎo
second(s)

Xiànzài jǐdiǎn?
What time is it now?

Yī diǎn.
(It's) 1:00.

Xià cì jiàn!
See you next time!

Děng huìr jiàn!
See you later!

Huítóu jiàn!
See you soon!

shénme shíhou
when

shéi
who

Wèi?
Hello? (on the phone)

Wǒ xuéle Zhōngwén liǎng nián.
I studied Chinese for two years.

Wǒ xué guò Zhōngwén.
I've studied Chinese before.

Wǒmen qù kàn diànyǐng.
We're going to a movie.

Tāmen kāichē lái wǒde jiā.
They are driving to my home.

UNIT 7
Asking directions

In this Unit, you'll learn how to ask directions and get around town. That means that you'll learn a lot of useful vocabulary for places and spatial relationships. You'll also learn some important new grammar for expressing direction, location, and so on.

————————— Lesson 25 (words) —————————

WORD LIST 1

càishìchǎng	*food market*
diànyǐngyuàn	*cinema, movie theater*
bǎihuò gōngsī	*department store*
fúzhuāng diàn	*clothing store*
shūdiàn	*bookstore*
jiāyòng diànqì diàn	*electronics store (lit., home appliances store)*
xiédiàn	*shoe store*
shāngdiàn	*shop, store*
gōngyuán	*park*
yóujú	*post office*
pàichūsuǒ	*police station*
fànguǎn/cānguǎn	*restaurant*
fàndiàn	*hotel*
huǒchēzhàn	*train station*
jīchǎng	*airport*
jiàotáng	*church*
yínháng	*bank*

| zhèlǐ | *here* |
| nàli | *there* |

NUTS & BOLTS 1
ZHÈLǏ *(HERE)* AND NÀLI *(THERE)*

You've already seen how the demonstrative pronouns **zhè** *(this)* and **nà** *(that)* combine with nouns with the help of measure words:

Zhè zhī bǐ shì wǒde.
This pen is mine.

Nà ge fángzi hěn dà.
That house is very big.

When these demonstrative pronouns are combined with **lǐ**, which literally means *place*, they become location expressions: **zhèlǐ** *(here)* and **nàli** *(there)*.

Keep in mind that **nàli** *(there)* is different from **nǎli** *(where)*, which you learned in Unit 5. Notice the difference in tones. **Nàli** comes from **nà** *(that)* while **nǎli** comes from **nǎ** *(which)*.

In formal speech, the full forms **zhèlǐ** and **nàli** are used to indicate location:

Wǒ zài zhèlǐ.
I'm here. (lit., I'm at this place.)

Tāde péngyou zài nàli.
His friend is over there (lit., His friend is at that place).

Nàli shì tāde jiā.
That's his home. (lit., That place is his home.)

In colloquial Chinese, these forms are usually expressed as **zhèr** and **nàr** respectively:

Wǒ zhù zài zhèr.
I live here.

Tāde péngyou zài nàr.
His friend is over there.

PRACTICE 1

Translate the following sentences from Chinese into English.

1. Nǐ shénme shíhou lái?
2. Wǒ lái zhèlǐ, nǐ qù nàli.
3. Wǒde shū zài nàli.
4. Zhèlǐ shì wǒde jiā.
5. Tā zài nàli chīfàn.
6. Wǒ qù nàli kàn diànyǐng.

WORD LIST 2

jiē	*street*
lùkǒu	*corner*
hónglǜdēng	*traffic light*
shízì lùkǒu	*intersection*
rénxíngdào	*sidewalk*
rénxíng dìdào	*underpass*
lìjiāoqiáo	*overpass*
chūzūchē	*taxi*
gōngchē	*bus*
gōngchēzhàn	*bus stop*
chē/qìchē	*car*
mótuōchē	*motorcycle*
zìxíngchē	*bicycle*
huǒchē	*train*
huǒchēzhàn	*train station*
dìtiě	*subway*
dìtiězhàn	*subway station*
chuán	*ship*

| fēijī | *airplane* |
| cóng | *from* |

NUTS & BOLTS 2
OTHER LOCATION EXPRESSIONS

Of course, **zhèlǐ** *(here)* and **nàli** *(there)* are not the only words used to indicate location. Here are some other location expressions that are a bit more specific:

qiánbiān	*in front of*
hòubiān	*behind*
pángbiān	*next to*
shàngbiān/shàng	*on*
lǐbiān/lǐ	*in, inside*
wàibiān	*outside*
xiàbiān/xià	*under*
zuǒbiān	*(on) the left side of*
yòubiān	*(on) the right side of*
zhōngjiān	*between*

Typically, these location words are used along with the preposition **zài** *(in, on, at)* to form larger, more specific location phrases. And just like time expressions, location expressions are always placed before the main verb.

When combined with **zài**, location words are usually preceded by a noun that helps to identify exactly where someone or something is situated. Occasionally, the noun can be omitted if you are indicating a general place or direction: **Tā zài wàibiān** *(He's outside)*. But usually, the noun is required to help specify a precise location: **Tā zài yínháng wàibiān** *(He's outside the bank)*. The resulting word pattern (**zài** + noun + location word) is the template upon which most location phrases are formulated in Chinese.

The following examples show how this grammatical construct is used to pinpoint the location of people, animals, and objects in a variety of contexts:

Nà zhī māo zài yǐzi xiàbiān.
The cat is under the chair.

Wǒde shū zài zhuōzi shàngbiān.
My book is on the table.

Tāde xuéxiào zài gōngyuán pángbiān.
His school is next to the park.

Wáng xiānsheng zài Zhāng xiǎojiě hòubiān.
Mr. Wang is behind Miss Zhang.

Tāmen zài wàibiān gōngzuò.
They are working outside.

Wǒ xiànzài zài jiālǐ xuéxí Zhōngwén.
I'm studying Chinese at home now.

Tāde māo xǐhuan zài shāfā shàng shuìjiào.
Her cat likes to sleep on the sofa.

Wǒde fángzi zài shāngdiàn yòubiān.
My house is on the right side of the shop.

Diànhuàjiān zài cānguǎn wàibiān.
The telephone booth is outside the restaurant.

Cèsuǒ zài wòshì lǐ.
The toilet is inside/in the bedroom.

Wǒde chē zài qiáo shàngbiān huàile.
My car broke down on the bridge.

Wǒ māma de bàngōngshì zài pàichūsuǒ pángbiān.
My mother's office is next to the police station.

Dìtiězhàn zài yóujú hé yínháng zhōngjiān.
The subway station is between the post office and the bank.

Note that, in the last example, **zhōngjiān** links two nouns, **yóujú** *(post office)* and **yínháng** *(bank)*. Whenever something is spatially located between two other things, their relationship is described in Chinese using the grammatical structure **zài** A **hé** B **zhōngjiān** *(lit., at A and B between)*.

When location and time expressions are both used in a sentence, the time expression usually comes first, then the location word, and finally the main verb. For example:

Wǒ měitiān qù gōngyuán pángbiān de xuéxiào shàngxué.
I go to school next to the park every day.

Nà ge xiǎo péngyou měitiān zài wǒmen fángzi qiánbiān wán.
That child plays in front of our house every day.

When a location word is used with a personal pronoun, the pronoun is traditionally followed by the particle **de: Tāde māma zài tā de qiánbiān** *(His mother is in front of him)*. The resulting word order assumes the following pattern: **zai** + pronoun + **de** + location word.

In this case, **de** turns **tā** into a possessive pronoun and the location word **qiánbiān** acts as a noun *(lit., (his) front)* rather than as a preposition *(in front)*. In colloquial conversation, however, **de** is usually dropped and the pronoun is used on its own: **Tāde māma zài tā qiánbiān** *(His mother is in front of him)*.

Here are some additional sentences that highlight how location words are used in combination with personal pronouns in Chinese:

Wǒde péngyou zài wǒ (de) pángbiān.
My friend is next to me.

Lǎoshī zhàn zài tāmen (de) hòubiān.
The teacher is standing behind them.

PRACTICE 2
Take a look at the following diagram, which shows eight people **zuò** *(sitting)* in two rows at a movie theater. Choose the appropriate location word in each of the following sentences.

Movie Screen			
Xiǎo Měi	Guó Zhōng	Měi Lì	Xīn Míng
Húng Huá	Zhèng Dōng	Xiù Chūn	Xué Míng

1. *Xiao Mei is sitting* _____ (qiánbiān/hòubiān/zuǒbiān) *Hung Hua.*

2. *Hung Hua is sitting* _____ (qiánbiān/hòubiān/zuǒbiān) *Zheng Dong.*

3. *Zheng Dong is sitting* _____ (zhōngjiān/hòubiān/zuǒbiān) *Hung Hua and Xiu Chun.*

4. *Mei Li is sitting* _____ (yòubiān/zhōngjiān/zuǒbiān) *Guo Zhong.*

5. *Xin Ming is sitting* _____ (yòubiān/zhōngjiān/zuǒbiān) *Mei Li.*

6. *Xiu Chun is sitting* _____ (pángbiān/zhōngjiān/qiánbiān) *Zheng Dong.*

7. *Xue Ming is sitting* _____ (qiánbiān/hòubiān/zuǒbiān) *Xin Ming.*

8. *Guo Zhong is sitting* _____ (yòubiān/zhōngjiān/zuǒbiān) *Xiao Mei.*

Tip!

The verb *to take (a form of transportation)* can be translated as **dā** or **zuò** in Chinese. Here are several examples of how these words are used to convey a sense of travel:

Wǒ měitiān zuò gōngchē shàngxué.
I take the bus to school every day.

Tā zuótiān zuò fēijī lái.
He came here by plane yesterday.

Wǒmen dā huǒchē shàngbān.
We go to work by train.

Lǎoshī bù xǐhuan dā dìtiě.
The teacher doesn't like to take the subway.

There is a subtle difference between **dā** and **zuò**. **Dā** is usually used when one takes public transportation, while **zuò** is used for both public and private transportation. To illustrate, if you take your friend's car to work, you would say **Wǒ zuò tāde chē shàngbān** (*I take his car to work*). But, if you take the subway, you would say **Wǒ dā dìtiě shàngbān** (*I take the subway to work*).

Please note that in cases where someone is going somewhere by bicycle, motorcycle, or horse, the verb **qí** is used rather than **dā** or **zuò**.

Wǒ qí zìxíngchē shàngbān.
I ride a bike to work./I go to work by bicycle.

Tā qí mǎ shàngxué.
He rides a horse to school.

ANSWERS

PRACTICE 1: 1. When will you come here? **2.** I'll come here. You go there. **3.** My book is over there. **4.** This is my home. (lit., Here is my home.) **5.** He/She is eating over there. **6.** I am going there to watch a movie.

PRACTICE 2: 1. qiánbiān; 2. zuǒbiān; 3. zhōngjiān; 4. yòubiān;
5. yòubiān; 6. pángbiān; 7. hòubiān; 8. yòubiān

───────── Lesson 26 (phrases) ─────────

PHRASE LIST 1

zài shāngdiàn wàibiān	*outside the shop*
zài lùkǒu	*on the corner*
zài cānguǎn lǐbiān	*in the restaurant*
zài nàli	*over there*
zài fùjìn	*it's nearby*
Yǒu duō yuǎn?	*How far?*
hěn jìn	*very near*
hěn yuǎn	*very far*
yǒu diǎn yuǎn	*a little further*
liǎng tiáo jiē	*two blocks*
zài fàndiàn pángbiān	*next to the hotel*
shàng chē	*to get on (a vehicle)*
xià chē	*to get off (a vehicle)*
zǒu lù	*on foot*
guò mǎlù	*to cross the street*
wènlù	*to ask directions (lit., to ask the road)*
kàn dìtú	*to read a map*

NUTS & BOLTS 1

YǑU DUŌ YUǍN? *(HOW FAR?)*

You've already learned a few question words with **duō** *(how)*, for
example **duōshǎo** *(how many/how much)* and **duōjiǔ** *(how long)*.
When talking about location and distance, a very useful question
phrase using **duō** is **yǒu duō yuǎn** *(how far)*. In Chinese, this
phrase is preceded by **cóng ... dào ...** *(from ... to ...)*, which indicates the two locations that determine the distance being measured. So the formula is: **Cóng** A **dào** B **yǒu duō yuǎn?** *(lit., From
A to B, how far is it?)*

For example:

Cóng zhèlǐ dào huǒchēzhàn yǒu duō yuǎn?
How far is it from here to the train station?

Cóng yínháng dào fànguǎn yǒu duō yuǎn?
How far is it from the bank to the restaurant?

Cóng zhèlǐ kāichē dào yīyuàn yǒu duō yuǎn?
How far is it from here to the hospital by car?

Cóng zhèlǐ zǒulù dào xuéxiào yǒu duō yuǎn?
How far is it from here to the school on foot?

Cóng zhèlǐ dào nà dào qiáng yǒu duō yuǎn?
How far is it from here to that wall?

To answer, simply replace **duō yuǎn** with a specified distance, measured in **mǐ** *(meters)* or **gōnglǐ** *(kilometers)*, or with a specific period of time:

Cóng zhèlǐ kāichē dào yīyuàn yǒu duō yuǎn?
How far is it from here to the hospital by car?

–Cóng zhèlǐ kāichē dào yīyuàn yǒu liǎng gōnglǐ.
–It's two kilometers from here to the hospital by car.

Cóng yínháng dào fànguǎn yǒu duō yuǎn?
How far is it from the bank to the restaurant?

–Cóng yínháng dào fànguǎn dàgài zǒu shí wǔ fēnzhōng.
–It takes about fifteen minutes to walk from the bank to the restaurant.

PRACTICE 1
Translate the following questions into Chinese:

1. *How far is it from the park to the bank?*
2. *How far is it from here to the post office?*

3. *How far is it from your home to the school?*

4. *How far is it from his school to the museum* (bówùguǎn)?

5. *How far is it from the hotel to the train station?*

6. *How far is it from here to the food market?*

7. *How far is it from here to the airport by car?*

8. *How far is it from your home to the bus stop?*

PHRASE LIST 2

yìzhí wǎng qián zǒu	*go straight ahead*
wǎng zuǒ zhuǎn	*turn left*
wǎng yòu zhuǎn	*turn right*
guǎi ge wān	*(turn) around the corner*
zài zuǒbiān	*to/on the left*
zài yòubiān	*to/on the right*
zhè biān	*this way*
duìmiàn	*across the street/on the other side of the street*
zài dàlóu qiánbiān	*in front of the building*
zài dàlóu hòubiān	*behind the building*
zài fùjìn	*around there*
zài yínháng hé yóujú zhōngjiān	*between the bank and the post office*
zài qiáo shàngbiān/shàng	*on the bridge*

NUTS & BOLTS 2

EXPRESSING DIRECTION OR MOTION WITH LOCATION PHRASES

You've already learned a lot of ways of expressing location in Chinese: **qiánbiān** *(in front of)*, **hòubiān** *(behind)*, **zuǒbiān** *(left side)*, **yòubiān** *(right side)*, **wàibiān** *(outside)*, **lǐbiān** *(inside)*, **shàngbiān** *(on)*, **pángbiān** *(next to)*, and **zhōngjiān** *(between)*.

Don't forget that these location expressions are usually used along with **zài** *(in, at, on)*, and they're placed immediately after the object noun, rather than before it as in English. In other words, the English phrase *in front of the bus stop* would be translated literally as *the bus stop in front of* in Chinese, or zài gōngchēzhàn qiánbiān.

Here are some examples to show you how this word pattern (zài + noun/pronoun + location word) is typically used in Chinese:

Tā zài yínháng qiánbiān děng nǐ.
He's waiting for you in front of the bank.

Huǒchēzhàn zài yínháng hòubiān.
The train station is behind the bank.

You can also express direction or motion with location phrases. To do so, you must use them in sentences containing dynamic verbs that indicate an activity is taking place in or around the location.

For example, the phrase **zài yínháng hòubiān** *(behind the bank)* can be used in Chinese to describe a state of being or static sense of location: **Tā zài yínháng hòubiān** *(He's behind the bank)*. But it can also describe direction or motion when immediately followed by a verb that denotes kinetic action: **Tā zài yínháng hòubiān zǒu** *(He's walking behind the bank)*. As you can see, direction or motion is expressed by placing the location phrase in a sentence whose word pattern is: subject + zài + (noun) + location word + verb.

Here are some additional examples that show how this works:

Tā zài (mǎlù) duìmiàn zǒu.
He's walking on the opposite side of the street.

Tāmen zài gōngyuán pángbiān kāichē.
They're driving next to/alongside the park.

Tā zài jiàoshì lǐ shuìjiào.

She slept in the classroom.

Nà tiáo gǒu zài fángzi wàibiān pǎo.

The dog ran outside of the house.

Wǒ zài xuéxiào pángbiān děng nǐ.

I'll wait for you next to the school.

Nǐ bǎ yǐzi fàng zài zhuōzi hé diànshì zhōngjiàn.

You put the chair between the table and the television.

PRACTICE 2

Translate the words in parentheses and fill in the blanks to describe the location of each person in the following sentences:

1. Huáng xiānsheng zài Huáng tàitai _____ *(next to)* tiàowǔ.

2. Měilì zhàn zài wǒde _____ *(in front of)*.

3. Tāde jiā _____ *(behind)* méiyǒu gōngyuán.

4. _____ *(left side)* shì wèishēngjiān.

5. Yínháng zài fànguǎn _____ diànyǐngyuàn _____ *(between)*.

6. Wǒde péngyou zài xuéxiào _____ *(inside)* yóuyǒng.

7. Lǎoshī zài _____ *(outside)* děng zhe wǒmen.

8. Nà tiáo gǒu zài zhuōzi _____ *(under)* shuìjiào.

ANSWERS

PRACTICE 1: 1. Cóng gōngyuán dào yínháng yǒu duō yuǎn?
2. Cóng zhèlǐ dào yóujú yǒu duō yuǎn? **3.** Cóng nǐ(de) jiā dào xuéxiào yǒu duō yuǎn? **4.** Cóng tāde xuéxiào dào bówùguǎn yǒu duō yuǎn? **5.** Cóng fàndiàn dào huǒchē zhàn yǒu duō yuǎn? **6.** Cóng zhèlǐ dào càishìchǎng yǒu duō yuǎn? **7.** Cóng zhèlǐ kāichē dào jīchǎng yǒu duō yuǎn? **8.** Cóng nǐ(de) jiā dào gōngchē zhàn yǒu duō yuǎn?

PRACTICE 2: 1. Huáng xiānsheng zài Huáng tàitai pángbiān tiàowǔ. (Mr. Huang is dancing next to Mrs. Huang.) **2.** Měilì zhàn zài wǒde qiánbiān. (Meili is standing in front of me.) **3.** Tāde jiā hòubiān méiyǒu gōngyuán. (There is no park behind his/her house.) **4.** Zuǒbiān shì wèishēngjiān. (There is a toilet on the left side.) **5.** Yínháng zài fànguǎn hé diànyǐngyuàn zhōngjiān. (The bank is between the restaurant and the cinema.) **6.** Wǒde péngyou zài xuéxiào lǐ/lǐbiān yóuyǒng. (My friend is swimming inside the school.) **7.** Lǎoshī zài wàibiān děng zhe wǒmen. (The teacher is waiting for us outside.) **8.** Nà tiáo gǒu zài zhuōzi xiàbiān/xià shuìjiào. (That dog is sleeping under the table.)

--- **Lesson 27 (sentences)** ---

SENTENCE LIST 1

Qǐngwèn xǐshǒujiān zài nǎli?	*May I ask where the restroom is?*
Huǒchēzhàn zài nǎli?	*Where's the train station?*
Zuì hǎo de fànguǎn zài nǎli?	*Where's the best restaurant?*
Wǒ zài nǎ ge zhàn xià chē?	*At what stop do I get off?*
Bówùguǎn zài nǎli?	*Where's the museum?*
Zài nǎli mǎi piào?	*Where are (the) tickets sold? (lit., Where to buy tickets?)*
Wǒ zài nǎli huàn chē?	*Where do I change trains/subways/buses?*
Huǒchēzhàn zài yóujú qiánbiān.	*The train station is in front of the post office.*
Fàndiàn zài jiàotáng hòubiān.	*The hotel's behind the church.*
Gōngchēzhàn zài qiáo xiàbiān.	*The bus stop is under the bridge.*
Dōngfāng Lù zài nǎli?	*Where is Dongfang Road?*
Tā zài fáng lǐ.	*She's in the room.*
Wáng tàitai zhù zài Shànghǎi.	*Mrs. Wang lives in Shanghai.*
Wǒ xiànzài zài Měiguó.	*I'm in the U.S. now.*

NUTS & BOLTS 1
USING LǏ AND ZÀI IN LOCATION EXPRESSIONS

As you have seen, **zài** on its own is a "catch-all" preposition that can be translated as *in, to, on, at,* and so on, depending on context. **Zài** is used with location phrases and the question word **nǎli** *(where)*. It can also be used on its own with geographical locations, such as cities and countries.

Wǒ xiànzài zài Měiguó.

I'm in the U.S. now.

Tāmende dàxué zài Hāěrbīn.

Their university is in Harbin.

However, if you want to emphasize that something is contained within a given space, you can add **lǐ** (which also means *in*) to **zài**. This is similar to the English distinction between *in* and *inside* or *within*. Note that the word order is **zài** + noun + **lǐ**.

Tā zài fáng lǐ.

She is inside the room.

Yàoshi zài hézi lǐ.

The keys are inside the box.

Háizimen zài chē lǐ./Háizimen zài chē shàng.

The children are inside the car./The children are in the car. (lit., The children are on the car.)

PRACTICE 1
Let's review basic location expressions. Re-arrange the following words and phrases so that they form meaningful sentences in Chinese.

1. shàngkè/wǒde lǎoshī/zài bówùguǎn
2. měitiān/nà ge rén/chīfàn/zài zhèlǐ

3. měi ge lǐbài sān/tā hé péngyou/tiàowǔ/zài nàli
4. shuìjiào/zài zhèlǐ/shéi/?

SENTENCE LIST 2

Shāngdiàn pángbiān yǒu liǎng jiā yínháng.	*There are two banks next to the shop.*
Yǒu méiyǒu piányi de lǚguǎn?	*Is there an inexpensive hotel?*
Fùjìn yǒu méiyǒu yīyuàn?	*Is there a hospital nearby?*
Zài zhèli yǒu méiyǒu gōngchē qù Běijīng Lù?	*Is there a bus to Beijing Road from here?*
Zhèlǐ yǒu méiyǒu Zhōngguó fànguǎn?	*Are there any Chinese restaurants here?*
Wǒ jiā fùjìn méiyǒu yóujú.	*There is no post office near my home.*
Bówùguǎn qiánbiān yǒu diànhuàtíng.	*There is a telephone booth in front of the museum.*
Gōngchēzhàn méiyǒu rén.	*Nobody is at the bus stop./There are no people at the bus stop.*
Wǒde fángzi hòubiān yǒu yí ge gōngyuán.	*There is a park behind my house.*
Zhè ge fángzi yǒu liǎng ge dà wòfáng, yí ge xiàndàihuà de chúfáng.	*There are two big bedrooms and one modern kitchen in this house.*
Lóuxià yǒu rén zhǎo nǐ.	*Someone is looking for you downstairs.*

NOTES:
The indefinite pronoun *someone/somebody* is usually translated as **yǒu rén** in Chinese, which literally means *there is a person*.

NUTS & BOLTS 2
YǑU *(THERE IS/THERE ARE)*
You already know that **yǒu** *(to have)* can indicate possession in Chinese. But as several of the examples above demonstrate, **yǒu** can also mean *there is* or *there are*. In other words, **yǒu** can also indicate the existence of something.

There's a difference in usage to keep in mind, though. When the subject of **yǒu** is a personal pronoun or a living object, then **yǒu** is being used to indicate possession and can be translated as *to have*. But if the subject is a place or a location phrase, then **yǒu** is being used to indicate existence and can be translated as *there is* or *there are*. Take a look at this contrast:

Wǒ yǒu liǎng zhī māo.

I have two cats.

Zhuōzi shàng yǒu liǎng zhī māo.

There are two cats on the table.

Here are some more examples of the existential **yǒu**. Don't forget that the negative of **yǒu**, both as a possessive and an existential, is **méiyǒu**.

Zhèlǐ yǒu yì jiā fēicháng hǎo de cānguǎn.

There's a great restaurant here.

Zhèlǐ méiyǒu Zhōngguórén.

There are no Chinese people here.

Zhè ge chéngshì méiyǒu hǎo de bówùguǎn.

There's no good museum in this city.

Zhōngguó yǒu lǎohǔ ma?

Are there any tigers in China?

Yínháng lǐ yǒu tíkuǎnjī ma?

Is there an ATM at the bank?

Two quantity phrases that you may want to use with the existential **yǒu** are: **hěn duō** (*a lot, many, much*) and **yì diǎndiǎn** (*a few, a little*), which literally means *very few*.

Nǐde shūjià shàng yǒu hěn duō CD.

There are a lot of CDs on your shelf.

Bēizi lǐ zhǐ yǒu yì diǎndiǎn shuǐ.

There is only a little water in the glass.

PRACTICE 2

Give the Chinese translation of each of the English sentences in parentheses, using the existential **yǒu** or **méiyǒu** as appropriate. A partial Chinese translation is already given.

1. xuéxiào qiánbiān gōngchē zhàn. *(There is a bus stop in front of the school.)*

2. lù shàng hěn duō chē. *(There are a lot of cars on the road.)*

3. zhuōzi pángbiān liǎng bǎ yǐzi. *(There are two chairs next to the table.)*

4. tāde fángzi hòubiān yì kē shù. *(There is a tree behind his house.)*

5. yǐzi xiàbiān sān běn shū. *(There are three books under the chair.)*

6. jiàoshì lǐbiān xuésheng. *(There is no student in the classroom.)*

7. huǒchēzhàn rén. *(There are no people at the train station./Nobody is at the train station.)*

ANSWERS

PRACTICE 1: 1. Wǒde lǎoshī zài bówùguǎn shàngkè. (My teacher attends class at the museum.) **2.** Nà ge rén měitiān zài zhèlǐ chīfàn. (That person eats here every day.) **3.** Tā hé péngyou měi ge lǐbài sān zài nàli tiàowǔ. (He/She and his/her friends dance there every Wednesday.) **4.** Shéi zài zhèlǐ shuìjiào? (Who sleeps here?)

PRACTICE 2: 1. Xuéxiào qiánbian yǒu gōngchēzhàn. **2.** Lù shàng yǒu hěn duō chē. **3.** Zhuōzi pángbiān yǒu liǎng bǎ yǐzi. **4.** Tāde fángzi hòubiān yǒu yì kē shù. **5.** Yǐzi xiàbiān yǒu sān běn shū. **6.** Jiàoshì lǐbiān méiyǒu xuésheng. **7.** Huǒchēzhàn méiyǒu rén.

CONVERSATION 1
Listen as Jess asks directions.

> Jess: Láojià, qǐngwèn Guāngmíng Lù zěnme zǒu?
> Lùrén: Nín yìzhí wǎng qián zǒu, zài dì sì ge lùkǒu
> wǎng zuǒ zhuǎn, zǒu sān ge lùkǒu. Guāngmíng
> Lù jiù zài nínde yòubiān.
> Jess: Xièxie!
> Lùrén: Búkèqì.

(Jess zhōngyú zhǎo dào le Guāngmíng Lù.)

> Jess: Láojià, qǐngwèn yī lù gōngchēzhàn zài nǎli?
> Lùrén: Nín kànjiàn qiánbiān nà zuò báisè de dàlóu
> ma? Gōngchēzhàn jiù zài nà zuò dàlóu de
> qiánbiān.
> Jess: Xièxie!

(Jess zhōngyú zhǎo dào le gōngchēzhàn.)

> Jess: Láojià, wǒ yào qù zhè ge dìzhǐ, qǐngwèn wǒ zài
> nǎ yí zhàn xiàchē?
> Lùrén: Nín zài dì wǔ ge zhàn xiàchē.
> Jess: Xièxie!

> Jess: *Excuse me, may I ask how to get to Guangming Road?*
> Passerby: *Go straight ahead. Turn left at the fourth intersection*
> *and walk three blocks. Guangming Road is on your*
> *right hand side.*
> Jess: *Thank you!*
> Passerby: *You're welcome.*

(Jess finally finds Guangming Road.)

>   Jess: *Excuse me, may I ask where the number one bus stop is?*
>
> Passerby: *Do you see the white building ahead? The bus stop is in front of the building.*
>
>   Jess: *Thank you!*

(Jess finally locates the bus stop.)

>   Jess: *Excuse me, I need to go to this address. At which stop should I get off?*
>
> Passerby: *You get off at the fifth stop.*
>
>   Jess: *Thank you!*

NOTES

Remember that **láojià** means *excuse me,* and can be used to get someone's attention if you want to ask a question.

Lùkǒu literally means *mouth of the road.* It can be translated as either *intersection* or *block.*

NUTS & BOLTS 1
CÓNG . . . DÀO *(FROM . . . TO . . .)*
In Lesson 26, you learned how to use **cóng . . . dào . . .** *(from . . . to . . .)* with the question phrase **yǒu duō yuǎn** *(how far)* and in answers indicating a specific distance or time.

However, **cóng . . . dào . . .** can also be used on its own and without a reference to a specified time or distance.

Simply combine **cóng** *(from)* with the word **dào** *(to)* to form the expression **cóng** A **dào** B *(from A to B).*

Cóng zhèlǐ dào huǒchēzhàn zěnme zǒu?
How do I get to the train station from here? (lit., From here to the train station how (to) go?)

Cóng fēijīchǎng dào fàndiàn zěnme zǒu?

How do I get to the hotel from the airport?

Tāmen cóng Chéngdū bān dào Chóngqìng.

They moved from Chengdu to Chongqing.

PRACTICE 1
Translate the following sentences into English:

1. Cóng huǒchēzhàn dào nǐde jiā yǒu duō yuǎn?
2. Cóng xuéxiào dào dìtiězhàn zěnme zǒu?
3. Cóng zhèlǐ dào yīyuàn yǒu duō yuǎn?
4. Cóng wǒde jiā dào xuéxiào yǒu sān gōnglǐ.
5. Cóng fàndiàn dào yínháng yǒu duō yuǎn?
6. Cóng yóujú dào càishìchǎng zěnme zǒu?
7. Cóng zhèlǐ wǎng yòu zhuǎn.

CONVERSATION 2
Jess asks Wang Hai how to get to Jinshan Park. She also wants his recommendation for a good Chinese restaurant.

> **Jess:** Wáng Hǎi, nǐ zài zhèlǐ zhùle duō jiǔ?
> **Hai:** Wǒ cóng sān suì kāishǐ zhù zài zhèlǐ, xiànzài chābùduō yǒu shíbā nián le.
> **Jess:** Nǐ shénme dìfang yě huì qù ma?
> **Hai:** Dāngrán.
> **Jess:** Wǒ míngtiān qù Jīnshān Gōngyuán jiàn yí ge péngyou, nǐ zhīdào zěnme qù ma?
> **Hai:** Nǐ cóng zhèlǐ zuò sān lù gōngchē, dào Rénmín Dàshà ménkǒu xiàchē, ránhòu huàn dìtiě, zài Jīnshān Yīyuàn xiàchē. Jīnshān Gōngyuán jiù zài yīyuàn de pángbiān.
> **Jess:** Cóng zhèlǐ zuò gōngchē dào Jīnshān Gōngyuán yǒu duō yuǎn?

Hai: Dàgài èrshí fēnzhōng. Nǐ bú huì kàn bú jiàn.
Jess: Jīnshān Gōngyuán fùjìn yǒu cānguǎn ma? Wǒ xiǎng gēn péngyou zài nàli chī wǔfàn.
Hai: Cóng gōngyuán wǎng zuǒ zǒu, guòle qiáo, mǎlù duìmiàn shì yí zuò báisè de dàlóu. Nǐ huì kànjiàn Jīnshān Cānguǎn. Tāmende cài búcuò, érqiě jiàqián bú guì.

Jess: *Wang Hai, how long have you been living here?*
Hai: *I've been living here since I was three. It's almost been 18 years now.*
Jess: *Are you familiar with every part of the city? (lit., Do you know how to go everywhere?)*
Hai: *Of course.*
Jess: *I'm going to see a friend in Jinshan Park tomorrow. Do you know how to get there?*
Hai: *You take the number three bus from here and get off in front of the Renmin Building. Then you transfer to the subway and get off at Jinshan Hospital. Jinshan Park is next to the hospital.*
Jess: *How long does it take to get to Jinshan Park from here?*
Hai: *About twenty minutes. You can't miss it.*
Jess: *Is there a restaurant near the park? I want to have lunch there with my friend.*
Hai: *From the park, walk left and cross over a bridge; across the street, there is a white building. You will see Jinshan Restaurant. The food there is good, and (what's more) it's not expensive.*

NOTES
Zhīdào is a verb that means *to know a fact/to know something*. To say that you know a book, a movie, or a person in the sense of being familiar with it, use **rènshi**.

Let's look at other verbs that can be translated as *to know*:

Wǒ zhīdào zěnme qù nàli.
I know how to get there.

Wǒ hěn shúxī zhèlǐ./Wǒ hěn shúxī zhè ge qū.
I know this neighborhood very well. (lit., I'm very familiar with here/this area.)

Wǒ huì shuō yì diǎndiǎn Zhōngwén.
I know how to speak a little Chinese.

Kāishǐ is a verb meaning *to start.* You can use it along with another verb.

Huǒchē kāi le.
The train started to move.

Tāmen kāishǐ jiǎng le.
They began talking.

Kāishǐ xiàyǔ le.
It started to rain.

Chābùduō is an adverb that means *almost.* When combined with **yǒu,** it means *approximately* or *about,* as in the phrase **chābùduō yǒu liù suì** *(approximately/about six years old).*

Huàn means *to change.* Placed before a form of transportation such as a car, bus, train, etc., it means to transfer from one vehicle to another. For example:

Wǒ zài zhèlǐ huàn gōngchē.
I transfer to the bus here.

Érqiě is a conjunction that means *moreover* or *what's more* . . . You can use it when you're adding information to something that you've just said.

NUTS & BOLTS 2
SHÌ *(TO BE)*

As you know, the verb **shì** means *to be*. Like **yǒu,** it's often used to express existence:

Wǒde xuéxiào qiánbiān shì yì tiáo hěn kuān de mǎlù.
There is a very wide road in front of my school.

Nà ge fángzi hòubiān shì yì tiáo hé.
There is a river behind the house.

Lóuxià shì zhěnsuǒ.
There is a clinic downstairs.

Note the word order in these sentences. In Chinese, location phrases precede the verb **shì,** and the subject comes at the end of each sentence. So, **nà ge fángzi hòubiān shì yì tiáo hé** translates literally as *that house behind (there) is a river.* Also note that the verb **yǒu** can be substituted for **shì** in the three examples above. You have the choice of saying either **lóuxià shì zhěnsuǒ** or **lóuxià yǒu zhěnsuǒ.**

But **shì** and **yǒu** are not always interchangeable, and there is a fundamental difference between the two. Basically, it all comes down to whether you're asserting the existence of one or more things. **Shì** can only be used to assert the existence of one thing, as in the three examples above. **Yǒu** can also assert the existence of one thing.

Nà ge fángzi hòubiān shì yì tiáo hé.
There is a/one river behind the house.

Nà ge fángzi hòubiān yǒu yì tiáo hé.
There is a/one river behind the house.

But if you're talking about the existence of two or more things, you can only use **yǒu.**

Nà ge fángzi hòubiān yǒu sān tiáo hé.

There are three rivers behind the house.

Lóuxià yǒu sān jiā zhěnsuǒ.

There are three clinics downstairs.

Wǒde bàngōngshì fùjìn yǒu liǎng jiā hěn hǎo de cānguǎn.

There are two good restaurants near my office.

PRACTICE 2

Rewrite the following sentences by substituting **shì** for **yǒu** where possible. Write the letter *N* next to those sentences where a substitution cannot be made.

1. Fángzi qiánbiān yǒu yí ge gōngyuán.
2. Gōngyuán qiánbiān yǒu sān kē shù.
3. Qiáo xiàbiān yǒu yì tiáo hé.
4. Fàndiàn zuǒbiān yǒu yì tiáo hěn cháng de jiē.
5. Huǒchē shàng yǒu hěn duō rén.
6. Zhōngguó yǒu hěn duō rén.

Culture note

When speaking to people outside your family, it is impolite to approach or interrupt them without using certain polite forms of speech in Chinese. For example, if you're asking for directions or for help, it is customary to start your request with the words **láojià** (*excuse me*) and **qǐngwèn** (*may I ask*): **Láojià, qǐngwèn nín huǒchēzhàn zài nǎli?** (*Excuse me, may I ask where the train station is?*) Likewise, if you don't understand or didn't hear what someone said and want them to repeat it, you need to begin your request with the word **duìbuqǐ**, which means *I'm sorry*: **Duìbuqǐ, qǐng zài shuō yí cì** (*I'm sorry, please say it again*). Generally, these words are considered too formal or too polite to be used among family members and close friends, so they are usually reserved only for addressing strangers or people with whom you do not have a close relationship.

ANSWERS

PRACTICE 1: 1. How far is it from the train station to your home? **2.** How can I get to the subway station from the school? **3.** How far is it from here to the hospital? **4.** It's three kilometers from my home to the school. **5.** How far is it from the hotel to the bank? **6.** How can I get to the food market from the post office? **7.** Turn right (from) here.

PRACTICE 2: 1. Fángzi qiánbiān shì yí ge gōngyuán. **2.** N. **3.** Qiáo xiàbiān shì yì tiáo hé. **4.** Fàndiàn zuǒbiān shì yì tiáo hěn chǎng de jiē. **5.** N. **6.** N.

UNIT 7 ESSENTIALS

Láojià.

Excuse me.

Gōngchēzhàn zài qiáo xiàbiān.

The bus stop is under the bridge.

Yàoshi zài hézi lǐ.

The keys are inside the box.

Wǒ xiànzài zài Měiguó.

I'm in the U.S. now.

Bówùguǎn qiánbiān yǒu diànhuàtíng.

There is a telephone booth in front of the museum.

Yǒu méiyǒu piányi de lǚguǎn?

Is there an inexpensive hotel?

Lóuxià yǒu rén zhǎo nǐ.

Someone is looking for you downstairs.

Zhèlǐ méiyǒu Zhōngguórén.

There are no Chinese people here.

Wǒ hěn shúxī zhèlǐ./Wǒ hěn shúxī zhè ge qū.

I know this neighborhood very well. (lit., I'm very familiar with here/this area.)

Cóng fēijīchǎng dào fàndiàn zěnme zǒu?

How do I get from the airport to the hotel?

Wǒ zhīdào zěnme qù nàli.

I know how to get there.

Tāmen kāishǐ jiǎng le.

They began talking.

Wǒ zài zhèlǐ huàn gōngchē.

I transfer to the bus here.

Nà ge fángzi hòubiān shì yì tiáo hé.

There is a river behind the house.

Wǒde bàngōngshì fùjìn yǒu liǎng jiā hěn hǎo de cānguǎn.

There are two good restaurants near my office.

UNIT 8
At a restaurant

In this Unit, you'll learn vocabulary words and expressions that will come in handy when you want to order food in a restaurant. You'll also add to your knowledge of Chinese grammar by learning how to make suggestions, give commands, and form requests. Plus, you'll learn how to express what you want, and how to ask negative questions.

So, let's get started!

──────────── Lesson 29 (words) ────────────

WORD LIST 1

zǎocān	*breakfast*
wǔcān	*lunch*
wǎncān	*dinner, supper*
yèxiāo/xiāoyè	*late night snack*
tiándiǎn	*dessert*
kāfēi	*coffee*
chá	*tea*
qìshuǐ	*soda*
niúnǎi	*milk*
táng	*sugar*
shíwù	*food*
guǒzhī	*juice*
píjiǔ	*beer*
jiǔ	*wine, alcohol*
hújiāo	*pepper*
yán	*salt*

jiàngyóu	*soy sauce*
jièmo	*mustard*
là	*hot, spicy*
lěng	*cold*
hǎochī	*delicious*

NUTS & BOLTS 1
MAKING SUGGESTIONS: HǍO MA?

When you want to make a suggestion or recommendation in Chinese, you typically place the phrase **hǎo ma?** at the end of a declarative sentence.

Hǎo ma? can be translated as *what do you think?* or *is that okay with you?* or other similar expressions. Here are some examples to illustrate how this works:

Zánmen qù chī Rìběn cài, hǎo ma?
Let's go eat Japanese food. Is that okay with you?

Nǐ míngtiān qù kàn yīshēng, hǎo ma?
Go see a doctor tomorrow, okay?

Notice that these phrases can be translated into English as suggestions with *let's*, as softened commands, and so on.

Zánmen is an inclusive way of saying *we* or *us* in Chinese, implying *you and I* or *all of us* as opposed to *just us and not you*. For example: *You and I, we are going to China* (inclusive) vs. *We are going to China, but you are not* (exclusive). **Zánmen** is often translated as *let's* and is used mostly in Beijing and other parts of northern China.

If you agree with a suggestion that uses **hǎo ma,** use the phrase **hǎo.** If you disagree, however, your answer depends on the suggestion. One option is to use the phrase **wǒ bù xiǎng** *(I don't want)*. For example, if you disagree with the first suggestion listed above, you could say **wǒ bù xiǎng chī Rìběn cài** *(I don't want to eat Japanese food)*. If the suggestion is **zánmen qù kàn zhè ge diànyǐng, hǎo ma?** *(let's go see this movie, okay?)*, you could say **wǒ bù xiǎng kàn zhè ge diànyǐng** *(I don't want to go see this movie)*.

Zánmen qù nà jiā xīn cānguǎn, hǎo ma?

Let's go to the new restaurant, okay?

-Hǎo ba.

-Yes, let's go.

-Wǒ bù xiǎng qù nà jiā xīn cānguǎn.

-No, I don't want to/I'd rather not go to the new restaurant.

PRACTICE 1
Translate the following suggestions into Chinese.

1. *Let's eat Chinese food tonight. What do you think?*

2. *Let's dance, shall we?*

3. *Let's take the bus, okay?*

4. *Let's go to a movie tomorrow, okay?*

5. *Let's go over there, shall we?*

6. *Let's go swimming next Monday. Is that okay with you?*

7. *Let's watch TV together, okay?*

WORD LIST 2

tāng	*soup*
ròu	*meat*
niúpái	*steak*
niúròu	*beef*
zhūpái	*pork chop(s)*
jī	*chicken*
jīròu	*chicken meat (boneless)*
huǒtuǐ	*ham*

yú	*fish*
xiā	*shrimp*
lóngxiā	*lobster*
dàn	*egg(s)*
shūcài	*vegetables*
bāoxīncài	*cabbage*
hóngluóbo	*carrot*
qíncài	*celery*
huángguā	*cucumber*
mǎlíngshǔ/tǔdòu	*potatoes*
shālā	*salad*
miàntiáo	*noodles*
diǎnxīn	*dim sum*
shuǐguǒ	*fruit*
miànbāo	*bread*
huángyóu	*butter*

NUTS & BOLTS 2
MORE COMMANDS AND REQUESTS

You learned in Lesson 17 that a command can be formed in Chinese simply by using a verb without any subject in a sentence. You can soften the tone of a command by using the particle **ba** after the verb.

Zǒu!

Leave! (Get out!)

Zǒu ba.

Leave. (Go ahead and leave.)

Shuì!

Sleep!

Shuì ba.

Go to sleep.

As you know, negative commands are formed by adding **bié** (or **búyào**) in front of the verb.

Bié shuì ba.
Don't sleep.

Bié zǒu!
Do not leave!

Bié děng le. Nǐ xiān chī ba.
Don't wait. You eat first.

You can also form a third-person command in Chinese by putting **ràng . . . ba** around a declarative sentence. This phrase can be translated into English as *let . . .*

Ràng tā kàn nǐde shū ba.
Let him see/read your book.

Ràng tāmen xiān zǒu ba.
Let them go first.

Ràng nǐde nǚ'ér xiān chī ba.
Let your daughter eat first.

PRACTICE 2
Translate the following commands into Chinese.

1. *Let's dance.*

2. *Let your daughter and her friend go to that restaurant this Sunday.*

3. *You eat first.* (softer tone)

4. *Let them go to school to study Chinese.*

5. *Give him two yuan.* (softer tone)

6. *Go to sleep.* (softer tone)

7. *Let's go swimming tomorrow.*

8. *Leave.* (softer tone)

ANSWERS

PRACTICE 1: **1.** Zánmen jīntiān wǎnshang chī Zhōngguó cài, hǎo ma? **2.** Zánmen tiàowǔ, hǎo ma? **3.** Zánmen zuò gōngchē, hǎo ma? **4.** Zánmen míngtiān (qù) kàn diànyǐng, hǎo ma? **5.** Zánmen qù (zài) nàli, hǎo ma? **6.** Zánmen xià ge xīngqī/lǐbài yī qù yóuyǒng, hǎo ma? **7.** Zánmen yìqǐ kàn diànshì, hǎo ma?

PRACTICE 2: **1.** Zánmen tiàowǔ ba. **2.** Ràng nǐde nǚ'ér hé tāde péngyou zhège xīngqī rì qù nà jiā cānguǎn ba. **3.** Nǐ xiān chī ba. **4.** Ràng tāmen qù xuéxiào xué Zhōngwén ba. **5.** Gěi tā liǎng kuài qián ba. **6.** Shuì ba. **7.** Zánmen míngtiān qù yóuyǒng ba. **8.** Zǒu ba.

──────────── Lesson 30 (phrases) ────────────

PHRASE LIST 1

yì bǎ dāo	*a knife*
yì zhī tāngchí/sháozi	*a spoon*
yì zhī chāzi	*a fork*
yì bēi kāfēi	*a cup of coffee*
yì bēi chá	*a cup of tea*
yì bēi nǎichá	*a cup of milk tea (tea with milk)*
yì tiáo cānjīn	*a napkin*
yí ge pánzi	*a plate*
yí ge bēizi	*a cup/glass*
yì shuāng kuàizi	*a pair of chopsticks*
yì wǎn tāng	*a bowl of soup*
yí kuài miànbāo	*a piece of bread*
yì píng jiǔ	*a bottle of wine*
yì píng hóngjiǔ	*a bottle of red wine*
yì píng báijiǔ	*a bottle of white spirits*

yì bēi jiǔ	*a glass of wine*
yì wǎn mǐfàn	*a bowl of rice*
yì hé niúnǎi	*a carton of milk*
yí guàn mógu	*a can of mushrooms*
yì bāo mǐ	*a bag of rice*
yì bāo miàn	*a bag of noodles*
yì xiāng fāngbiànmiàn	*a box of instant noodles*

NUTS & BOLTS 1
MODAL VERBS

A modal verb is a verb that you can use along with another verb, as in <u>want</u> to eat or <u>must</u> learn. **Yào** *(to want/need)* and **xiǎng** *(to want/would like)* can both be used as modal verbs in Chinese to express a willingness to do something or a wish for something to happen. As the following examples demonstrate, the verb **yào** indicates a stronger sense of desire:

Wǒ yào zhù zài xuéxiào fùjìn.

I (really) want to live near school.

Wǒ xiǎng hē yì bēi kāfēi.

I'd like to drink a cup of coffee.

Tā xiǎng yào yì bēi chá.

He wants to have a cup of tea.

Note that **yào** can be used as both a main verb (meaning *to have* or *to need)* or as a modal verb (meaning *to want)* in Chinese. In the third example above, **yào** is the main verb, and **xiǎng** is the modal verb. Combined, they mean *want(s) to have.*

Another common modal verb is **kěyǐ,** which means *can, may* or *to be able to* in the sense of being permitted or allowed to do something. The modal verb **néng(gòu),** on the other hand, is used to mean *can* or *to be able to* when referring to one's ability or proficiency in performing an action.

Here are some examples that illustrate how these modal verbs are used in Chinese:

Wǒmen xiànzài kěyǐ chī le. Měi ge rén dōu lái le.
We can eat now. Everyone has arrived.

Wǒ nénggòu zài wǔ fēnzhōng zhīnèi chī wán liǎng wǎn miàntiáo.
I can eat two bowls of noodles in five minutes.

Tā jīntiān wǎnshang bù néng lái le.
He can't come tonight. (He won't be able to come tonight.)

Wǒ kěyǐ cháng dào zhè ge cài lǐbiān yǒu jiāng.
I can taste ginger in this dish.

Nǐ huì zhǔ Zhōngguó cài ma?
Can you cook Chinese food?

Wǒ huì kāichē. Dànshì, yīnwèi wǒ méiyǒu jiàzhào, suǒyǐ wǒ bù kěyǐ kāichē.
I can drive. But, since I don't have a license, I can't drive.

Note that in the last two examples, *can* is translated as **huì** in Chinese when it means *know how to*. Also note that when **néng(gòu)** is negated by adding the negative particle **bù**, the resulting verb form **bù néng(gòu)** is always shortened to **bù néng**.

Bìxū is another commonly used modal verb in Chinese. It is translated as *have to* or *must* and is used to indicate necessity or an obligation to do something.

Wǒ xiànzài bìxū kāishǐ zuòfàn le.
I have to start cooking now.

Wǒmen bìxū duō mǎi yìxiē zhūròu zuò wǎnfàn. Wǒmen jiā lǐ de ròu bú gòu le.
We have to buy more pork for dinner. We don't have enough meat at home. (lit., Our home doesn't have enough meat.)

PRACTICE 1

Translate the following sentences into Chinese:

1. *I would like to have a glass of wine.*
2. *I don't feel well. I can't drink coffee.*
3. *I want to go to China next year.*
4. *I'd like to have a knife.*
5. *I would like to drink soup.*
6. *Can you give me some tea?*
7. *He wants to go to a movie tomorrow night.*
8. *We must buy more beef today.*

PHRASE LIST 2

Gěi wǒ . . .	*Bring me . . . /Give me . . .*
Wǒ xiǎng yào . . .	*I would like to have . . .*
Nǐ kěyǐ gěi wǒ . . . ma?	*May I have . . . ? (lit., Could you give me . . . ?)*
yìxiē shuǐguǒ	*some fruit*
Zài gěi wǒ yì tiáo cānjīn.	*(Give me) another napkin. (lit., Give me a napkin again.)*
Zài gěi wǒ yí ge chāzi hé yì bǎ dāo.	*(Give me) another fork and knife. (lit., Give me a fork and a knife again.)*
zài lái yì píng jiǔ	*another bottle of wine*
zài lái yìdiǎn nà ge	*a little more of that*
zài lái yìdiǎn miànbāo	*a little more bread*
zài lái yìdiǎn ròu	*a little more meat*
Nǐmen yǒu . . . ?	*Do you have . . . ?*
Wǒ yào . . .	*I need/want . . .*
Nǐ yào . . . ?	*Do you need/want . . . ?*
Máfan nǐ gěi wǒmen . . .	*Please bring us . . .*
Qǐng nǐ jiézhàng!	*Check please!*

NUTS & BOLTS 2
Negative questions

As in English, Chinese questions can be posed both in the affirmative and in the negative forms:

Nǐ xǐhuan yú ma?
Do you like fish?

Nǐ bù xǐhuan yú ma?
Don't you like fish?

To answer a negative question in English, you have a choice between showing agreement *(No, I don't.)* and disagreement *(Yes, I do!).* In Chinese, however, these answers take on a different form. To show agreement, start with the positive word **shì** *(yes),* and then repeat the (negative content of the) question, so that you literally reply: *Yes, I don't like fish.* To show disagreement, start with the negative phrase **bú shì** *(no),* and follow it with a sentence that rephrases the question in a positive way, so literally: *No, I like fish.* You may find this pattern confusing, because it's quite the opposite of English. But if you think about it, it's really very logical!

Nǐ bù xǐhuan yú ma?
Don't you like fish?

–Shì. Wǒ bù xǐhuan yú.
–No, I don't like fish. (lit., Yes. I don't like fish.)

–Bú shì. Wǒ xǐhuan yú.
–Yes, I like fish. (lit., No. I like fish.)

PRACTICE 2
Translate the answers in parentheses into Chinese:

1. Nǐ bù chī zǎocān ma? *(No, I don't eat breakfast.)*
2. Nǐ bù chī zǎocān ma? *(Yes, I do eat breakfast.)*

3. Tāmen bù qù xuéxiào ma? *(No, they don't go to school.)*

4. Tāmen bù qù xuéxiào ma? *(Yes, they do go to school.)*

5. Nǐde māma méiyǒu zuòfàn ma? *(Yes, my mother did cook.)*

6. Nǐde māma méiyǒu zuòfàn ma? *(No, my mother didn't cook.)*

7. Nà ge Měiguórén bú huì shuō Zhōngwén ma? *(Yes, that American does know how to speak Chinese.)*

8. Nà ge Měiguórén bú huì shuō Zhōngwén ma? *(No, that American doesn't know how to speak Chinese.)*

ANSWERS

PRACTICE 1: 1. Wǒ xiǎng yào yì bēi jiǔ. **2.** Wǒ bù shūfu. Wǒ bù néng hē kāfēi. **3.** Wǒ míngnián yào qù Zhōngguó. **4.** Wǒ xiǎng yào yì bǎ dāo. **5.** Wǒ xiǎng hē tāng. **6.** Nǐ kěyǐ gěi wǒ yìxiē chá ma? **7.** Tā míngtiān wǎnshang yào kàn diànyǐng. **8.** Wǒmen jīntiān bìxū duō mǎi yìxiē niúròu.

PRACTICE 2: 1. Shì. Wǒ bù chī zǎocān. **2.** Bú shì. Wǒ chī zǎocān. **3.** Shì. Tāmen bù qù xuéxiào. **4.** Bú shì. Tāmen (huì) qù xuéxiào. **5.** Bú shì. Wǒde māma zuòle fàn. **6.** Shì. Wǒde māma méiyǒu zuòfàn. **7.** Bú shì. Nà ge Měiguórén huì shuō Zhōngwén. **8.** Shì. Nà ge Měiguórén bú huì shuō Zhōngwén.

--------------------- **Lesson 31 (sentences)** ---------------------

SENTENCE LIST 1

Gěi wǒ yì bēi chá hé yìxiē chūnjuǎn.	Bring me a cup of tea and some spring rolls.
Qǐng nǐ gěi wǒ liǎng fèn zǎocān.	May I have breakfast for two?/Please give me breakfast for two.
Qǐng nǐ gěi wǒ càidān.	May I have a menu?/Please give me a menu.
Máfan nǐ gěi wǒ yìxiē hújiāo.	Could you give me some pepper (please)?
Nǐmen yǒu shénme hē de?	What do you have to drink?

Qǐng nǐ ná yí ge chāzi gěi wǒ.	*May I have a fork?/Please give me a fork.*
Nǐ zěnme zhǔ zhè ge ròu?	*How do you cook the meat?*
Nǐ kěyǐ jiāo wǒ zěnme yòng kuàizi ma?	*Can you teach me how to use chopsticks?*
Wǒ xiǎng zài yào yì wǎn mǐfàn.	*I would like to have another bowl of rice.*
Qǐng bú yào fàng tài duō yóu.	*Please don't put too much oil (in it).*
Wǒ shì chīsù de.	*I'm a vegetarian.*
Wǒ kěyǐ shuā kǎ ma?	*Can I pay by credit card?*

NUTS & BOLTS 1
POLITE REQUESTS

As you know, it is polite to add the word **qǐng** *(please)* before a request or command. You can also add **qǐng nǐ/nín** to the beginning of a sentence in order to say *Please . . .* or *May I . . .*

Qǐng nín gěi wǒ nínde míngpiàn.
May I have your business card?/Please give me your business card.

Qǐng nǐ gěi wǒ yì bēi rè kāishuǐ.
May I have a glass of hot water?/Please give me a glass of hot water.

Another common way to make a polite request in English is to use the conditional *could.* In Chinese, this is done by using **máfan nǐ/nín,** which literally means *to bother you.* It can be translated as *could you . . . ?* in English.

Máfan nǐ gěi wǒ yì bēi chá hé yìxiē chūnjuǎn.
Could you bring me a cup of tea and some spring rolls (please)?

Máfan nǐ gěi wǒ yìxiē hújiāo.
Could you give me some pepper (please)?

PRACTICE 1

Translate the following sentences into Chinese.

1. *May I have a bowl of noodles?*
2. *May I have two bottles of wine?*
3. *Could you give me some butter?*
4. *May I have a napkin?*
5. *May I have a menu?*
6. *Could you give me a pair of chopsticks?*

SENTENCE LIST 2

Nǐ hē de tài kuài.	*You're drinking too quickly.*
Tāmende cài zuò de fēicháng hǎo.	*Their dishes are very good.*
Nǐ ná kuàizi ná de búcuò.	*You handle chopsticks very well. (lit., You hold chopsticks pretty well.)*
Wǒde māma shāocài shāo de hěn hǎo.	*My mother cooks very well.*
Zhè ge cānguǎn de chúshī shāocài shāo de bù hǎo.	*The chef in this restaurant doesn't cook well.*
Tā měi dùn fàn dōu chī de tài kuài.	*He eats too fast at every meal.*
Tā gēn tāde xiānsheng shēnghuó de hěn kuàilè.	*She lives happily with her husband.*
Niúròu zhǔ de tài lǎo le.	*The beef is (cooked) too tough.*
Niúròu zhǔ de hěn nèn.	*The beef is (cooked) very tender.*
Chá tài tàng le. Tā děi hē de hěn xiǎoxīn.	*The tea is too hot. He needs to drink it carefully.*

NUTS & BOLTS 2

ADVERBIAL EXPRESSIONS WITH DE

So far, you have learned the use of the particle **de** with possessives and adjectives. There's also an adverbial particle **de,** which is used between a verb and an adjective to form an adverbial expression that describes how an action is performed. **De** is always placed immediately after the verb in this construction. In colloquial Chinese, the adverbs **hěn** *(very)* or **tài** *(too)* are commonly added before the adjective in this type of sentence. Here are some examples:

Tā chī de hěn kuài.
He eats very quickly.

Nǐ shuō de hěn hǎo.
You speak very well.

Nǐde māma shuō de tài kuài.
Your mother speaks too fast.

If an object follows the verb, then the verb needs to be repeated, and the object must be placed between the duplicated verbs in the following manner: verb + object + duplicated verb + **de**.

Wǒ shuō Zhōngwén shuō de hěn bù hǎo.
I don't speak Chinese very well. (lit., I speak Chinese not very well.)

Tā chī tiándiǎn chī de hěn kuài.
He eats dessert very quickly.

With verb-object verbs, this means that just the verb **(tiào)** is repeated, not the full two-syllable verb-object verb **(tiàowǔ)**.

Note that the **de** (得) that is used adverbially is written differently in Chinese characters from the **de** (的) used with possessives and adjectives, although both have the same pronunciation.

PRACTICE 2
Translate the following sentences into Chinese.

1. *I like to eat vegetables.*
2. *My mother cooks very well.*
3. *Her student speaks Chinese very well.*
4. *He walks very slowly.*
5. *My teacher speaks very fast.*
6. *You eat fish too quickly.*
7. *She doesn't dance too well.*
8. *I drink too slowly.*

ANSWERS
PRACTICE 1: 1. Qǐng nǐ gěi wǒ yì wǎn miàntiáo. **2.** Qǐng nǐ gěi wǒ liǎng píng jiǔ. **3.** Máfan nǐ gěi wǒ yìxiē huángyóu. **4.** Qǐng nǐ gěi wǒ yì tiáo cānjīn. **5.** Qǐng nǐ gěi wǒ càidān. **6.** Máfan nǐ gěi wǒ yì shuāng kuàizi.

PRACTICE 2: 1. Wǒ xǐhuan chī shūcài. **2.** Wǒ(de) māma zuòfàn zuò de hěn hǎo. **3.** Tāde xuésheng shuō Zhōngwén shuō de hěn hǎo. **4.** Tā zǒu de hěn màn. **5.** Wǒde lǎoshī shuō de hěn kuài. **6.** Nǐ chī yú chī de tài kuài. **7.** Tā tiàowǔ tiào de bú tài hǎo. **8.** Wǒ hē de tài màn.

––––––––––– Lesson 32 (conversations) –––––––––––

CONVERSATION 1
Jess and her friend Hai are going to a Chinese restaurant to have lunch.

> **Jess:** Wǒ yǒu diǎn è le. Wǒmen qù nǎli chīfàn?
> **Hai:** Nǐ xǐhuan chī Zhōng cài háishì xī cài?

Jess: Wǒ xǐhuan chī Zhōng cài. Nà jiā cānguǎn kàn qǐlái búcuò. Wǒmen jiù zài nàli chīfàn ba.

Hai: Hǎo ba.

(Tāmen zài zhuōzi pángbiān zuò xiàlái.)

Hai: Nǐ xǐhuan diǎn shénme dōngxi? Jīròu háishì niúròu?

Jess: Wǒ ài chī sùcài hé báiròu, bǐrú jīròu huòzhě yú. Tāmen yǒu shālā ma?

Hai: Zhōng cānguǎn shì méiyǒu shālā de. Rúguǒ nǐ xǐhuan cài de huà, wǒmen kěyǐ diǎn yì dié chǎocài, zěnme yàng?

Jess: Hǎo. Méi wèntí.

Jess: *I'm hungry. Where should we go to eat?*

Hai: *Do you want Chinese or Western food?*

Jess: *I like Chinese food. That place looks pretty good. Let's go there to eat.*

Hai: *Alright.*

(They sit at a table.)

Hai: *What would you like to order? Chicken or beef?*

Jess: *I like (lit., love) vegetable dishes and white meat, like chicken or fish. Do they have salad?*

Hai: *Chinese restaurants don't have salad. If you like vegetables, we could order a stir-fried dish, how's that?*

Jess: *Okay. That's fine.*

NUTS & BOLTS 1

HUÒZHĚ/HÁISHÌ *(OR)*

In Chinese, two different words, **huòzhě** and **háishì,** are used to express the concept of *or.* **Huòzhě** is usually used to form statements, linking two nouns or larger phrases:

Wǒ huì qù Shànghǎi huòzhě Běijīng.
I'll go to Shanghai or Beijing.

Nǐ hē huòzhě wǒ hē dōu kěyǐ.
Either you or I can drink it. (lit., You drink or I drink, both are fine.)

In questions, either **háishì** or **huòzhě** may be used, but they don't mean quite the same thing. **Háishì** is used in questions that suggest a preference for one choice or the other.

Nǐ xǐhuan wǒ háishì tā?
Do you like me or him?

Nǐ jīntiān qù háishì míngtiān qù?
Do you go today or tomorrow?

Nǐ xǐhuan píngguǒ háishì júzi?
Do you like apples or oranges?

When **huòzhě** is used in questions, the implication is that there is no preference between one choice and the other, or that there is no control over the choice. For example, you could ask about items on a menu using **huòzhě**. You would also use **huòzhě** to ask about states of being over which there is no control:

Càidān yǒu mǐfàn huòzhě miàntiáo ma?
Is there rice or noodles on the menu?

Nǐ juéde lěng huòzhě rè ma?
Do you feel cold or hot?

PRACTICE 1
Translate the following sentences into Chinese.

1. *Do you want chicken (meat) or beef?*
2. *I'll go to China in January or March.*

3. *Are you British or American?*

4. *Do you want to eat noodles or bread?*

5. *I would like to have a bowl of rice or a bowl of noodles.*

6. *Do you have a fork or spoon?*

7. *I can eat meat or vegetables. (Either is fine.)*

8. *Shall I pay with cash or by credit card?*

CONVERSATION 2

Fúwùyuán: Qǐngwèn nǐmen yào diǎn shénme cài?

Hai: Nǐmen jīntiān de wǔcān yǒu shénme cài?

Fúwùyuán: Wǒmen jīntiān yǒu hěnduō bùtóng de cài, bǐrú hóngshāo ròu, gōngbǎo jīdīng, mápó dòufu, huíguōròu hé sìjìdòu.

Hai: Yǒu yú ma?

Fúwùyuán: Wǒmende hóngshāo lǐyú búcuò. Nǐmen yào chángyicháng ma?

Hai: Hǎo. Wǒmen yào yí ge hóngshāo lǐyú, yí ge sìjìdòu, hái yào yí ge cài tāng hé liǎng wǎn mǐfàn.

Fúwùyuán: Nǐmen yào shénme yǐnliào ma?

Hai: Gěi wǒmen liǎng bēi júzi zhī.

Waitress: *What would you like to eat?*

Hai: *Can you tell me what you have for lunch today?*

Waitress: *Today we have a lot of different dishes, such as braised pork, Kung Pao chicken, Mapo tofu, twice-cooked pork, and string beans.*

Hai: *Do you have fish?*

Waitress: *Our braised carp is quite good. Would you like to taste it?*

Hai: *Okay. We'd like the braised carp, stir-fried string beans, a vegetable soup, and two bowls of rice.*

Waitress: *Would you like any drinks?*

Hai: *Give us two glasses of orange juice (please).*

NUTS & BOLTS 2
Expressing quantities
The phrases **hěn duō** and **bù shǎo** can be used to express *many, a lot* or *quite a few*. The phrases **yìxiē** and **hěn shǎo** are used in Chinese to express *some* and *very few* respectively. As you can see from the following examples, they always precede the noun they modify, and no measure word is necessary.

Wǒ yǒu bù shǎo gǒu.

I have many dogs.

Wǒmen zài yànhuì shàng chīle hěn duō dōngxi.

We ate a lot of food at the banquet. (lit., We ate a lot of things at the banquet.)

Zhōngguó yǒu hěn duō rén.

There are a lot of people in China.

Tā yǒu yìxiē wèntí.

He has some questions.

Hěn shǎo kèrén lái wǔhuì.

Very few guests came to the dance party.

PRACTICE 2
Fill in the blanks in the following sentences by translating the words in parentheses, and then give the English translation for the entire sentence.

1. Wǒ xiǎng yào _____ *(some)* miànbāo.

2. Qǐng nǐ gěi wǒ _____ *(some)* huángyóu.

3. Shànghǎi yǒu _____ *(many)* hěn hǎo de cānguǎn.

4. Nà ge dàxué yǒu _____ *(many)* Zhōngguórén.

5. _____ *(Very few)* rén qù nà jiā cānguǎn chīfàn.

Culture note

When the waiter in a Chinese restaurant asks you what kind of drink you would like, he expects you to request soda, beer, juice, or wine. Of course, you could ask only for **chá** *(tea)*, which is always served hot rather than cold and always without sugar in China.

Generally, the person who hosts a Chinese meal is the one to pour tea for everyone else at the table. When someone pours tea for you, it is customary to give a silent gesture of thanks by tapping your index and middle fingertips on the table or by bending these two fingers and tapping the table with the first or second joint closest to the fingertips. Tradition has it that, a long time ago, an emperor ventured among his people dressed as a commoner. His two aides, who were obliged to keep his true identity a secret, paid silent homage by "bowing" to him with their fingers whenever he poured tea for them in public.

In addition to drinking tea, Chinese dining etiquette centers mainly around the use of chopsticks, which are the sole eating utensils used on a daily basis throughout China both in restaurants and at home. Using chopsticks is always a challenging task for Westerners who are accustomed to knives and forks. It takes not only dexterity but an understanding of cultural rules to help one handle chopsticks both properly and politely.

A number of rules apply at all times to the use of chopsticks. For example, when you hold your chopsticks, make sure your index finger doesn't point at someone at the table since pointing is considered rude in China. Also, when taking food from a commonly shared plate, always work the side of a plate nearest you and refrain from reaching for a choice morsel that happens to be on a side of the plate facing other people. Never pass your chopsticks over someone else's hands when reaching for food, but wait for that person to finish taking his or her food before selecting your own. In addition, never lick your chopsticks since this is considered to be bad table manners.

When you take food from a shared plate, it is tradition to place the food you have taken atop your individual bowl of rice and then bring the bowl close to your lips. You then pass the food from the bowl to your mouth using your chopsticks. Chopsticks are also used to maneuver any solid food in soup, which is customarily sipped from a bowl.

When you've finished eating, it is good etiquette to place your chopsticks neatly together next to your bowl. If you're in a restaurant, you can either place your chopsticks flat across the top of your bowl or across your plate to signal the waiter that you're done with your meal. Under no circumstances should you ever leave your chopsticks standing upright in a bowl of rice or play with them like drumsticks.

If invited to someone's home for a meal, you should ask or wait to be told where to sit at the table rather than seat yourself. In most Chinese households, guests are held in high esteem and are seated at a specific side of the table to show respect.

ANSWERS

PRACTICE 1: 1. Nǐ yào jīròu háishì niúròu? **2.** Wǒ huì zài yī yuè huòzhě sān yuè qù Zhōngguó. **3.** Nǐ shì Yīngguórén háishì Měiguórén? **4.** Nǐ yào chī miàntiáo háishì miànbāo? **5.** Wǒ xiǎng yào yì wǎn mǐfàn huòzhě yì wǎn miàntiáo. **6.** Nǐ yǒu chāzi huòzhě tāngchí/sháozi ma? **7.** Wǒ kěyǐ chī ròu huòzhě shūcài. **8.** Wǒ fù xiànjīn háishì shuākǎ?

PRACTICE 2: 1. yìxiē, I would like (to have) some bread. **2.** yìxiē, Please give me some butter. **3.** hěn duō/bù shǎo, There are many very good restaurants in Shanghai. **4.** hěn duō/bù shǎo, There are many Chinese (students) at that university. **5.** Hěn shǎo, Very few people go eat at that restaurant.

UNIT 8 ESSENTIALS

Zánmen qù chī Rìběn cài, hǎo ma?

Let's go eat Japanese food. Is that okay with you?

Bié děng le. Nǐ xiān chī ba.

Don't wait. You eat first.

Ràng nǐde nǚ'ér xiān chī ba.

Let your daughter eat first.

Wǒ xiǎng hē yì bēi kāfēi.

I'd like (to drink) a cup of coffee.

Wǒmen xiànzài kěyǐ chī le. Měi ge rén dōu lái le.

We can eat now. Everyone has arrived.

Tā jīntiān wǎnshang bù néng lái le.

He can't come tonight. (He won't be able to come tonight.)

Wǒ xiànzài bìxū kāishǐ zuòfàn le.

I have to start cooking now.

Zài gěi wǒ yí ge chāzi hé yì bǎ dāo.

(Give me) another fork and knife. (lit., Give me a fork and a knife again.)

Qǐng nǐ jiézhàng!

Check please!

Nǐ bù xǐhuan yú ma?

Don't you like fish?

Shì. Wǒ bù xǐhuan yú.

No, I don't like fish. (lit., Yes. I don't like fish.)

Máfan nǐ gěi wǒ yìxiē hújiāo.

Could you give me some pepper (please)?

Qǐng nǐ gěi wǒ yì bēi rè kāishuǐ.

May I have a glass of hot water?/Please give me a glass of hot water.

Wǒ kěyǐ shuā kǎ ma?

Can I pay by credit card?

Nǐ ná kuàizi ná de búcuò.

You handle chopsticks very well. (lit., You hold chopsticks pretty well.)

Niúròu zhǔ de tài lǎo le.

The beef is (cooked) too tough.

Tā chī de hěn kuài.

He eats very quickly.

UNIT 9
Work and school

This Unit focuses on work and school, so you'll learn a lot of useful vocabulary and expressions for talking about your studies or your job. In addition, you'll learn how to talk about the future and make comparisons, and how to express suggestions similar to *ought to* or *should* in English. Unit 9 also teaches ordinal numbers like *first, second,* and so on, as well as some important conjunctions, or linking words, that you can use to form more complex sentences.

———————— Lesson 33 (words) ————————

WORD LIST 1
Let's start with some vocabulary that will come in handy around the office.

diànhuà	*telephone*
chuánzhēnjī	*fax machine*
diànnǎo	*computer*
bàngōngshì	*office*
dǎyìnjī	*printer*
shūjià	*bookshelf*
wénjiàn	*document, file*
dǎng'àn	*file*
dǎng'àn guì	*filing cabinet*
gōngsī	*company*
huìyì	*meeting*
xīnshuǐ	*salary*
lǎobǎn	*boss*

tóngshì	*colleague*
gùyuán	*employee*
gōngzuò rényuán/yuángōng	*staff*
jiàqī	*holiday, vacation*
jiānzhí	*part-time job*

NUTS & BOLTS 1

YĪNGGĀI *(SHOULD, OUGHT TO)*

The word **yīnggāi** is placed before a main verb in Chinese to make a suggestion or give advice, like the English *should* or *ought to*. As the following sentences illustrate, this construction is used to tell someone that it is their duty to do something because of obligation or correctness. It is typically used when criticizing someone's actions.

Nǐ yīnggāi zuò gōngkè.
You should do your homework.

Tā yīnggāi tīng māma de huà.
He should listen to his mother.

Tāmen yīnggāi xiǎoxīndiǎn.
They ought to be more careful.

Yīnggāi can also be separated from the main verb by an adverb that indicates, for example, when or how something should be done:

Nǐ yīnggāi mǎshàng zuò fēijī qù Běijīng.
You should take a plane to (go to) Beijing immediately.

Xuésheng yīnggāi měitiān zhǔnshí shàngxué.
Students should get to school on time every day.

Nǐ yīnggāi gèng nǔlì gōngzuò.
You should work harder.

If you want to negate a sentence with **yīnggāi,** add the negative particle **bù** immediately before **yīnggāi** rather than before the main verb.

Nǐ bù yīnggāi chídào.
You shouldn't be late.

Nǐ bù yīnggāi zài wǎncān qián chī qiǎokèlì.
You shouldn't eat chocolate before dinner.

Rúguǒ tāmen méiyǒu qián, jiù bù yīnggāi qù lǚxíng.
They shouldn't travel if they don't have money.

Nà ge rén zuì le, tā bù yīnggāi kāichē.
That person is drunk. He shouldn't drive.

PRACTICE 1
Rewrite the following sentences using **yīnggāi** *(should)* or **bù yīng-gāi** *(shouldn't)* as indicated:

1. Wǒ chídào. *(shouldn't)*

2. Tāde péngyou qù xuéxiào xué Zhōngwén. *(should)*

3. Tā jīntiān dǎ diànhuà gěi nǐ. *(should)*

4. Tā yǒu sān tiān de jiàqī. *(should)*

5. Gōngsī mǎi liǎng bù dǎyìnjī. *(should)* (bù is the measure word for dǎyìnjī)

WORD LIST 2
Now let's look at some vocabulary for school.

jiàoshì	*classroom*
xiàozhǎng	*principal*
dàxué	*university*
yánjiūyuàn/yánjiūsuǒ	*graduate school*
yánjiūshēng	*graduate student*

bìyè	*to graduate*
xì	*department (college level)*
zhuānyè/zhǔxiū	*major*
zhéxué	*philosophy*
wàiyǔ	*foreign language*
shēngwù	*biology*
wùlǐ	*physics*
huàxué	*chemistry*
lìshǐ	*history*
cānkǎoshū	*reference book*
kèběn	*textbook*
túshūzhèng	*library card*
xiàoyuán	*campus*
shūdiàn	*bookstore*
shíyànshì	*laboratory*
kèwài huódòng	*extracurricular activities*
chéngjī	*academic performance*
kǎoshì	*examination, test*

NUTS & BOLTS 2
MAKING COMPARISONS

To express differences in size, age, quantity, distance, and so on, you can use the following construction: A **bǐ** B + adjective.

This construction is the equivalent of the English comparative that uses *more* or the ending *-er*. So, *she is older than he is* would literally be *she* **bǐ** *he old* in Chinese. Notice that the verb *to be* is not used in this construction.

Ta bǐ wǒ dà.
She is older/bigger than I (am).

Wǒ bǐ nǐ gāo.
I am taller than you.

Zhè běn shū bǐ nà běn shū guì.

This book is more expensive than that one.

Yīngtáo bǐ píngguǒ xiǎo.

Cherries are smaller than apples.

Tāmen bǐ wǒmen niánqīng.

They are younger than we are.

Běijīng bǐ Shànghǎi yuǎn.

Beijing is farther than Shanghai.

Tāmende cǎodì bǐ nǐmende lǜ.

Their lawn is greener than yours.

To express the exact degree of difference between two nouns, words specifying age or amount are placed immediately after the adjective:

Wǒ bǐ nǐ dà sān suì.

I am three years older than you.

Nà ge nánhái bǐ tāde jiějie qīng shí bàng.

That boy is ten pounds lighter than his older sister.

Chéngdū bǐ Guǎngzhōu jìn jǐ bǎi gōnglǐ.

Chengdu is several hundred kilometers closer than Guangzhou.

The degree of difference can also be described in broader terms by placing the adverb **hěn** immediately before the comparative adjective. In this case, **hěn** is translated as *much*.

Nǐ bǐ wǒ gāo hěn duō.

You are much taller than I (am.)

Nà ge nánhái bǐ tāde jiějie qīng hěn duō.

That boy is much lighter than his older sister.

Zhè piàn cǎodì bǐ nà piàn lǜ hěn duō.

This lawn is much greener than that one.

In Chinese, you can also make comparisons between how a particular action is performed. In other words, you can compare adverbs rather than adjectives. The construction you use to do this is: A + verb + **de bǐ** + B + adverb. So, *Mary sings more beautifully than John* would literally be *Mary sings* **de bǐ** *John beautifully* in Chinese.

Wǒ zǒu de bǐ nǐ kuài.

I walk more quickly than you do.

Tā shuō de bǐ tāde mèimei màn.

She speaks more slowly than her younger sister.

Tā bèi shī bèi de bǐ lǎoshī liúlì.

He recited the poem more eloquently than (his) teacher.

Remember that, in Chinese, adjectives do not change form when they are used as adverbs.

PRACTICE 2
Fill in the blanks to make the appropriate comparisons based on the information and English clues provided.

1. Wáng xiǎojiě yìbǎi èr shí bàng. Zhāng xiǎojiě yìbǎi bàng. Wáng xiǎojiě _____ Zhāng xiǎojiě zhòng. *(heavier)*

2. Wǒ shí bā suì. Tā shí qī suì. Wǒ bǐ tā _____. *(older)*

3. Tāde mèimei piàoliang. Wǒde mèimei bú piàoliang. Tāde mèimei bǐ wǒ de mèimei _____. *(prettier)*

4. Tāde xīnshuǐ bù gāo. Wǒ de xīnshuǐ gāo. _____ bǐ _____ gāo. *(higher)*

5. Zhè ge rén zuò de hěn màn. Nà ge rén zuò de hěn kuài. _____ bǐ _____ kuài. *(faster)*

6. Wǒde xuésheng de chéngjī búcuò. Tāde xuésheng de chéngjī bù hǎo. Wǒde xuésheng de chéngjī bǐ tāde xuésheng de chéngjī _____. *(better)*

7. Tāde xuéxiào de xiàoyuán dà. Wǒde xuéxiào de xiàoyuán xiǎo. Wǒde xuéxiào de xiàoyuán bǐ tāde xuéxiào de xiàoyuán _____. *(smaller)*

8. Tāde kèběn hěn duō. Wǒde kèběn bù duō. _____ bǐ _____ duō. *(more)*

ANSWERS
PRACTICE 1: 1. Wǒ bù yīnggāi chídào. (I shouldn't be late.) **2.** Tāde péngyou yīnggāi qù xuéxiào xué Zhōngwén. (His/Her friend should go to a school to study Chinese.) **3.** Tā jīntiān yīnggāi dǎ diànhuà gěi nǐ. (He/She should give you a call today.) **4.** Tā yīnggāi yǒu sān tiān de jiàqī. (He/She should have three vacation days.) **5.** Gōngsī yīnggāi mǎi liǎng bù dǎyìnjī. (The company should buy two printers.)

PRACTICE 2: 1. Wáng xiǎojiě bǐ Zhāng xiǎojiě zhòng. (Miss Wang is heavier than Miss Zhang.) **2.** Wǒ bǐ tā dà. (I'm older than he/she is.) **3.** Tāde mèimei bǐ wǒde mèimei piàoliang. (His/Her younger sister is prettier than mine.) **4.** Wǒde xīnshuǐ bǐ tāde xīnshuǐ gāo. (My salary is higher than his/hers.) **5.** Nà ge rén zuò de bǐ zhè ge rén kuài. (That person works faster than this person.) **6.** Wǒde xuésheng de chéngjī bǐ tāde xuésheng de chéngjī hǎo. (My students' academic performance is better than his/her students' academic performance.) **7.** Wǒde xuéxiào de xiàoyuán bǐ tāde xuéxiào de xiàoyuán xiǎo. (My school's campus is smaller than his/hers.) **8.** Tāde kèběn bǐ wǒ(de) duō. (He/She has more books than I do. [lit., His/Her textbooks are more than mine.])

PHRASE LIST 1
Here are some useful expressions for talking about your job.

jiābān	*to work overtime*
qǐng bìngjià	*to take sick leave*
qǐng (shì) jià	*to take personal leave*
dǎ diànhuà	*to make a phone call*
fā chuánzhēn	*to send a fax*
jì xiàlái	*to jot something down*
kāihuì	*in a meeting/to have a meeting*
jiǎng diànhuà	*on the phone*
liúyán	*to leave a message*
yùyuē/yuē	*to make an appointment*
chūchāi	*to take a business trip*
fàngjià	*on vacation, time off*
zuìhòu qīxiàn	*deadline*

NUTS & BOLTS 1
THE DOUBLE CONJUNCTION YÒU . . . YÒU

In English, if you want to use two adjectives or adverbs together to give a description of how something is or how something is done, you simply connect them with *and*. In Chinese, you use the double conjunction yòu . . . yòu. This literally means *again . . . again,* but you can translate it as *and*:

Tā yòu dà yòu gāo.
He is big and tall.

Here are some more examples:

Nà ge rén zuò de yòu kuài yòu hǎo.
That man works quickly and well.

Zhè ge huìyì yòu cháng yòu mèn.
This meeting was long and boring.

Wǒde gōngzuò yòu yǒu tiǎozhànxìng yòu huā shíjiān.
My job is quite challenging and time-consuming.

PRACTICE 1

Use the double conjunction **yòu . . . yòu** to combine each pair of sentences into a single comparative statement:

1. Tāde lǎobǎn cōngmíng. Tāde lǎobǎn hǎo.

2. Wǒde bàngōngshì dà. Wǒde bàngōngshì piàoliang.

3. Nà ge guójiā xiǎo. Nà ge guójiā qióng *(poor)*.

4. Zhè ge huìyì hěn cháng. Zhè ge huìyì hěn mèn.

5. Xuéxiào de kèwài huódòng hěn duō. Xuéxiào de kèwài huódòng hěn hǎowán *(fun)*.

6. Shíyànshì de shèbèi *(equipment)* hěn xīn. Shíyànshì de shèbèi hěn hǎo.

PHRASE LIST 2

Now let's look at some useful expressions for school.

shàngkè	*to attend (a) class*
pángtīng	*to audit a class*
kǎoshì	*exam, to take an exam*
pái dì yī míng	*to be placed first*
fàngxué	*after-school hours*
shēnqǐng	*to apply*
fùxí	*to review a lesson*
yùxí	*to prepare for a lesson*
sīrén bǔxí	*private tutoring*
shàngwǎng	*to go online*
jiāo gōngkè	*to submit homework*

nǐde chéngjī	*your academic performance*
shàng dàxué	*to attend university*
zhù zài sùshè lǐ	*to live in the dorm*
zài shítáng lǐ chīfàn	*to eat in the cafeteria*

NUTS & BOLTS 2
ORDINAL NUMBERS

You already know cardinal numbers—numbers like *one, sixteen,* and *forty-five,* which show quantity or are used to count. Ordinal numbers are used to describe order, so they correspond to the English *first, sixteenth,* and *forty-fifth.* Quite simply, cardinal numbers are transformed into ordinal numbers in Chinese by adding the prefix **dì.**

yī *(one)*	**dì yī** *(first)*
èr *(two)*	**dì èr** *(second)*
sān *(three)*	**dì sān** *(third)*
sì *(four)*	**dì sì** *(fourth)*

Here are a few examples that show how ordinal numbers are typically used in Chinese sentences. Notice the use of measure words between the ordinal numbers and the nouns they modify. Also notice the word order of the descriptive phrases and the use of **de.**

Wǒ shì zhè ge gōngsī de dì yī ge yuángōng.

I'm the first person to work for this company. (lit., this company's first staff member)

Tā shì dì yī ge xué Zhōngwén de Měiguórén.

He is the first American to study Chinese. (lit., the first-to-study-Chinese American)

PRACTICE 2
Translate the following sentences into English:

1. Tā shì wǒ dì yī ge lǎobǎn.

2. Wǒmende dì yī ge yuángōng shì Yīngguórén.

3. Zài zhè ge xuéxiào lǐ, wǒ shì dì yī ge huì shuō Zhōngwén de Měiguórén.

4. Tā dì èr ge nǚpéngyou (*girlfriend*) shì Zhōngguórén.

5. Tā pái dì sì míng.

ANSWERS
PRACTICE 1: 1. Tāde lǎobǎn yòu cōngmíng yòu hǎo. (His boss is intelligent and good.) **2.** Wǒde bàngōngshì yòu dà yòu piàoliang. (My office is large and beautiful.) **3.** Nà ge guójiā yòu xiǎo yòu qióng. (That country is small and poor.) **4.** Zhè ge huìyì yòu cháng yòu mèn. (This meeting was long and boring.) **5.** Xuéxiào de kèwài huódòng yòu duō yòu hǎowán. (The extracurricular activities at school are many and fun.) **6.** Shíyànshì de shèbèi yòu xīn yòu hǎo. (The laboratory's equipment is new and good.)

PRACTICE 2: 1. He/She is my first boss. **2.** Our first staff member was British. **3.** I'm the first American who knows how to speak Chinese at this school. **4.** His second girlfriend was Chinese. **5.** He/She placed fourth.

———————— Lesson 35 (sentences) ————————

SENTENCE LIST 1

Tā míngtiān huì huí gōngsī.	*She will be back in the office tomorrow.*
Nǐ míngnián huì qù Měiguó dúshū ma?	*Will you go to America to study next year?*
Wǒmen xià ge yuè bìyè.	*We'll graduate next month.*

Wǒ bìyè zhīhòu bù dú yánjiūyuàn.	*I won't be going to graduate school after graduation.*
Hěn duō xuésheng míngtiān kǎoshì.	*Many students will take the/an exam tomorrow.*
Xuéxiào xià ge lǐbài yī fàngjià.	*The school will be closed next Monday.*
Xuésheng xià ge yuè kāishǐ shàngkè.	*Students will begin going to school next month.*
Zhè ge xuéxiào jiǔyuè zhāoshēng.	*This school will recruit students in September.*
Tāde gōngsī xià ge lǐbài guānbì.	*His company will go out of business next week.*
Nǐ huì zhǎo qítā gōngzuò ma?	*Will you look for another job?*
Tā xià ge lǐbài èr huì gēn lǎobǎn chūchāi.	*She will take a business trip with her boss next Tuesday.*

NUTS & BOLTS 1

FUNCTIONS OF HUÌ

You have already been exposed to **huì,** which has different meanings in Chinese depending on how it is used. Here is a review of two of its main functions.

As you learned in Lesson 21, one of the primary functions of **huì** is to express the possibility that an action will take place in the future. When placed immediately before the main verb in a sentence, **huì** is the equivalent of *will* in English. It expresses a future action that is likely or <u>probable</u>, but of course not guaranteed since it hasn't happened yet. If you want to stress that something is <u>possible</u>, use **kěnéng** *(maybe, perhaps)*. This is the equivalent of *may.*

Wǒ míngtiān huì qù Shànghǎi.
I'll (probably) go to Shanghai tomorrow.

Tā děng yíhuìr huì gěi nǐ.

He will (most likely) give it to you in a while.

Tā kěnéng huì lái.

She may come.

In the previous Unit, you learned that **huì** can also be used as a modal verb, in which case it means *can* in the sense of *know how to*.

Wǒ huì shuō Zhōngwén.

I can (know how to) speak Chinese.

Wǒ bú huì shuō Zhōngwén.

I can't (don't know how to) speak Chinese.

Huì can also be used as a main verb, in which case it means *to know how*.

PRACTICE 1

Match each Chinese sentence in the column on the left with the correct English translation on the right.

1. Nǐ míngtiān huì shàngxué ma?	a. *I will (probably) go to bed in a while.*
2. Tā bú huì shuō Yīngwén.	b. *Will he (possibly) come tonight?*
3. Wǒ děng yíhuìr (a while) huì qù shuìjiào.	c. *He won't attend university next year.*
4. Wǒ míngtiān bú shàngxué.	d. *Will you (most likely) go to school tomorrow?*
5. Zhāng lǎoshī huì kāichē.	e. *She will go study in the U.S. next month.*

6. Tā jīntiān wǎnshang huì lái ma?	f. *He doesn't know how to speak English.*
7. Tā míngnián bú shàng dàxué.	g. *Teacher Zhang knows how to drive.*
8. Tā xià ge yuè qù Měiguó dúshū.	h. *I won't go to school tomorrow.*

SENTENCE LIST 2

Tāde bàba hé wǒde māma yíyàng dà.	*His father is as old as my mother. (His father is at the same age as my mother.)*
Zhè ge xuéxiào hé nà ge xuéxiào yíyàng hǎo.	*This school is as good as that school.*
Tāde xīnshuǐ hé nǐde yíyàng gāo.	*Her salary is as high as yours.*
Tāde gōngsī yǒu nǐde zhème dà.	*His company is as big as yours.*
Wǒde jiàqī méiyǒu nǐde nàme duō.	*My vacation is not as long as yours.*
Jīnnián de kǎoshì hé qùnián de yíyàng nán.	*The examination this year is as difficult as it was last year.*
Jīnnián de kǎoshì méiyǒu qùnián de róngyì.	*This year's examination is not as easy as last year's.*
Zài Měiguó, sīlì xiǎoxué de xuéfèi hé sīlì dàxué de xuéfèi yíyàng guì.	*In the U.S., the tuition fee at private elementary schools is as expensive as at universities.*
Wénkē de xuéfèi méiyǒu lǐkē de nàme guì.	*Tuition fees for the humanities majors are not as expensive as for the sciences.*
Yīngwén méiyǒu Zhōngwén nàme nán xué.	*English is not as difficult to learn as Chinese.*
Zhè běn shū hé nà běn shū yíyàng yǒu yìsi.	*This book is as interesting as that one.*

Tāde shēngwù lǎoshī de *His biology teacher gives as much*
gōngkè hé huàxué lǎoshī *homework as his chemistry teacher.*
de yíyàng duō.

NUTS & BOLTS 2
MAKING EQUAL COMPARISONS

There are two ways in Chinese to express equal comparisons, corresponding to the English construction *as...as*. The first is to use **yǒu . . . zhème/nàme** to show that separate entities share the same characteristics and are comparatively very similar.

Wǒ yǒu nǐ nàme gāo.
I am as tall as you.

Nǐ yǒu wǒ zhème gāo.
You are as tall as I am.

Zhè ge hézi yǒu nà ge nàme dà.
This box is as big as that one.

Whether you use **zhème** or **nàme** depends on the relative location of the speaker. As you can see from the examples above, **zhème** is used to refer to someone or something close to the speaker, while **nàme** is used to refer to someone or something that is farther away from the speaker. In other words, **zhème** is used in the sentence **Nǐ yǒu wǒ zhème gāo** *(You are as tall as I am)* because it modifies the word *I*, which refers to the speaker himself. On the other hand, **nàme** is used in the sentence **Wǒ yǒu nǐ nàme gāo** *(I am as tall as you)* because it modifies the word *you*, which is separate and apart from the speaker.

The second way of expressing equal comparisons in Chinese is by using the word **yíyàng** *(same)* to form the grammatical construct:
A + **hé** + B + **yíyàng** + adjective.

This indicates a more precise level of exact comparison and literally means that two things are the same:

Wǒ hé nǐ yíyàng gāo.

I am as tall as you. (We are the same height.)

Wǒde wèikǒu hé nǐde yíyàng dà.

My appetite is as big as yours. (Our appetites are equally big.)

Zhè kē shù hé zhè ge fángzi yíyàng lǎo.

The tree is as old as the house. (The tree and the house are the same age.)

Likewise, there are two different ways in Chinese to show similarity when comparing two different actions or activities. You can use either of the following constructions:

A + verb + **de** + **yǒu** + B + **zhème/nàme** + adverb

or

A + **hé** + B + verb + **de** + **yíyàng** + adverb

Wǒ chī de yǒu nǐ nàme kuài.

I eat as quickly as you do.

Wǒ hé nǐ chī de yíyàng kuài.

I eat as quickly as you do. (You and I eat at the same speed.)

Both of these forms are equally correct and are used interchangeably in colloquial Chinese. Here are some more examples:

Tā pǎo de hé tāmen yíyàng kuài.

She runs as fast as they do.

Wǒde māma zuòfàn zuò de hé chúshī yíyàng hǎo.

My mother cooks as well as a professional chef.

There are different rules in Chinese for negating equal comparisons. In constructions that use the verb **yǒu**, simply replace **yǒu** with **méiyǒu** in order to form the negative. But in constructions that don't use **yǒu,** place the negative particle **bù** in front of **yíyàng** + adjective/adverb.

Wǒ méiyǒu nǐ nàme gāo.

I'm not as tall as you.

Wǒ hé nǐ bù yíyàng gāo.

I'm not as tall as you. (You and I are not the same height.)

Wǒ chī de méiyǒu nǐ nàme kuài.

I don't eat as quickly as you do.

Wǒ hé nǐ chī de bù yíyàng kuài.

I don't eat as quickly as you do. (You and I do not eat at the same speed.)

PRACTICE 2

Using the word or phrase in parentheses, rewrite and combine each pair of sentences into a single comparative statement. Then translate your answers.

1. Wǒ shuō Zhōngwén hěn kuài. Tā shuō Zhōngwén hěn kuài. (yíyàng)

2. Wǒde bàba hěn gāo. Nǐde bàba hěn gāo. (yǒu . . . zhème/nàme)

3. Nà ge rén de fángzi hěn piàoliang. Wǒde péngyou de fángzi hěn piàoliang. (yǒu . . . zhème/nàme)

4. Huáng xiānsheng zǒu de hěn kuài. Wáng xiǎojiě zǒu de hěn kuài. (yíyàng)

5. Nà bù chē hěn guì. Zhè bù chē hěn guì. (yíyàng)

6. Zhāng lǎoshī hěn hǎo. Lǐ lǎoshī hěn hǎo. (yíyàng)

7. Jiānádà *(Canada)* hěn dà. Zhōngguó búshì hěn dà. (méiyǒu . . . zhème)

8. Tāde chéngjī hěn hǎo. Wǒde chéngjī hěn hǎo. (yíyàng)

ANSWERS
PRACTICE 1: 1. d; **2.** f; **3.** a; **4.** h; **5.** g; **6.** b; **7.** c; **8.** e

PRACTICE 2: 1. Wǒ shuō Zhōngwén hé tā yíyàng kuài. (I speak Chinese as quickly as he/she does.) **2.** Wǒde bàba yǒu nǐde bàba nàme gāo. (My father is as tall as your father.) **3.** Nà ge rén de fángzi yǒu wǒde péngyou de fángzi nàme piàoliang. (That person's house is as pretty/beautiful as my friend's house.) **4.** Huáng xiānsheng zǒu de hé Wáng xiǎojiě yíyàng kuài. (Mr. Huang walks as fast as Miss Wang.) **5.** Nà bù chē hé zhè bù chē yíyàng guì. (That car is as expensive as this car.) **6.** Zhāng lǎoshī hé Lǐ lǎoshī yíyàng hǎo. (Teacher Zhang is as good as Teacher Li.) **7.** Zhōngguó méiyǒu Jiānádà nàme dà. (China is not as big as Canada.) **8.** Tāde chéngjī hé wǒde chéngjī yíyàng hǎo. (His/Her academic performance is as good as my academic performance.)

─────────── Lesson 36 (conversations) ───────────

CONVERSATION 1

Wang Hai and Jess are talking about their plans after graduation.

Hai: Jié Xī, nǐ bìyè zhīhòu dǎsuàn zěnyàng?

Jess: Wǒ dǎsuàn liú zài Zhōngguó gōngzuò yì nián, zhīhòu qù lǚxíng, ránhòu cái huí guó. Nǐ ne?

Hai: Wǒ xiǎng zài Zhōngguó jiāo liǎng sān nián Yīngwén, chǔ yìdiǎn qián, zài shēnqǐng chūguó dúshū. Tīngshuō zài Měiguó dúshū, shēnghuófèi hěn gāo.

Jess: Nà yào kàn nǐ zài nǎ yí ge chéngshì, dà chéngshì de shēnghuófèi bǐ xiǎo zhèn de gāo, hěn duō dàxuéshēng dōu yào zuò jiānzhí bāngbǔ yí xià.

Hai: Nà wǒ xiànzài kāishǐ yào shěng yìdiǎn qián le. Nǐ xiǎng zuò shénme gōngzuò?

Jess: Wǒ yě xiǎng zài zhèlǐ jiāo Yīngwén, hěn duō Zhōngguó xuésheng dōu xǐhuan xué hǎo Yīngwén.

Hai: Nǐde Zhōngwén shuō de hěn hǎo, miànshì de shíhou yídìng huì yǒu bāngzhù.

Jess: Xièxie!

Hai: *Jess, what do you plan to do after graduation?*

Jess: *I'm planning to stay in China for a year. Then I'll travel, and after that I'll go back to my own country. How about you?*

Hai: *I want to teach English in China for two or three years. Meanwhile, I'll save some money and apply to study abroad. I hear that life is very expensive in the U.S.*

Jess: *Well, it depends on which city you live in. The cost of living in a big city is higher than in a small town, and a lot of undergraduates have part-time jobs to help cover the expenses.*

Hai: *Then I have to start saving money now. What's your plan for staying in China?*

Jess: *I'd also like to teach English here. A lot of Chinese students want to improve their English.*

Hai: *You speak Chinese very well. It will definitely help you when you interview for a job.*

Jess: *Thanks!*

NOTES

The verb **dǎsuàn** *(to plan)* can be used with another verb to mean *to plan to do something.*

The verb **liú** *(to stay)* is usually combined with the preposition **zài** to indicate where one is staying or intends to stay.

The word **ránhòu** can be translated as *then* or *afterwards.*

The verb **chǔ** (or **cún**) means *to save* or *to store up,* as in money, food, and so on.

The verb **chūguó** may be translated as *to leave one's own country* or *to go abroad*.

The word **nà** is used as a conversational flavoring word in the same way as *well* . . . It can also be used to mean *in this case* or *in that case*.

NUTS & BOLTS 1
THE INTERROGATIVE WÈISHÉNME *(WHY)*

In previous lessons, you learned how a number of interrogatives are used in Chinese to ask basic questions like *how, what, where, who,* and *which.* Another important interrogative is **wèishénme,** which means *why.* In questions, **wèishénme** can take one of several different positions. It can be placed at the head of a sentence immediately in front of the subject, or else it can come right after the subject:

Wèishénme nǐ bù xǐhuan kàn diànyǐng?
Why don't you like going to the movies?

Nǐ wèishénme bù xǐhuan kàn diànyǐng?
Why don't you like going to the movies?

In cases where a time period is specified, there are a few different word order possibilities with respect to **wèishénme,** the subject, and the time expression:

wèishénme + subject + time expression + verb

subject + time expression + **wèishénme** + verb

time expression + subject + **wèishénme** + verb

Wèishénme nǐ jīntiān chídào?
Why were you late today?

Nǐ jīntiān wèishénme chídào?
Why were you late today?

Jīntiān nǐ wèishénme chídào?
Why were you late today?

The choice depends on what you want to stress. Put the word that is receiving the most emphasis first. If **wèishénme** starts the sentence, you are emphasizing that you want to know *why* something happened. If the subject comes first, then you're emphasizing that you want to know why *a particular person* is responsible for doing something. And if the time expression begins the sentence, you are emphasizing that you want to know why someone did something *at a particular time*. Take another look at our examples. The underlined word is the element of the question that is being emphasized.

Wèishénme nǐ jīntiān chídào?
Why were you late today?

Nǐ jīntiān wèishénme chídào?
Why were you late today?

Jīntiān nǐ wèishénme chídào?
Why were you late today?

PRACTICE 1
Use **wèishénme** to turn the following statements into questions:

1. Wǒmen bú qù Měiguó dúshū le.

2. Tā míngtiān bú shàngbān.

3. Jīntiān xiàwǔ fàngxué zhīhòu wǒmen bú yìqǐ fùxí.

4. Wǒde lǎobǎn xǐhuan yuángōng jiābān.

5. Wǒde xīnshuǐ méiyǒu nǐde gāo.

6. Zhāng xiǎojiě bìyè zhīhòu bù gōngzuò.

7. Nǐmen yīnggāi zhǔnshí shàngxué.

8. Wǒ yào yìbǎi kuài qián.

CONVERSATION 2

Jess and Wang Hai are talking about university life.

Jess: Zǎoshang hǎo! Zuótiān zài xuéxiào méiyǒu kànjiàn nǐ, nǐ dào nǎli qùle?

Hai: Zuótiān wǒ xiàkè hòu qù bāng wǒde biǎodì bǔxí.

Jess: Zhēn de? Wèishénme?

Hai: Yīnwèi tāde chéngjī bú tài hǎo, míngnián tā yào kǎo dàxué, suǒyǐ tā māma yào wǒ guòqù bāngmáng.

Jess: Guàibude zuìjìn nǐ zǒu de zhème cōngmáng. Tā xiǎng dú shénme zhuānyè?

Hai: Tā xǐhuan zhéxué. Kěshì, tā māma yào tā dú gōngchéng.

Jess: Wèishénme Zhōngguó jiāzhǎng dōu xiǎng zǐnǚ dú gōngchéng, yīkē, fǎlǜ?

Hai: Búshì měi yí ge jiāzhǎng dōu zhèyàng de. Xiàng wǒ fùmǔ, tāmen jiù méiyǒu yào wǒ dú lǐkē. Wǒ yīnwèi xǐhuan yǔwén, suǒyǐ xiànzài dú wàiyǔ xì.

Jess: Rúguǒ měi yí ge fùmǔ dōu hé nǐde bàba māma yíyàng kāimíng jiù hǎo le.

Jess: Good morning! I didn't see you after school yesterday. Where did you go?

Hai: I went to tutor my cousin.

Jess: Really? Why?

Hai: Since his academic performance is not very good and he has to take the college entrance exam next year, his mother wants me to help him.

Jess: No wonder you've been leaving school so quickly lately. What major does he intend to pick?

Hai: *He likes philosophy. But his mother wants him to study engineering.*

Jess: *Why do so many Chinese parents want their children to study engineering, medicine, or law?*

Hai: *Not every parent thinks that way. Take my parents; they didn't ask me to study science. I like languages, so I now study in the foreign language department.*

Jess: *It would be great if every parent were as open-minded as your parents!*

NUTS & BOLTS 2
THE CONJUNCTIONS YĪNWÈI *(BECAUSE)* AND SUŎYǏ *(THEREFORE)*

Questions that use the word **wèishénme** *(why)* are often answered with **yīnwèi . . .** *(because . . .)*. For example:

Wèishénme nǐ bú qù kàn diànyǐng?

Why don't you go to the movie?

–Yīnwèi wǒ hěn máng.

–Because I am very busy.

Yīnwèi is also often used with the word **suǒyǐ** *(therefore, consequently)* to convey a sense of cause and effect. This results in a two-part sentence in which **yīnwèi** first establishes a reason, and then **suǒyǐ** identifies the consequence. This can be translated into English as *since . . . , because . . . , . . . so, . . . therefore,* and so on.

Yīnwèi méiyǒu rén bāng wǒ, suǒyǐ wǒ zìjǐ zuò.

Since no one's going to help me, I'll do it myself.

Yīnwèi tā méiyǒu dúshū, suǒyǐ tā bùjígé.

He didn't study, so he failed the exam.

PRACTICE 2

Match the Chinese sentences in the column on the left with their English translations on the right.

1. Tā yīnwèi méiyǒu qián, suǒyǐ bù kěyǐ shàng dàxué.	a. *Since he's late, he can't take the exam.*
2. Yīnwèi méiyǒu dìtiě, suǒyǐ wǒ yào zǒulù shàngbān.	b. *Since she doesn't have money, she can't attend university.*
3. Tā yīnwèi chídào, suǒyǐ bù kěyǐ kǎoshì.	c. *We don't like him, so we won't go tonight.*
4. Yīnwèi xuéxiào lí wǒ jiā yuǎn, suǒyǐ wǒ zhù zài sùshè.	d. *Since they are good friends, they ride to school together.*
5. Yīnwèi tiānqì bù hǎo, suǒyǐ wǒ bù xiǎng qù yóuyǒng le.	e. *There was no subway, so I had to go to work on foot.*
6. Wǒmen yīnwèi bù xǐhuan tā, suǒyǐ jīntiān wǎnshang wǒmen bú qù le.	f. *Since the weather isn't good, I don't want to go swimming.*
7. Yīnwèi tāmen shì hǎo péngyou, tāmen yìqǐ zuò chē shàngxué.	g. *The school is far from my home, so I live in the dorm.*

Culture note

Chinese parents usually steer their children in the direction of practical, well-respected professions, and therefore recommend that they study law, medicine, or one of the sciences. Parents feel that this guarantees their children a good job after graduating from college.

Because so much depends on how well one does at school, the pressure to succeed is great, and students learn at an early age to take their studies quite seriously. Generally speaking, admission to schools is very competitive in China and, once you are enrolled, you have to study very hard. From elementary school onward, curricula are performance-based and high grades and long hours of study are prerequisites for success. Chinese students are given a lot of homework, even at the elementary school level, and must constantly prepare for tests, quizzes, and dictations that are administered quite frequently throughout the school year.

The school year in China is also longer than the typical school year in the United States. It is divided into two consecutive semesters that begin in September and end in mid-July.

High school students have a particularly rigorous schedule since they must take a yearly public examination called **gāokǎo** *(lit., high exam)* in order to be admitted to a university. In order to do well on this examination, many students take special cramming classes after the regular school day ends.

Such an intense regimen of study leaves little time for extracurricular activities. Extracurricular activities do exist in China, but in smaller quantity and with far less variety than at American schools. Extracurricular activities are mainly limited to sports, singing, and the playing of musical instruments, and are designed for talented students, which means that not everyone has the opportunity to enjoy them.

ANSWERS

PRACTICE 1: 1. Wèishénme nǐmen bú qù Měiguó dúshū le? (Why don't you (pl.) go to the U.S. to study?) **2.** Tā wèishénme míngtiān bú shàngbān? (Why won't he/she go to work tomorrow?) **3.** Wèishénme jīntiān xiàwǔ fàngxué zhīhòu wǒmen bú yìqǐ fùxí? (Why don't we review the lessons together after school this afternoon?) **4.** Nǐde lǎobǎn wèishénme xǐhuan yuángōng jiābān? (Why does your boss like the staff to work overtime?) **5.** Nǐde xīnshuǐ wèishénme méiyǒu wǒde gāo? (Why isn't your salary higher than mine?) **6.** Wèishénme Zhāng xiǎojiě bìyè zhīhòu bù gōngzuò? (Why won't Miss Zhang work after graduation?) **7.** Wǒmen wèishénme yīnggāi zhǔnshí shàngxué? (Why should we go to school on time?) **8.** Nǐ wèishénme yào yìbǎi kuài qián? (Why do you need a hundred yuan?)

PRACTICE 2: 1. b; **2.** e; **3.** a; **4.** g; **5.** f; **6.** c; **7.** d

UNIT 9 ESSENTIALS

Nǐ yīnggāi gèng nǔlì gōngzuò.

You should work harder.

Tāmen bǐ wǒmen niánqīng.

They are younger than we are.

Zhè ge huìyì yòu cháng yòu mèn.

This meeting was long and boring.

Wǒde gōngzuò yòu yǒu tiǎozhànxìng yòu huā shíjiān.

My job is quite challenging and time-consuming.

shàngkè

to attend (a) class

Wǒ shì zhè ge gōngsī de dì yī ge yuángōng.

I'm the first person to work for this company. (lit., this company's first staff member)

Tā míngtiān huì huí gōngsī.

She will be back in the office tomorrow.

Tā xià ge lǐbài èr huì gēn lǎobǎn chūchāi.

She will take a business trip with her boss next Tuesday.

Tā kěnéng huì lái.

She may come.

Jīnnián de kǎoshì hé qùnián de yíyàng nán.

The examination this year is as difficult as it was last year.

Yīngwén méiyǒu Zhōngwén nàme nán xué.

English is not as difficult to learn as Chinese.

Nǐ yǒu wǒ zhème gāo.

You are as tall as I am.

Wǒ chī de yǒu nǐ nàme kuài.

I eat as quickly as you do.

Wǒ méiyǒu nǐ nàme gāo.

I'm not as tall as you.

Wǒ hé nǐ bù yíyàng gāo.

I'm not as tall as you. (You and I are not the same height.)

Wèishénme nǐ jīntiān chídào?

Why were you late today?

Yīnwèi wǒ hěn máng.

Because I was very busy.

Yīnwèi méiyǒu rén bāng wǒ, suǒyǐ wǒ zìjǐ zuò.

Since no one's going to help me, I'll do it myself.

UNIT 10
Sports and leisure activities

Are you ready for your last Unit of Chinese? Since you've put so much hard work into this course, we'll end on an enjoyable and relaxing topic: sports, recreational activities, hobbies, and things people do for fun. That means that you'll learn a lot of new vocabulary that will come in handy when you talk about your interests, plan social events, or just plain relax.

For grammar, you'll learn useful constructions for talking about sports and games, and you'll also learn indefinites like *anyone, anything, someone, something,* and so on. This last Unit will also highlight *if* conditional constructions and other expressions that will help make your Chinese sound more natural.

Are you ready?

——————— Lesson 37 (words) ———————

WORD LIST 1
Here is some vocabulary that will come in handy when you want to talk about sports.

yùndòng	*sports*
lánqiú	*basketball*
bàngqiú	*baseball*
qūgùnqiú	*hockey*
zúqiú	*soccer (football)*
Měishì zúqiú	*(American) football*
yǔmáoqiú	*badminton*

páiqiú	*volleyball*
wǎngqiú	*tennis*
mànpǎo/huǎnbùpǎo	*jogging*
qí zìxíngchē	*cycling*
yújiā	*yoga*
yuǎnzú	*hiking*
yóuyǒng	*swimming*
yěyíng/lùyíng	*camping*
Májiàng	*Mahjong*
Tàijíquán	*Taiji/Tai Chi*

NUTS & BOLTS 1

THE VERB DǍ QIÚ *(TO PLAY BALL)*

The expression **dǎ qiú** can be translated as *to play ball,* and it refers to games that require using one's hands to manipulate a ball. The expression literally translates as *to hit (a) ball.*

Wǒ zuótiān dǎ qiú.
I played ball yesterday.

Tāmen xǐhuan dǎ qiú.
They like to play ball.

You can specify a particular type of game by replacing **qiú** with the name of the game. Here are some examples of the games you can use with the basic verb **dǎ:**

dǎ bàngqiú	*to play baseball*
dǎ wǎngqiú	*to play tennis*
dǎ lánqiú	*to play basketball*
dǎ yǔmáoqiú	*to play badminton*
dǎ pīngpāngqiú	*to play table tennis*

dǎ Májiàng	to play Mahjong
dǎ Tàijíquán	to do Taiji/Tai Chi

Note that the game of soccer (football) is not included in the list above. Since soccer is played with the feet, the verb **tī** *(to kick)* is substituted for **dǎ** *(to hit)*. As a result, **tī zúqiú** means *to play soccer.* Here are a few more example sentences with both **dǎ** and **tī**:

Wǒmen zǒngshì zài gōngyuán tī zúqiú.
We always play soccer in the park.

Háizimen fàngxué zhīhòu dǎ lánqiú.
The children play basketball after school.

Nǐ huì dǎ wǎngqiú ma?
Do you play tennis? (lit., Do you know how to play tennis?)

Wǒ hěn xǐhuan dǎ pīngpāngqiú, dànshì wǒ dǎ de bùhǎo.
I love to play table tennis, but I'm not very good at it. (lit., I like to play table tennis very much, but I don't play well.)

PRACTICE 1
Match each Chinese word or expression with its equivalent in English:

1. dǎ wǎngqiú	a. *cycling*
2. dǎ yǔmáoqiú	b. *yoga*
3. yuǎnzú	c. *to play basketball*
4. dǎ lánqiú	d. *to play (American) football*
5. tī zúqiú	e. *hiking*
6. dǎ Měishì zúqiú	f. *to play badminton*

| 7. qí zìxíngchē | g. *to play tennis* |
| 8. yújiā | h. *to play soccer* |

WORD LIST 2

Here are some helpful words you can use when talking about hobbies.

àihào	*hobbies*
kàn shū	*reading*
shī	*poetry*
xiǎoshuō	*novel*
yīnyuè	*music*
gǔdiǎn yīnyuè	*classical music*
liúxíng yīnyuè	*pop music*
diànyǐng	*film, movie*
xiězuò	*writing*
diàoyú	*fishing*
biānzhī	*knitting*
pēngrèn	*cooking*
lǚxíng	*travel*
huàhuà	*painting*
chànggē	*singing*

NUTS & BOLTS 2
USES OF BǍ

As you know, basic word order in Chinese is the same as it is in English: subject + verb + object. But it's possible to move the object of a sentence in front of the verb by adding the word **bǎ**. This gives you the word order: subject + **bǎ** + object + verb (+ **le**). The verb must always follow the object in sentences with **bǎ**.

Wǒ chīle píngguǒ.

I ate the/an apple.

Wǒ chīle nà ge píngguǒ.

I ate the apple. (lit., I ate that apple.)

Wǒ bǎ píngguǒ chīle.

I ate the apple.

Wǒ bǎ nà ge píngguǒ chīle.

I ate the apple. (lit., I ate that apple.)

Remember that, in Chinese, there is no real equivalent for the English word *the*. However, **bǎ** can be used to make your reference more specific, as in **Wǒ bǎ píngguǒ chīle** *(I ate the apple)*. However, the words *this* **(zhè ge)** and *that* **(nà ge)** are usually used in place of *the* in Chinese. If you want to tell someone *I ate the apple,* you can say **Wǒ chīle zhè ge píngguǒ** *(lit., I ate this apple)* or **Wǒ chīle nà ge píngguǒ** *(lit., I ate that apple)*. Of course, these sentences can also take on their literal meanings.

Bǎ is also used in more complex constructions. Compare these two examples:

Tā ná zhe nà běn shū.

He is holding that book.

Tā bǎ nà běn shū cóng shūjià shàng ná zǒu.

He took that book away from the shelf. (lit., He [bǎ] that book from the shelf take off.)

The first example is simple, and the English is a literal translation of the Chinese. If, however, you want to explain specifically how his action of taking resulted in the book being off of the shelf, you need to use the word **bǎ,** followed by the complex phrase **nà běn shū cóng shūjià shàng ná zǒu,** which can literally be translated as *that book from the shelf take off.*

Generally speaking, the word **bǎ** (which literally means *to grasp*) is introduced to show the intention or consequence of a deliberate action, or it can clarify the location, time frame, or manner in which something is purposely done. These constructions are often built very differently in Chinese than they are in English, but comparing a few examples both with and without **bǎ** will help make them clearer.

Wǒ nále zhè xiē xiézi.
I took these shoes.

Wǒ bǎ zhè xiē xiézi ná huí jiā lǐ lái.
I took these shoes home.

Wǒ chīle wǎncān.
I ate dinner.

Wǒ huāle yí ge zhōngtóu bǎ wǎncān chī wán.
I spent an hour finishing eating dinner.

Nà ge xuésheng gǎile dá'àn.
The student changed his answer.

Nà ge xuésheng bǎ dá'àn gǎile sān cì.
The student changed his answer three times.

Wǒ xǐle pánzi.
I washed the plate.

Wǒ bǎ pánzi xǐ de hěn gānjìng.
I washed the plate clean.

One issue to keep in mind is that **bǎ** is only used in contexts with some kind of action verb where there's a tangible result, such as **ná** *(to take)*, **chī** *(to eat)*, or **xǐ** *(to wash)*. In our last example above, *wash* expresses a tangible activity, and the result of the washing is that the plates are clean. So you wouldn't use **bǎ** with a verb that expresses a state or a psychological condition, such as **xǐhuan** *(to like)* or **ài** *(to love)*. Nor would you use it with sensory verbs such as **gǎndào** *(to feel)*, **zhīdào** *(to know)*, **kànjiàn** *(to see)*, or **tīngdào** *(to hear)*; with ordinary verbs such as **shì** *(to be)* or **yǒu** *(to have)*; or with verbs that describe movement to and from a location such as **lái** *(to come)* or **qù** *(to go)*.

PRACTICE 2

Each of the following sentences has been broken down into its grammatical components to help you identify the subject, object, verb, and time phrase. Restate these sentences using **bǎ**, and don't forget to change the word order. Then see if you can give an English translation. As an example, the answer to the first one is:

Wǒmen zuótiān bǎ jiā lǐ de shuǐ hē guāng le. *(Yesterday we drank all the water at home.)*

Guāng literally means *all used up, all gone.*

Subject	Time Phrase	Action	Object
1. Wǒmen	zuótiān	hē guāng le	jiā lǐ de shuǐ
2. Nǐ	yīnggāi	ná zǒu	nà bǎ yǐzi
3. Tā		huā guāng le	qián
4. Nà ge rén		zuò hǎo le *(made)*	zhè ge dàngāo
5. Wǒ	jīntiān	kàn wán le *(finish)*	nǐde shū

ANSWERS

PRACTICE 1: **1.** g; **2.** f; **3.** e; **4.** c; **5.** h; **6.** d; **7.** a; **8.** b

PRACTICE 2: **2.** Nǐ yīnggāi bǎ nà bǎ yǐzi ná zǒu (le). (You ought to take away that chair.) **3.** Tā bǎ qián huā guāng le. (He/She spent/used up all his/her money.) **4.** Nà ge rén bǎ zhè ge dàngāo zuò hǎo le. (That person made this cake.) **5.** Wǒ jīntiān bǎ nǐde shū kàn wán le. (I finished reading your book today.)

PHRASE LIST 1
Here are some phrases related to leisure activities and entertainment.

kàn diànyǐng	*to go to a movie/the movies*
qù hǎitān	*to go to the beach*
kàn xìjù	*to see a play*
kàn diànshì	*to watch TV*
wán de kāixīn	*to have fun*
qù tǐyùguǎn	*to go to a stadium*
zuò yùndòng	*to play a sport*
wán yóuxì	*to play a game*
dǎ chéng píngshǒu	*to tie the score*
tán gāngqín	*to play the piano*
lā xiǎotíqín	*to play the violin*
dǎ gǔ	*to play the drums*
chuī dízi	*to play the flute*

NUTS & BOLTS 1
EXPRESSING FREQUENCY WITH CÌ OR BIÀN
You can use the word **cì** or **biàn** *(times)* along with a number to express how many times something happened. The word order is number + **cì/biàn,** and this phrase is positioned after the verb.

Wǒ qùle sān cì.
I went three times.

Lǎoshī shuōle liǎng biàn.
The teacher said it twice. (lit., The teacher spoke twice.)

Note that **biàn** is usually used to describe how many times a completed action has been done (for example, the teacher's action of saying something was completed twice), while **cì** can generally be used with any event.

If an object that comes after the verb is not a personal pronoun or a place name, the phrase 'number + **cì/biàn**' comes between the verb and the object.

Wǒ jīntiān huànle sì cì yīfu.
I've changed clothing four times today.

Tā zhè ge lǐbài fāle liǎng cì shāo.
He had a fever twice this week.

In cases where the object is a personal pronoun or place name, the phrase 'number + **cì/biàn**' comes after the pronoun or place name.

Wǒ jiàn guò tā yí cì.
I saw him once.

Tāmen qùle Shànghǎi liǎng cì.
They went to Shanghai twice.

PRACTICE 1
Match the Chinese sentences in the right column with the English translations on the left.

1. *I have seen his teacher twice.*	a. Wǒ yí ge lǐbài yóu liǎng cì yóuyǒng.
2. *They have been to China once.*	b. Tā měitiān dǎ liǎng cì diànhuà gěi māma.
3. *I swim twice a week.*	c. Wǒ jiàn guò tāde lǎoshī liǎng cì.

4. *She has been late ten times this year.*	d. Wǒ jīntiān zǎoshang chīle sān cì.
5. *He gives his mother a call twice every day.*	e. Qǐng nǐ zài shuō yí cì.
6. *Please say it (once) again.*	f. Tāmen qù guò Zhōngguó yí cì.
7. *I ate three times this morning.*	g. Tā jīnnián chídào le shí cì.

PHRASE LIST 2
Here are some phrases that express duration and frequency.

hěn jiǔ	*a long time*
hěn duō cì	*many times*
jǐ cì	*several times*
cónglái méiyǒu . . .	*never*
yì nián	*one year*
liǎng ge lǐbài	*two weeks*
sān ge yuè	*three months*
jǐ tiān	*several days*
wǔ nián	*five years*
yì fēnzhōng	*one minute*
bàn ge xiǎoshí	*half an hour*
liǎng ge zhōngtóu	*two hours*

NUTS & BOLTS 2
EXPRESSING DURATION
Phrases that express how long an activity lasted are generally placed after the verb in Chinese, at the end of the sentence:

Wǒmen děngle yí ge zhōngtóu.
We waited for an hour.

Tā zǒule liǎng nián.

He traveled for two years.

As with the phrase 'number + **cì/biàn**,' in cases where an object follows the verb and the object is neither a personal pronoun nor a place name, the expression of duration is put between the verb and the object, and the object goes last.

Wǒ xuéle sān nián Zhōngwén.

I have studied Chinese for three years.

Tā kànle wǔ ge zhōngtóu diànshì.

She watched TV for five hours.

If the object is a personal pronoun or place name, the expression of duration comes after the object.

Tā děngle wǒ bàn ge xiǎoshí.

He waited for me for half an hour.

Wǒde péngyou láile Niǔ Yuē yí ge lǐbài.

My friend has come to New York for a week.

PRACTICE 2

Match the Chinese sentences in the column on the left with the English translations on the right.

1. Tāmen xuéle liǎng nián Zhōngwén.	a. *My mother and father have danced for an hour.*
2. Wǒde péngyou qùle Zhōngguó sān ge yuè.	b. *I have been living in the U.S. for a year.*
3. Māma hé bàba tiàole yí ge zhōngtóu wǔ.	c. *They played ball for an hour today.*

4. Wǒ zài Měiguó zhùle yì nián.	d. *They have studied Chinese for two years.*
5. Wǒde dìdi wánle bàn ge xiǎoshí diànnǎo yóuxì.	e. *My friend went to China for three months.*
6. Wǒ jīntiān wǎnshang dúle liǎng ge zhōngtóu shū.	f. *I read for two hours tonight.*
7. Tā chàngle sān ge zhōngtóu gē.	g. *My younger brother has played computer games for half an hour.*
8. Tāmen jīntiān dǎle yí ge zhōngtóu qiú.	h. *She has been singing for three hours.*

Tip!

In English, the verb *to play* is used with all musical instruments: *play the flute, play the piano, play the violin,* and so on. In Chinese, however, different verbs are used for each instrument depending on how that instrument is actually played. Since a drum is hit or struck, the verb **dǎ** *(to hit)* is used in the expression **dǎ gǔ** *(to play the drums)*. Similarly, the verb used with a piano is **tán** *(to flick)*, **lā** *(to pull)* is used with a violin, and **chuī** *(to blow)* is used with a flute.

ANSWERS

PRACTICE 1: 1. c; **2.** f; **3.** a; **4.** g; **5.** b; **6.** e; **7.** d

PRACTICE 2: 1. d; **2.** e; **3.** a; **4.** b; **5.** g; **6.** f; **7.** h; **8.** c

―――――――――― Lesson 39 (sentences) ――――――――――

SENTENCE LIST 1

Wǒ shénme shū yě bú kàn.	*I don't read (any) books.*
Wǒ shéi yě bù xiǎng jiàn.	*I don't want to see anyone.*
Wǒ nǎli yě bù xiǎng qù.	*I don't want to go anywhere.*
Wǒ hěn lèi, shénme yě bù xiǎng zuò.	*I'm tired and don't want to do anything.*

Wǒ yǒu diǎn dōngxi gěi nǐ.	*I have something to give you.*
Wǒ xiànzài yǒukòng, shénme shíhou dōu kěyǐ péi nǐ qù.	*I'm free now and can go with you anytime.*
Shéi dōu kěyǐ jìn zhè ge dàxué dúshū.	*Anyone can (go) study at this university.*
Wǒ yǒu qián, zhù zài nǎli dōu kěyǐ.	*I have money and can live anywhere.*
Xiànzài shénme xuéxiào dōu yǒu diànnǎo kè le.	*Now there is a computer course in every school.*
Tāde chéngjī hěn hǎo, shénme dàxué dōu kěyǐ shēnqǐng.	*Her academic performance is very good, so she can apply to any university.*

NUTS & BOLTS 1
INDEFINITE PRONOUNS

Indefinite pronouns refer to people, places, and things that are not specifically identified. The indefinite pronouns *anyone, anything, anywhere,* and *anytime* are made in Chinese using question words + **yě/dōu**. **Dōu** is more commonly used than **yě**.

shéi *(who)*	**shéi yě/dōu** *(anyone)*
shénme dōngxi *(what thing)*	**shénme dōngxi yě/dōu** *(anything)*
shénme shíhòu *(when)*	**shénme shíhòu yě/dōu** *(anytime)*
nǎli *(where)*	**nǎli yě/dōu** *(anywhere)*

Let's see some example sentences:

Shéi dōu kěyǐ lái zhè ge wǔhuì.
Anyone can come to the party.

Nǐ shénme shíhou guòlái dōu kěyǐ.
You can come over anytime.

Wǒ shénme dōngxi dōu huì chī.
I'll eat anything.

Rúguǒ nǐ huì shuō Yīngwén, nǐ nǎli dōu kěyǐ qù.
If you know how to speak English, you can go anywhere.

The indefinites *someone/somebody* and *something* are not formed this way. *Someone/Somebody* is expressed by **yǒu rén,** and *something* by **(yì) diǎn dōngxi** or **(yì) xiē dōngxi:**

Yǒu rén qùle xuéxiào zhǎo Zhāng lǎoshī.
Someone went to the school to look for Teacher Zhang.

Wǒde shūbāo lǐ yǒu diǎn dōngxi.
There is something in my schoolbag.

The indefinites *nothing* or *nowhere* are expressed in Chinese by using **shénme dōngxi yě/dōu** *(anything)* or **nǎli yě/dōu** *(anywhere)* in a negative sentence. In this way they're very similar to the English *not . . . anything* and *not . . . anywhere:*

Jīntiān wǒ shénme dōngxi dōu méiyǒu chī.
Today I ate nothing. (lit., Today I anything didn't eat.)

Tāmen nǎli yě bú qù.
They go nowhere./They don't go anywhere.

Nobody is expressed in a similar way, using the indefinite pronoun **shénme rén yě/dōu** *(anyone)* and negation with **bù** or **méiyǒu.**

Wǒ zài jiàoshì lǐ shénme rén yě méiyǒu kànjiàn.
I saw nobody in the classroom./I didn't see anyone in the classroom.

Tā shénme rén yě bú shì.
She is nobody./She isn't anybody.

The indefinites **shéi yě/dōu** *(anyone)* and **shénme dōngxi yě/dōu** *(anything)* can also be translated into English as *everyone* and *everything:*

Shéi dōu xǐhuan wǒ.
Everyone loves me.

Shénme dōngxi zùihòu dōu hùi sǐ.
Everything eventually dies.

PRACTICE 1
Translate the following sentences in English.

1. Tā shénme shíhou dōu kěyǐ fàngjià.

2. Wǒ shénme yě bù zhīdào.

3. Shéi yě bù xiǎng chīfàn.

4. Wǒ māma shénme dōngxi yě méiyǒu mǎi.

5. Yǒu rén zài tāde fángzi lǐ.

6. Shéi yě bù zhīdào tā shì shéi.

7. Wǒ shénme dōngxi dōu xiǎng mǎi.

8. Tāmen nǎli dōu qù guò.

SENTENCE LIST 2

Rúguǒ nǐ yǒu kòng, kěyǐ lái wǒ jiā ma?	*If you're free, could you come to my home?*
Rúguǒ nǐ xǐhuan tī zúqiú, wèishénme bù gēn tāmen yìqǐ qù?	*If you like playing soccer, why don't you go with them?*
Rúguǒ nǐ zài chídào, jīnnián jiu bù kěyǐ kǎoshì.	*If you're late again, you can't take the exam this year.*
Rúguǒ wǒ shì nǐ, wǒ bú hùi qù.	*If I were you, I wouldn't go.*

Rúguǒ tāmen lái wǒmen de xuéxiào, wǒ huì dài tāmen cānguān xuéxiào.	*If they come to our school, I will give them a tour.*
Rúguǒ tā yíngle cǎipiào, tā huì mǎi yí ge fángzi.	*If he had won the lottery, he would have bought a house.*
Rúguǒ nǐ yǒu qián, nǐ huì mǎi shénme dōngxi?	*If you had money, what would you buy?*
Rúguǒ nǐ zhīdào tāde jiā nàme yuǎn, nǐ hái huì qù ma?	*If you had known that his home was so far away, would you still have gone?*
Rúguǒ nǐ xiǎng xué Zhōngwén, wǒ kěyǐ jiāo nǐ.	*If you want to learn Chinese, I can teach you.*
Rúguǒ nǐ jiānchí yào zǒu, wǒ búhuì zǔzhǐ nǐ.	*If you insist on leaving, I won't stop you (from doing it).*
Rúguǒ nǐ yǒu kùnnan, wǒmen huì bāng nǐ.	*If you have difficulty, we will help you.*

NUTS & BOLTS 2
EXPRESSING CONDITIONS WITH RÚGUǑ *(IF)*

The conjunction **rúguǒ** is the equivalent of the English word *if* and is used in Chinese to indicate a conditional relationship between an action or event and its consequence. In other words, **rúguǒ** is used to form conditional sentences that show what requirements must be met in order for something to happen, or how one action occurs as the consequence of another.

As in English, conditional sentences in Chinese are comprised of two clauses. One is the *if* or conditional clause (beginning with **rúguǒ**); the other is the main or consequence clause. **Rúguǒ** is typically placed at the head of a sentence, so this construction is similar to *if . . . then* in English, although *then* is not overtly expressed in Chinese.

Rúguǒ nǐ qù, wǒ bú qù.
If you go, (then) I won't go.

Rúguǒ nǐ yònggōng dúshū, nǐ huì chénggōng.
If you study hard, (then) you'll succeed.

If you want to express a possible future consequence of a condition, use the particle **huì** in the consequence clause.

Rúguǒ wǒ yǒukòng, wǒ huì dǎ pīngpāngqiú.
If I'm free, I'll play table tennis.

Rúguǒ tā kāi zhe diànshì, tā huì zhěngtiān zuò zài jiā lǐ kàn diànshì.
If she turns on the TV, she'll sit at home and watch it all day long.

Note that, unlike English, there is no conditional verb tense *(would, could,* etc.) in Chinese, so a conditional meaning in a sentence is therefore determined mainly by context. Occasionally, the word **le,** which is sometimes used to end a sentence, helps to emphasize a change in condition.

Rúguǒ wǒ qùnián méiyǒu kāishǐ zuò yùndòng, xiànzài wǒde shēntǐ kěnéng huì hěn chā.
If I hadn't started to exercise last year, my body would've been very weak now.

Rúguǒ nǐ méiyǒu pǎo de nàme kuài, jiù bú huì shòushāng le.
If you hadn't run so fast, you wouldn't have gotten hurt.

Rúguǒ tā yǒu qián, wǒ huì jiào tā mǎi yí ge fángzi.
If he had money, I would ask him to buy a house.

Rúguǒ wǒ huì dǎ qiú, wǒ huì gēn tāmen qù.
If I knew how to play ball, I'd go with them.

Rúguǒ tāmen rènzhēn dúshū, jiù bú huì bùjígé le.
If they had taken their studies seriously, they wouldn't have failed.

Rúguǒ nǐ xiǎoxīn, jiù bú huì nòng cuò le.
If you were careful, you wouldn't make mistakes.

Rúguǒ nǐ zuò qítā gōngzuò, nǐ jiù huì kāixīn yìdiǎn.
If you had a different job, you would be (a little) happier.

Rúguǒ tiānqì hǎo yìdiǎn jiù hǎo le.
It would be great if the weather were a little better.

Rúguǒ wǒ yǒu duō yìxiē qián jiù hǎo le.
It would be wonderful if I had more money.

PRACTICE 2
Match the Chinese sentences in the column on the left with the English translations on the right.

1. Rúguǒ nǐ xiǎng shěng *(save)* qián, nà nǐ jiù bù yīnggài mǎile nà liàng chē.	a. *If you had money, what would you like to do?*
2. Rúguǒ wǒmen yǒu liù ge rén, jiù kěyǐ dǎ lánqiú le.	b. *If we had six people, we could play basketball.*
3. Rúguǒ nǐ chídào, wǒmen huì bù děng nǐ.	c. *If the weather is bad today, I won't go swimming.*
4. Rúguǒ nǐ yǒu qián, nǐ xiǎng zuò shénme?	d. *If you're late, we'll leave without you. (lit., If you're late, we won't wait for you.)*
5. Rúguǒ jīntiān de tiānqì bù hǎo, wǒ bú huì qù yóuyǒng.	e. *If you wanted to save money, you shouldn't have bought that car.*

ANSWERS
PRACTICE 1: 1. He can take a day off anytime. **2.** I don't know anything. **3.** Nobody wants to eat. **4.** My mother didn't buy anything. **5.** Someone is in his/her house. **6.** Nobody knows who he/she is. **7.** I want to buy everything. **8.** They have gone everywhere.

PRACTICE 2: 1. e; **2.** b; **3.** d; **4.** a; **5.** c

CONVERSATION 1

Jess and Hai are talking about their hobbies.

Jess: Nǐ yǒukòng de shíhou xǐhuan zuò shénme?

Hai: Wǒ xǐhuan gēn péngyou qù dǎ qiú.

Jess: Nǐ xǐhuan dǎ shénme qiú? Lánqiú háishì bàngqiú?

Hai: Bàngqiú zài Zhōngguó bú tài liúxíng. Wǒ hé péngyou háishì bǐjiào xǐhuan dǎ lánqiú. Wǒmen tōngcháng yí ge lǐbài dǎ yí cì. Wǒ hái qù yóuyǒng. Xiàtiān de shíhou, chàbuduō měitiān dōu qù. Nǐ ne?

Jess: Wǒ shénme yùndòng dōu bù xǐhuan. Wǒ zhǐ xǐhuan kàn diànyǐng hé kànshū. Zài Měiguó, yīnwèi diànyǐng piào hěn guì, suǒyǐ, wǒ yí ge yuè zhǐ néng kàn yì liǎng cì. Zài zhèr, diànyǐng piào bǐjiào piányi, wǒ kěyǐ yí ge lǐbài qù kàn yí cì diànyǐng.

Hai: Nǐ zhīdào ma? Chéng lǐ yǒu yì jiā diànyǐngyuàn de piào bǐ zhèlǐ gèng piányi, tāmen fàng de diànyǐng yě hěn hǎo kàn.

Jess: Zhēn de ma? Nà nǐ xià cì dài wǒ qù ba.

Hai: Hǎo, méi wèntí.

Jess: What do you like to do when you have free time?

Hai: I like to play ball with my friends.

Jess: Which game do you play? Basketball or baseball?

Hai: Baseball is not popular in China. My friends and I like to play basketball instead. We usually play once a week. I also like swimming. During the summer, I swim almost every day. How about you?

Jess: I don't like sports. I only like going to the movies and reading. In the U.S., movie tickets are very expensive, so I was only able to go one or two times a month.

Since tickets are comparatively cheaper here, now I can go to the movies once a week.

Hai: *You know what? There's a movie theater in the city whose tickets are even cheaper than they are here, and the movies they show are very interesting.*

Jess: *Really? Can you take me there next time?*

Hai: *Sure! No problem.*

NOTES

Here is some helpful vocabulary. You should already be familiar with some of the words.

liúxíng *(to be popular, trendy)*

chàbuduō *(almost)*

piào *(ticket)*

chéng(shì) *(city)*

piányi *(cheap)*

dài *(to bring, to take)*

Zhēn de ma? *(Really?)*

NUTS & BOLTS 1

MAKING COMPARISONS WITH GÈNG *(EVEN)*

In English, you can clarify the degree of a comparison by using *even*, as in *even colder* or *even more expensive*. In Chinese, this is done with **gèng** using the construction A + **bǐ** + B + **gèng** + adjective. Here are some examples of how **gèng** combines with various comparative adjectives.

Wǒ bǐ tā gèng gāo.

I'm even taller than he is.

Zhè běn shū bǐ nà běn shū gèng hǎokàn.

This book is even more interesting than that one.

Dàxué lǐ lǎoshī bǐ yǐqiáng gèng shǎo.

There are even fewer teachers at the university than before.

Zhèlǐ de miàn diàn bǐ Shànghǎi de gèng dà.

The noodle shops here are even larger than those in Shanghai.

Wǒ xiǎng yào gèng xiǎo yìdiǎn de dàngāo.

I'd like an even smaller piece of cake.

Jiānglái zhèlǐ de rén huì gèng duō.

There will be even more people here in the future.

Yǐqián hé lǐ de yú gèng duō.

In the past, there were even more fish in the river.

PRACTICE 1

Translate the following sentences into English.

1. Jīnnián gèng duō Zhōngguó rén kàn Měiguó diànyǐng.

2. Tā mǎile chē hòu gèng qióng.

3. Wǒ yòngle *(paid)* gèng duō qián mǎi zhè běn shū.

4. Tāmen jīntiān zǎoshang lái de gèng zǎo *(early)*.

5. Nà ge dàxué xiànzài yǒu gèng duō Měiguó xuésheng.

6. Nǐ bǐ píngshí *(usual)* gèng xiǎoxīn.

7. Yīnwèi tā qùnián kǎoshì bù jígé, suǒyǐ tā jīnnián gèng yònggōng.

CONVERSATION 2

Jess and Hai are talking about their studies.

Hai: Kuài kǎoshì le. Wǒ dǎsuàn xiàwǔ qù túshūguǎn wēnxí, nǐ yào yìqǐ lái ma?

Jess: Wǒ bú qù le. Wǒ xǐhuan zìjǐ yí ge rén zài sùshè lǐ wēnxí. Túshūguǎn lǐ de rén tài duō, wǒ bù néng jízhōng jīngshén. Érqiě zuìjìn yuè lái yuè duō xuésheng qù túshūguǎn, wǒ hěn nán zhǎo dào zuòwèi.

Hai: Nǐ shuō de duì. Túshūguǎn zǒngshì zài kǎoshì qián hěn yōngjǐ. Hěn duō xuésheng yào zhǔnbèi kǎoshì de shíhou cái qù nàli. Dànshì, yīnwèi wǒ jiā lǐ tài chǎo, suǒyǐ wǒ xǐhuan qù túshūguǎn dúshū.

Jess: Nǐ píngshí zài nàr dāi duōjiǔ?

Hai: Zhè ge hěn nán shuō. Rúguǒ wǒ yǒu kè, wǒ měi cì dàgài zuò sān ge xiǎoshí. Bú yòng shàngkè de shíhou, wǒ kěyǐ zài nàr zuò yì zhěng tiān.

Jess: Kuài wǔ diǎn le. Wǒ yuē le péngyou qù kàn diànyǐng. Wǒ yào zǒu le. Míngtiān jiàn.

Hai: Míngtiān jiàn.

Hai: *It's almost time for exams. I'm planning to go to the library this afternoon to start reviewing my course notes. Do you want to go with me?*

Jess: *No. I'd prefer to stay in the dorm and study by myself. There are too many people at the library, and I can't concentrate. Furthermore, more and more students have been going to the library recently and I can't find a seat.*

Hai: *You're right. The library always gets really crowded before exam time. A lot of students don't go there until they have to prepare for their examinations. But I often like to study at the library because it's too noisy at home.*

Jess: *How long do you usually stay there?*

Hai: *It's hard to say. On days when I have classes, I probably stay at the library for three hours. When there's no class, I can stay there the whole day.*

Jess: *It's almost five o'clock! I made an appointment with friends to go to a movie, so I have to go now. See you tomorrow.*

Hai: *See you tomorrow.*

NOTES
Here is some more useful vocabulary:

zìjǐ *(self)*
jízhōng jīngshén *(to concentrate)*
nán *(difficult)*
chǎo *(noisy)*
dāi *(to stay)*
Zhè ge hěn nán shuō. *(It's hard to say.)*
dàgài *(approximately, about)*
yì zhěng tiān *(the whole day)*
Kuài kǎoshì le. *(It's almost time for exams.)*

Kuài . . . le is a phrase which literally means *quickly . . . as of now.*
When a verb is added between **kuài** and **le, kuai . . . le** takes on
the meaning of *it's almost time to do something.* The following examples show how this works:

Kuài xiàbān le.
It's almost time to leave work.

Kuài kāishǐ le.
It's almost time to start.

Kuài chīfàn le.
It's almost time to eat.

NUTS & BOLTS 2
INTENSIFYING COMPARISONS
In English, you can show a gradual increase or decrease in intensity with the phrases *more and more* or *less and less.* In Chinese, this
is done by combining **yuè lái yuè** with a descriptive adjective in
a sentence whose main verb expresses a state of being. Take a look
at these examples:

Tiānqì yuè lái yuè huài.

The weather is getting worse and worse.

Zài Niǔ Yuē, yào zhǎo yí ge piányi de gōngyù yuè lái yuè nán.

It's harder and harder to find a cheap apartment in New York.

Tāmen yuè lái yuè lèi.

They (gradually) became more and more tired.

Hú lǐ de qīngwā yuè lái yuè shǎo.

There are fewer and fewer frogs in this lake.

The phrase **yuè lái yuè** can also be combined with an adverb to express the change in intensity that an action undergoes over a given or implied period of time. In this case, the sentence must include an action rather than a state of being.

Tā pǎo de yuè lái yuè kuài.

He ran more and more quickly.

Nà xiē é fēi de yuè lái yuè gāo.

The geese flew higher and higher.

PRACTICE 2

Translate the following phrases into English.

1. Fángzi yuè lái yuè guì.

2. Tā zǒu de yuè lái yuè màn.

3. Tā zuò *(works)* de yuè lái yuè kuài.

4. Yuè lái yuè shǎo rén xiǎng zuò lǎoshī.

5. Yuè lái yuè duō Měiguórén xué Zhōngwén.

6. Yuè lái yuè duō Zhōngguó yímín *(immigrants)* lái Měiguó.

7. Xiàtiān yuè lái yuè rè.

ANSWERS

PRACTICE 1: 1. This year even more Chinese people are watching American movies. **2.** After he/she bought the car, he/she became even poorer. **3.** I paid even more to buy this book. **4.** They came even earlier this morning. **5.** The/That university has even more American students now. **6.** You've been even more careful than usual. **7.** Since he/she failed the exam last year, he/she is studying even harder this year.

PRACTICE 2: 1. Houses are becoming more and more expensive. **2.** He/She walks more and more slowly. **3.** He/She works faster and faster. **4.** Fewer and fewer people want to be a teacher. **5.** More and more Americans are learning to speak Chinese. **6.** More and more Chinese immigrants are coming to America. **7.** The summer is getting hotter and hotter.

UNIT 10 ESSENTIALS

dǎ lánqiú
to play basketball

dǎ Tàijíquán
to do Taiji/Tai Chi

Wǒmen zǒngshì zài gōngyuán tī zúqiú.
We always play soccer in the park.

Wǒ hěn xǐhuan dǎ pīngpāngqiú, dànshì wǒ dǎ de bùhǎo.
I love to play table tennis, but I'm not very good at it. (lit., I like to play table tennis very much, but I don't play well.)

Wǒ bǎ píngguǒ chīle.
I ate the apple.

Wǒ huāle yí ge zhōngtóu bǎ wǎncān chī wán.
I spent an hour finishing eating dinner.

Wǒ jīntiān huànle sì cì yīfu.
I've changed clothing four times today.

Wǒ xuéle sān nián Zhōngwén.
I have studied Chinese for three years.

Wǒde péngyou láile Niǔ Yuē yí ge lǐbài.
My friend has come to New York for a week.

Shéi dōu kěyǐ lái zhè ge wǔhuì.
Anyone can come to the party.

Nǐ shénme shíhou guòlái dōu kěyǐ.
You can come over anytime.

Wǒ shénme dōngxi dōu huì chī.
I'll eat anything.

Rúguǒ nǐ huì shuō Yīngwén, nǐ nǎli dōu kěyǐ qù.
If you know how to speak English, you can go anywhere.

Rúguǒ nǐ yǒu kòng, kěyǐ lái wǒ jiā ma?
If you're free, could you come to my home?

Rúguǒ nǐ méiyǒu pǎo de nàme kuài, jiù bú huì shòushāng le.
If you hadn't run so fast, you wouldn't have gotten hurt.

Zài Niǔ Yuē, yào zhǎo yí ge piányi de gōngyù yuè lái yuè nán.
It's harder and harder to find a cheap apartment in New York.

Tā pǎo de yuè lái yuè kuài.
He ran more and more quickly.

CHINESE IN ACTION

A. FORMAL WEDDING INVITATION AND REPLY

Jǐn dìng yú èr líng líng wǔ nián shí èr yuè shí bā rì(xīngqītīan) wèi zhǎngzǐ Yǒu Wéi yǔ Huáng Zhēn Zhēn xiǎojiě zài Shànghǎi Dà Jiàotáng jǔxíng hūnlǐ shì wǎn jiāzuò Dōngfāng lù yībǎi hào Shànghǎi Fàndiàn èr lóu jìng bèi xǐzhuó gōnghòu guānglín.

Lǐ Guāng jìng yuē

Hūnlǐ shíjiān:	Shàngwǔ shí diǎn–zhōngwǔ shí èr diǎn
Hūnlǐ dìdiǎn:	Nánjīng lù wǔ hào

Xiàwǔ sìshí gōnghòu
Bāshí rùxí
Lǐ Zhái diànhuà: 1234–567

The wedding ceremony of my eldest son Wei You and Miss Zhen Zhen Huang is scheduled to take place on Sunday, December 18, 2005, at the Shanghai Church. A wedding reception will be held on the same night on the second floor of the Shanghai Hotel, which is located at 100 Dongfang Road. We respectfully look forward to your honorable presence.

Guang Li sincerely invites you to attend

Wedding ceremony time:	*10 am-12 noon*
Wedding ceremony address:	*5 Nanjing Road*
Wedding reception:	*4 pm*
Wedding banquet:	*8 pm*
Li family's phone number:	*1234–567*

Generally, a printed reply card is not sent along with the wedding invitation. A guest usually replies by phone. When the guest arrives at the reception, he/she presents his/her gift—usually cash, placed in a red envelope along with a note—to the family that hosts the banquet. Here is one way to write the note that accompanies the gift:

Jǐn jù fēiyí fēngshēn hèjìng

(Name of the guest)
júgōng

Here is a small gift for you. (lit., An insignificant gift is presented to you.)

Humbly,
(Name of the guest)

NOTES
The name and the closing of a letter in Chinese have to be written in two lines in the bottom right-hand portion of the letter if the letter is written in a horizontal format. In China, letters can also be written in a vertical format, in which case the name and the closing are placed in the bottom left-hand corner in a manner parallel to English letter writing.

B. INFORMAL LETTER

Xiǎo Líng,

Shōu dào nǐde láixìn le, xièxie! Shíjiān guò de zhēn kuài. Wǒ yǐjīng xuéle Zhōngwén yì nián le. Zhè ge shǔjià wǒ dǎsuàn qù Zhōngguó lǚxìng liǎng ge yuè, érqiě dào Shànghǎi kàn nǐ hé nǐde jiārén. Wǒ xiǎng qù kànkan zài zhàopiānr lǐ de fēngjǐng. Wǒ yě xiǎng chángchang gè ge dìfang bùtóng de Zhōngguó shíwù. Nǐ kěyǐ gěi wǒ tūijiàn yìxiē dìfang ma?

Zhè shì wǒ dìyícì qù Zhōngguó. Nǐ kěyǐ gàosu wǒ yīnggāi dài shénme dōngxi qù Zhōngguó, yào zhùyì shénme ma? Liùyuè hé qīyuè qù Zhōngguó lǚxíng hǎo bù hǎo? Nǐ yào bú yào wǒ zài Měiguó dài shénme dōngxi gěi nǐ? Qǐng gàosu wǒ. Qǐng dài wǒ wènhòu nǐde jiārén.

Wǒ xīwàng hěn kuài shōu dào nǐ de huíxìn.

Zhù nǐ shēnghuó yúkuài!

Yǒu,
Jennifer Crowley
Shàng
Èr líng líng wǔ nián
yīyuè sānshí hào

Dear Xiao Ling,

I am glad to have received your letter. Thank you very much! Time goes so fast. I have been studying Chinese for a year. This summer, I plan to go to China for two months and would like to visit you and your family in Shanghai. I am eager to see the magnificent scenery that I have observed in photos. I would also like to try a variety of delicious Chinese foods from different regions throughout the country. Could you recommend some places I should visit during this trip?

This is my first trip to China. Could you tell me what I should take with me and what I should be aware of? Is it good to travel to China in June and July? Do you need anything from the U.S.? Please let me know if you want me to bring you something special. Kindly send my regards to your family.

I look forward to hearing from you soon.

I wish you all the best.

Your friend,
Jennifer Crowley

C. ADDRESSING AN ENVELOPE

Jì Shànghǎi Nánjīng Lù yī líng líng wǔ hào
Shànghǎi Dàxià shí bā lóu
Zhōng Měi Gōng Sī
Yóubiān yī líng líng líng yī
Lǐ Dà Tóng jīnglǐ shōu

        Běijīng Hǎidiàn Qū Jiěfàng Lù bā hào
        Guāngmíng Dàxià wǔ lóu wǔ shì
        Yóubiān èr líng líng líng sān
        Huáng Dōng fù

Huang Dong
Guangming Building 5th Fl Room 5
8 Jiefang Road
Beijing, Haidian Region
20003

        Zhong Mei Company
        Shanghai Building 18th Fl
        1005 Nanjing Road
        Shanghai
        10001
        (Attn: Manager Da Tong Li)

NOTES

Jì means *to send to* and identifies the address to which the letter is sent.

Shōu means *to receive* and indicates the recipient.

Fù means *to give* and functions here in a manner similar to the word *from* in English. It identifies the sender of the letter.

Yóubiān means *postal code/zip code.*

The envelope format in Chinese is very different from that in English. In Chinese, the addresses, including the return address, begin with the country name, then give the city, town or village name, followed by the street name, street address, name of the building, floor number, room number, zip code, and finally, the name of the sender or the recipient.

Importantly, unlike in English, the sender's address is placed at the bottom of the envelope and the recipient's is given in the upper left-hand corner.

D. EMAIL

Shōu jiàn rén:	**Chéng Lóng xiānsheng**
Fā xìn rén:	**John Robson**
Zhǔtí:	**Héyuē**
Fùběn chéng:	**Táng Tǒng xiānsheng**

Chén xiānsheng dà jiàn:

(body text)

John Robson shàng

To:	*Mr. Long Chen*
From:	*John Robson*
Subject:	*Contract*
c.c.:	*Mr. Tong Tang*

Dear Mr. Chen,

(body text)

Yours sincerely,
John Robson

SUPPLEMENTAL VOCABULARY

1. WEATHER

tiānqì	*weather*
Xiàyǔ.	*It's raining.*
Xiàxuě.	*It's snowing.*
Xiàbáo.	*It's hailing.*
Yǒu fēng.	*It's windy.*
Hěn rè.	*It's very hot.*
Hěn lěng.	*It's very cold.*
Qíngtiān.	*It's sunny.*
Duōyún.	*It's cloudy.*
Hěn měilì.	*It's very beautiful.*
fēngbào	*storm*
fēng	*wind*
tàiyáng	*sun*
léi	*thunder*
shǎndiàn	*lightning*
jùfēng[1]	*hurricane*
wēndù	*temperature*
dù	*degree*
yǔ	*rain*
xuě	*snow*
yún	*cloud*
wù	*fog*
yānwù	*smog*
yǔsǎn	*umbrella*

---

[1]Some regions of China have typhoons in the summer. The Chinese word for *typhoon* is táifēng.

2. FOOD

shíwù	*food*
wǎncān	*dinner*
wǔcān	*lunch*
zǎocān	*breakfast*
ròu	*meat*
jī(ròu)	*chicken (meat)*
niúròu	*beef*
zhūròu	*pork*
yú	*fish*
xiā	*shrimp*
lóngxiā	*lobster*
miànbāo	*bread*
dàn	*egg*
nǎilào/rǔlào	*cheese*
fàn	*rice (cooked), meal*
cài	*vegetable*
shēngcài/wōjù	*lettuce*
fānqié	*tomato*
húluóbo	*carrot*
huángguā	*cucumber*
làjiāo	*chili pepper*
shuǐguǒ	*fruit*
píngguǒ	*apple*
júzi	*orange*
xiāngjiāo	*banana*
lí	*pear*
pútáo	*grapes*
yǐnliào	*drink*
shuǐ	*water*
niúnǎi	*milk*
guǒzhī	*juice*

kāfēi	coffee
chá	tea
jiǔ	wine, alcohol
píjiǔ	beer
qìshuǐ	soft drink, soda
yán	salt
hújiāo	pepper
táng	sugar
fēngmì	honey
rè/lěng	hot/cold
tián/suān	sweet/sour

3. PEOPLE

rén	people, person, man
nánrén	man
nǚrén	woman
dàren/chéngrén	adult
xiǎohái'er/xiǎopéngyou	child
nánhái'er/nánhái(zi)	boy
nǚhái'er/nǚhái(zi)	girl
qīngshàonián	teenager
gāo/ǎi	tall/short
lǎo/niánqīng	old/young
pàng/shòu	fat/thin
yǒushàn/bùyǒushàn	friendly/unfriendly
kuàilè/shāngxīn	happy/sad
měilì/yīngjùn/nánkàn	beautiful/handsome/ugly
yǒubìng/jiànkāng	sick/healthy
qiáng/ruò	strong/weak
yǒumíng	famous
cōngmíng	intelligent
yǒu cáinéng	talented

4. AT HOME

zài jiā lǐ	*at home*
fángzi	*house*
gōngyù	*apartment*
fángjiān	*room*
kètīng	*living room*
fàntīng	*dining room*
chúfáng	*kitchen*
wòfáng/wòshì	*bedroom*
yùshì/wèishēngjiān	*bathroom*
méntīng	*hall*
bìchú/yīguì	*closet*
chuānghu	*window*
mén	*door*
zhuōzi	*table*
yǐzi	*chair*
shāfā/chángshāfā	*sofa/couch*
chuānglián	*curtain*
dìtǎn	*carpet*
diànshì	*television*
guāngdiéjī	*CD player*
dēng	*lamp*
dvd jī	*DVD player*
yīnxiǎng	*sound system*
huà/túhuà	*painting/picture*
jiàzi	*shelf*
lóutī	*stairs*
tiānhuābǎn	*ceiling*
qiáng	*wall*
dìbǎn	*floor*
dà/xiǎo	*big/small*
xīn/jiù	*new/old*

mùtóu/mùzhìde	*wood/wooden*
sùjiāo/sùjiāo zuò de	*plastic/made from plastic*

5. THE HUMAN BODY

réntǐ	*the human body*
tóu	*head*
liǎn	*face*
étóu	*forehead*
yǎngjing	*eye*
méimao	*eyebrow*
jiémáo	*eyelashes*
ěrduo	*ear*
bízi	*nose*
zuǐ/kǒu	*mouth*
yáchǐ	*tooth*
shétou	*tongue*
liǎnjiá	*cheek*
xiàba	*chin*
tóufa	*hair*
bózi	*neck*
xiōngkǒu	*chest*
xiōngbù	*breast*
jiānbǎng	*shoulders*
shǒubì	*arm*
zhǒu	*elbow*
shǒuwàn(r)	*wrist*
shǒu	*hand*
wèi/fù	*stomach/abdomen*
tuǐ	*leg*
xīgài	*knee*
huái	*ankle*
jiǎo	*foot*

shǒuzhǐ	*finger*
jiǎozhǐ	*toe*
pífū	*skin*
xuè/xiě	*blood*
nǎo	*brain*
xīn	*heart*
fèi	*lungs*
gǔtou	*bone*
jīròu	*muscle*
jiàn	*tendon*

6. TRAVEL AND TOURISM

lǚyóu jí lǚyóuyè	*travel and tourism*
guānguāngkè	*tourist*
lǚguǎn	*hotel*
qīngnián lǚguǎn	*youth hostel*
jiēdàitái	*reception desk*
bànlǐ dēngjì shǒuxù	*to check in*
fùzhàng hòu líkāi lǚguǎn	*to check out*
yùdìng	*reservation*
hùzhào	*passport*
lǚyóuchē/guānguāng bāshì	*tour bus*
lǚxíngtuán	*guided tour*
zhàoxiàngjī	*camera*
xìnxī zhōngxīn	*information center*
dìtú	*map*
xiǎocèzi	*brochure*
jìniànbēi	*monument*
qù guānguāng	*to go sightseeing*
qù pāizhào	*to take a picture*
Nǐ kěyǐ bāng wǒmen pāizhào ma?	*Can you take our picture? (lit., Can you help to take our picture?)*

7. IN THE OFFICE

zài bàngōngshì lǐ	*in the office*
bàngōngshì/bàngōnglóu	*office/office building*
xiězìtái/bàngōng zhuō	*desk*
diànnǎo/diànzǐ jìsuànjī	*computer*
diànhuà	*telephone*
chuánzhēnjī	*fax machine*
shūjià	*bookshelf*
dǎng'àn guì	*filing cabinet*
dǎng'àn	*file*
wénjiàn	*document, file*
lǎobǎn	*boss*
tóngshì	*colleague*
gùyuán	*employee*
gōngzuò rényuán	*staff*
gōngsī	*company*
mǎimài/shāngyè	*business*
gōngchǎng	*factory*
huìyìshì	*meeting room*
huìyì	*meeting*
yuēhuì	*appointment*
xīnjīn/xīnshuǐ	*salary*
gōngzuò	*job*
máng	*busy*
shàngbān	*to go to work*
zhuàn	*to earn*

8. AT SCHOOL

zài xuéxiào	*at school*
xuéxiào	*school*
dàxué	*university*
jiàoshì	*classroom*

kèchéng	*course*
lǎoshī/jiàoshī	*teacher*
jiàoshòu	*professor*
xuésheng	*student*
xuékē	*subject*
bǐjìběn	*notebook*
jiàokēshū	*textbook*
shùxué	*math*
lìshǐ	*history*
huàxué	*chemistry*
shēngwùxué	*biology*
wénxué	*literature*
yǔyán	*language*
yìshù	*art*
yīnyuè	*music*
tǐyùguǎn	*gym*
xiǎoxiū/kèjiān xiūxí	*recess*
cèyàn	*test*
jíbié	*grade*
chéngjīdān	*report card*
bìyè zhèngshū/wénpíng	*diploma*
xuéwèi	*degree*
kùnnan/róngyì	*difficult/easy*
xuéxí	*to study*
xué	*to learn*
kǎoshì	*exam*
kǎoshì jígé	*to pass*
kǎoshì bùjígé	*to fail*

9. SPORTS AND RECREATION

yùndòng jí yúlè	*sports and recreation*
zúqiú	*soccer (football)*

lánqiú	*basketball*
bàngqiú	*baseball*
Měishì zúqiú	*(American) football*
qūgùnqiú	*hockey*
wǎngqiú	*tennis*
yóuxì	*game*
duì/qiúduì/yùndòng duì	*team*
yùndòngchǎng	*stadium*
jiàoliàn	*coach*
yùndòngyuán	*player*
guànjūn	*champion*
qiú	*ball*
yuǎnzú	*to go hiking*
yěyíng/lùyíng	*to go camping*
zuò yùndòng	*to play a sport*
wán yóuxì	*to play a game*
yíng	*to win*
shū	*to lose*
dǎchéng píngjú	*to draw/tie*
	(lit., the match was drawn/tied)
kǎ	*cards*
zhuàngqiú/táiqiú	*pool, billiards*

10. NATURE

dàzìrán	*nature*
shù	*tree*
huā	*flower*
sēnlín	*forest*
shān	*mountain*
tiándì	*field, farm land*
hé	*river*
hú	*lake*

hǎiyáng	*ocean*
hǎi	*sea*
hǎitān	*beach*
shāmò	*desert*
yánshí	*rock*
shā	*sand*
tiān	*sky*
tàiyáng	*sun*
yuèliàng	*moon*
xīng	*star*
shuǐ	*water*
lùdì	*land*
zhíwù	*plant*
shānqiū	*hill*
chítáng	*pond*

11. COMPUTERS AND THE INTERNET

diànnǎo jí hùliánwǎng	*computers and the internet*
diànnǎo	*computer*
jiànpán	*keyboard*
yíngguāngpíng/píngmù	*monitor, screen*
dǎyìnjī	*printer*
huáshǔ/shǔbiāo	*mouse*
tiáozhìjiětiáoqì	*modem*
jìyìtǐ/cúnchǔqì	*memory*
guāngpán	*CD-ROM*
wéidú guāngdiéjī	*CD-ROM drive*
dǎng'àn	*file*
wénjiàn	*document, file*
diànlǎn	*cable*
shùmǎ yònghù xiànlù	*DSL*
hùliánwǎng	*internet*

wǎngzhàn	*website*
wǎngyè	*webpage*
diànyóu	*email*
liáotiānshì	*chatroom*
bókè/bùluógé /wǎngshàngrìzhì	*web log, blog*
jíshí xùnxī	*instant message*
fùjiàn	*attachment*
fā diànyóu	*to send an email*
fā wénjiàn	*to send a document/file*
zhuǎnjì	*to forward*
huífù	*to reply*
shānchú	*to delete*
cúnchǔ dǎng'àn	*to save a file*
dǎkāi wénjiàn	*to open a document/file*
guānbì wénjiàn	*to close a document/file*
fùshàng wénjiàn	*to attach a document/file*

12. FAMILY AND RELATIONSHIPS

jiātíng jí guānxì	*family and relationships*
māma	*mother*
bàba	*father*
érzi	*son*
nǚ'ěr	*daughter*
jiějie	*elder sister*
mèimei	*younger sister*
yīng'ér	*baby*
gēge	*elder brother*
dìdi	*younger brother*
xiānsheng/zhàngfu	*husband*
tàitai/qīzi	*wife*
gūmǔ (father's elder sister)	*aunt*

/gūgu (father's younger sister)

/gūmā (father's married sister)

/yímǔ (mother's elder sister)

/āyí (mother's younger sister)

/yímā (mother's married sister)

/bómǔ (father's elder brother's wife)

/shěnshen (father's younger brother's wife)

/jiùmǔ, jiùmā (mother's brother's wife)

bófù (father's elder brother) *uncle*

/shūshu (father's younger brother)

/jiùfù, jiùjiù (mother's brother)

/gūfù (father's sister's husband)

/yífù (mother's sister's husband)

nǎinai (father's mother) *grandmother*

/wàipó (mother's mother)

yéye (father's father) *grandfather*

/wàigōng (mother's father)

biǎojiě *cousin*
(father's sister or mother's sibling's daughter who is older than you)

/biǎomèi (father's sister or mother's sibling's daughter who is younger than you)

/biǎogē (father's sister or mother's sibling's son who is older than you)

/biǎodì (father's sister or mother's sibling's daughter who is younger than you)

/tángjiě (father's brother's daughter who is older than you)

/tángmèi (father's brother's daughter who is younger than you)

/tángxiōng (father's brother's son who is older than you)

/tángdì (father's brother's son who is younger than you)

yuèmǔ (wife's mother)   *mother-in-law*

/pópo (husband's mother)

yuèfù, yuèzhàng (wife's father)   *father-in-law*

/gōnggong (husband's father)

jìmǔ	*stepmother*
jìfù	*stepfather*
jìzǐ	*stepson*
jìnǚ	*stepdaughter*
nánpéngyou	*boyfriend*
nǚpéngyou	*girlfriend*
wèihūnfū	*fiancé*

wèihūnqī	*fiancée*
péngyou	*friend*
qīnqi	*relative*
ài	*to love*
rènshi	*to know (a person)*
jiàn	*to meet*
gēn . . . jiéhūn (to get married to . . .)	*to marry*
/jià (a woman to marry a man)	
/qǔ (a man to marry a woman)	
gēn . . . líhūn	*to divorce (someone)*
bàn líhūn	*to get a divorce*
jìchéng	*to inherit*

13. ON THE JOB

gōngzuò	*job*
gōng'ān/jǐngchá	*policeman, policewoman*
lǜshī	*lawyer*
yīshēng	*doctor*
gōngchéngshī	*engineer*
shāngrén/shíyèjiā	*business person*
tūixiāoyuán/shòuhuòyuán	*salesperson*
jiàoshī/lǎoshī	*teacher*
jiàoshòu	*professor*
yínhángjiā	*banker*
jiànzhùshī	*architect*
shòuyī	*veterinarian*
yáyī	*dentist*
mùjiàng	*carpenter*
jiànzhù gōngrén	*construction worker*

chūzūchē sījī	*taxi driver*
yìshùjiā	*artist*
zuòjiā	*writer*
guǎnzigōng	*plumber*
diàngōng	*electrician*
jìzhě	*journalist*
yǎnyuán	*actor, actress*
yīnyuèjiā	*musician*
nóngmín	*farmer*
mìshū/zhùlǐ	*secretary/assistant*
shīyè/dàiyè	*unemployed*
tuìxiū	*retired*
quánzhí	*full-time*
bànzhí	*part-time*
wěndìng de gōngzuò	*steady job*
shǔqīgōng	*summer job*

14. CLOTHING

yīfu	*clothes, clothing*
chènshān	*shirt*
kùzi	*pants*
niúzǎikù	*jeans*
T-xùshān/tìxùshān	*T-shirt*
xiézi	*shoe(s)*
wàzi	*sock(s)*
yāodài	*belt*
qiúxié/jiāodǐbùxié	*sneakers, tennis shoes*
liányīqún/lǐfú	*formal dress*
qúnzi	*skirt*
zhàoshān	*blouse*
tàozhuāng	*suit*
màozi	*hat*

shǒutào	*glove(s)*
wéijīn	*scarf*
duǎn shàngyī/jiākè	*jacket*
wàitào	*coat*
ěrhuán	*earring(s)*
shǒuzhuó	*bracelet*
xiàngliàn	*necklace*
yǎnjìng	*eyeglasses*
tàiyáng yǎnjìng	*sunglasses*
shǒubiǎo	*watch*
jièzhǐ/zhǐhuán	*ring*
nèikù	*underpants*
hànshān	*undershirt*
yóuyǒngkù	*bathing trunks, swimming trunks*
yóuyǒngyī	*bathing suit, swimsuit*
shuìyī	*pajamas*
miánbù	*cotton fabric*
pígé	*leather*
sī	*silk*
dēngxīnróng	*corduroy*
nílóng	*nylon*
huābiān	*lace*
hào/chǐmǎ	*size*
chuān	*to wear, to put on*

15. IN THE KITCHEN

zài chúfáng lǐ	*in the kitchen*
bīngxiāng	*refrigerator*
xǐcáo	*(kitchen) sink*
guìtái	*counter*
huǒlú	*stove*
kǎolú/kǎoxiāng	*oven*

wēibōlú	*microwave*
chúguì	*cupboard*
chōutì	*drawer*
pánzi	*plate*
bēi/bēizi	*cup*
wǎn	*bowl*
bōlibēi/bēizi	*glass*
kuàizi	*chopsticks*
tāngchí/sháozi	*spoon*
dāo	*knife*
chāzi	*fork*
guàn(tóu)/jīnshǔguàn	*can*
xiāng/hé	*box*
píng	*bottle*
zhǐbǎnxiāng	*carton*
kāfēijī	*coffee maker*
cháhú/hú	*teapot*
jiǎobànjī/zhàzhījī	*blender, juicer*
yùndǒu	*iron*
yùndǒu bǎn	*ironing board*
sàozhou	*broom*
xǐwǎnjī	*dishwasher*
xǐyījī	*washing machine*
hōnggānjī	*dryer*
zhǔ/shāo	*to cook* *(lit., to burn)*
xǐ pánzi	*to do the dishes* *(lit., to wash dishes)*
xǐ yīfu	*to do the laundry* *(lit., to wash clothing)*
qīngjiéjì	*dishwashing detergent*
xǐyīfěn/xǐyījīng	*laundry detergent*

| piǎobáijì | bleach |
| gānjìng/zāng | clean/dirty |

16. IN THE BATHROOM

zài yùshì lǐ	in the bathroom
yùshì/wèishēngjiān	bathroom
cèsuǒ/wèishēngjiān	toilet
xǐliǎnpén	sink (wash basin)
yùgāng/yùpén	bathtub
línyù	shower
jìngzi	mirror
yàoguì	medicine cabinet
máojīn	towel
wèishēngzhǐ	toilet paper
xǐfàjīng	shampoo
féizào	soap
línyùyè	bath gel
guāhúgāo	shaving cream
tìdāo	razor
xǐzǎo	to take a shower/bath
guā húzi	to shave
gǔlóngshuǐ	cologne
xiāngshuǐ	perfume
chúchòujì	deodorant
bēngdài	bandage
fěn	powder

17. AROUND TOWN

chéngzhèn yóulǎn	sightseeing around town
chéngzhèn	town
chéng(shì)	city, urban
cūnzhuāng	village

chē	*car*
gōngchē	*bus*
huǒchē	*train*
chūzūchē	*taxi*
dìtiě	*subway, metro*
jiāotōng	*traffic*
dàlóu/dàshà	*building*
gōngyù dàlóu	*apartment building*
túshūguǎn	*library*
cānguǎn/fànguǎn	*restaurant*
shāngdiàn	*store*
jiē	*street*
gōngyuán	*park*
huǒchēzhàn	*train station*
fēijīchǎng	*airport*
fēijī	*airplane*
shízì lùkǒu	*intersection*
lùdēngzhù/dēnggǎn	*lamppost*
lùdēng	*streetlight*
yínháng	*bank*
jiàotáng	*church*
miàoyǔ/sìyuàn	*temple*
qīngzhēnsì	*mosque*
rénxíngdào	*sidewalk*
miànbāodiàn	*bakery*
ròudiàn	*butcher shop*
kāfēidiàn	*café, coffee shop*
yàofáng	*drugstore, pharmacy*
chāojí shìchǎng	*supermarket*
shìchǎng	*market*
xiédiàn	*shoe store*
fúzhuāngdiàn	*clothing store*

diànzǐ qìjiàn shāngdiàn	*electronics store*
shūdiàn	*bookstore*
bǎihuò shāngdiàn	*department store*
shìzhǎng	*mayor*
shìzhèngfǔ/shìzhèng dàlóu	*city hall, municipal building*
mǎi	*to buy*
qù mǎi dōngxi	*to go shopping*
jìn	*near*
yuǎn	*far*
jiāoqū/shìjiāo	*suburban*
nóngcūn/xiāngxià	*rural*

18. ENTERTAINMENT

yúlè	*entertainment*
diànyǐng	*movie, film*
qù kàn diànyǐng	*to go to the movies*
kàn diànyǐng	*to see a movie*
diànyǐngyuàn	*movie theater, cinema*
jùyuàn	*theater*
kàn xìjù	*to see a play*
gējù	*opera*
yīnyuèhuì	*concert*
jùlèbù	*club*
mǎxì	*circus*
piào	*ticket*
bówùguǎn	*museum*
huàláng	*gallery*
měishùguǎn	*art museum, gallery*
huà	*painting*
diāokè/diāosù	*sculpture*
diànshì jiémù	*television program*

kàn diànshì	*to watch television*
xǐjù	*comedy*
jìlùpiān	*documentary*
xìjù	*drama*
shū	*book*
zázhì	*magazine*
kàn shū	*to read a book*
kàn zázhì	*to read a magazine*
tīng yīnyuè	*to listen to music*
gēqǔ	*song*
yuèduì	*band*
xīnwén	*the news*
qīngtán jiémù/fǎngtán jiémù	*talk show*
xuǎntái	*to choose channels*
zhuǎntái	*to change channels*
wán de gāoxìng	*to have fun*
mèn	*to be bored, boring*
yǒuqù/hǎowán	*funny*
yǒu yìsi	*interesting*
lìng rén xīngfèn	*exciting*
kěpà	*scary*
shèjiāo jùhuì	*party*
wǔhuì	*dance party*
fànguǎn/fàndiàn	*restaurant*
qù wǔhuì	*to go to a party*
bàn wǔhuì	*to have a party*
tiàowǔ	*to dance*

INTERNET RESOURCES

The following is a list of websites that students of Chinese might find interesting and useful.

www.livinglanguage.com	Living Language's site offers online courses, descriptions of supplemental learning material, resources for teachers and librarians, and much more.
cn.yahoo.com	Yahoo! for users in China
tw.yahoo.com	Yahoo! for users in Taiwan
hk.yahoo.com	Yahoo! for users in Hong Kong
sg.yahoo.com	Yahoo! for users in Singapore
www.baidu.com	A popular Chinese search engine. It also includes a Wikipedia-like encyclopedia.
www.google.cn	Google in Chinese
news.google.cn	Google news in Chinese
home.dangdang.com	A popular online bookseller in China.
www.amazon.cn	Amazon.com for China
www.onlinenewspapers.com	A site that will link you to newspapers from all around the world.

www.cctv.com	China Central Television. The website of a top broadcast network in China.
www.chinese-tools.com	A comprehensive site that includes an extensive dictionary in **pīnyīn,** English, and Chinese characters, additional tools for your computer, a forum, travel information, etc. Even learn how your name would be written in Chinese characters!
zhongwen.com	This website features information on Chinese characters and culture, including guides to writing Chinese characters, information on Chinese surnames, helpful links, and so on.
www.china.org.cn	The China Internet Information Center. The official government portal for news, cultural information, history, etc., from China.
www.qq.com	A widely used instant messaging service in China.
www.sina.com	A well-known information portal for Chinese speakers.

SUMMARY OF
CHINESE GRAMMAR

1. PRONUNCIATION AND THE *PĪNYĪN* SYSTEM
a. 23 initial sounds

b	like *b* in *bear*
p	like *p* in *poor*
m	like *m* in *more*
f	like *f* in *fake*
d	like *d* in *dare*
t	like *t* in *take*
n	like *n* in *now*
l	like *l* in *learn*
z	like *ds* in *yards*
c	like *ts* in *its*
s	like *s* in *sibling*
zh	like *dge* in *judge*
ch	like *ch* in *church*
sh	like *sh* in *hush*
r	like *r* in *rubbish*
j	like *dy* in *and yet*
q	like *ty* in *won't you*

x	like *sh* in *shoe*
g	like *g* in *get*
k	like *c* in *cow*
h	like *h* in *help*
w	like *w* in *wet*
y	like *y* in *yellow*

Note that the comparison of Chinese sounds to English sounds is only approximate.

b. 36 final sounds

a	like *a* in *ma*
ai	like *y* in *my*
ao	like *ou* in *pout*
an	like *an* in *élan*
ang	like *ong* in *throng*
o	like *o* in *or*
ou	like *oa* in *float*
ong	like *ong* in *long*
e	like *er* in *nerve*
ei	like *ay* in *day*
en	like *un* in *under*

eng	like *ung* in *mung*
i (after z, c, s, zh, ch, sh)	like *r* in *thunder*
i	like *ee* in *see*
ia	like *yah*
iao	like *eow* in *meow*
ian	like *yan*
iang	like *yang*
ie	like *ye* in *yes*
iu	like *yo* in *yo-yo*
iong	like *young*
in	like *in* in *sin*
ing	like *ing* in *sing*
u	like *u* in *flu*
ua	like *ua* in *suave*
uai	like *wi* in *wide*
uan	like *wan*
uang	like *wong* with a strong *u* at the beginning
uo	like *wo* in *won't*
ui	like *weigh*
un	like *won* but with a shorter *o* sound

ü	like *eu* in *rheumatic*
üan	like *ü* plus the *en* like in *pen*
üe	like *ü* plus the *e* like in *debt*
ün	like *ü* plus *n*
er	like *are*

c. Tones

There are four tones in Chinese. They are marked above the vowel of each syllable. In the case of diphthongs, the tone is marked over a single vowel in the following order of priority: *a, o, e, i, u*. When *i* and *u* combine to form a diphthong, the tone marker is placed over the second vowel.

Take the vowel *a* as an example:

First tone	ā
Second tone	á
Third tone	ǎ
Fourth tone	à

Here are a few examples of diphthongs:

ai	
First tone	āi
Second tone	ái

Third tone	ǎi
Fourth tone	ài

ui	
First tone	uī
Second tone	uí
Third tone	uǐ
Fourth tone	uì

iu	
First tone	iū
Second tone	iú
Third tone	iǔ
Fourth tone	iù

d. Neutral tone

Some syllables are "toneless" or pronounced with a neutral tone. There is no tone marker above the vowel of such a syllable. Examples of toneless syllables are particles *ma* and *ne*, which are always written and pronounced with a neutral tone.

For example:
Nǐ hǎo ma?	How are you?
Wǒ hěn hǎo. Nǐ ne?	I am fine. How about you?

e. Tone changes

1. Double third tones
When two syllables with third tones are next to each other, the first syllable with a third tone is usually pronounced as a half third tone, which sounds like a second tone. The *pīnyīn* tone mark remains the same.

Nǐ hǎo ma?   How are you?

2. *Yī* (one) and *bù* (not)
Yī undergoes three different types of tone changes.

When *yī* is used in counting, as part of a larger number, at the end of a word, or as an ordinal number, it is pronounced with a first tone.

yī, èr, sān	one, two, three
xīngqī yī	Monday
dì yī	the first
yī qī qī liù nián	year 1776

If it precedes a syllable with the fourth tone, *yī* is pronounced as *yí*.

yí cì	one time, once
yíwàn	ten thousand

If it precedes a syllable with the first, second, or third tone, *yī* is pronounced as *yì*.

yìqiān	one thousand
yìzhí	all along

Bù has two types of tone changes.

When *bù* is used alone, at the end of a word, or when it precedes a first, second, or third tone syllable, it remains unchanged and is pronounced *bù*.

Bù! Wǒ bù chī.	No! I won't eat it.
Wǒ bù zhīdào.	I don't know.

When it precedes a syllable with the fourth tone, it is written and pronounced as *bú.*

Wǒ bú huì qù.	I won't go.

f. Use of apostrophe

When a syllable starting with *a, o,* or *e* immediately follows another syllable, an apostrophe is added to keep the two syllables separate and prevent any confusion of meaning.

píng'ān (*píng + ān,* not *pín +gān*)	safe
pèi'ǒu (*pèi + ǒu,* not *pè + iǒu*)	spouse
Cháng'é (*cháng + é,* not *chán + gé*)	the moon goddess

2. PARTS OF SPEECH
a. Numerals

Cardinal numbers are used to indicate quantity and numbering.

yī	one
èr	two
sān	three
bǎi	hundred

Ordinal numbers are used to indicate order and sequencing.

dì yī	the first
dì èr	the second

b. Nouns

Nouns in Chinese denote people and objects, as well as abstract concepts, such as time, direction, and location.

For example:

Wǒ shì xuésheng.	I am a student.
Xiànzài shì sān diǎn.	Now it's three o'clock.
Wǒ zhù zài Shànghǎi guǎngchǎng.	I live in Shanghai Square.
Tàiyáng zài dōngfāng shēngqǐ.	The sun rises in the east.

A noun can modify another noun or can be modified by an adjective.

Zhè shì Zhōngguó píjiǔ.	This is Chinese beer.
Tā shì hǎo háizi.	He/She is a good boy/girl. (lit., He/She is a good child.)

Chinese does not make use of articles with nouns, unlike English (a/an, the). To say "She is <u>a</u> teacher" in Chinese, simply say *tā shì lǎoshī* (lit., she is teacher).

However, there are different ways in Chinese to translate the English "a/an" and "the" when it is absolutely necessary. Neither of them are exactly equivalent to the uses of English articles.

Use a numerical qualifier, followed by the measure word, to suggest the meaning of "a/an."

Gěi wǒ yì běn shū.	Give me one/a book.

Use the demonstrative pronoun *nà* (that) to suggest the meaning of "the."

Nà ge nánháizi qù yóuyǒng le.	The boy went swimming. (lit., That boy went swimming.)

c. Pronouns

Pronouns take the place of nouns and fall into categories such as personal, possessive, demonstrative, and indefinite in Chinese.

Often, pronouns are implied, rather than being actually stated in Chinese. The English word "it," for example, is not translated in Chinese expressions of time. For example: *liǎng diǎn* (lit., two o'clock) means "it is two o'clock."

d. Measure words

A measure word is a word used obligatorily between a number word and a noun.

sì ge rén	four people
liǎng běn shū	two books

e. Adjectives

Adjectives modify nouns and describe characteristics of people and things. An adjective is placed before the noun it modifies. The particle *de* is usually added between disyllabic adjectives and the nouns they are modifying, but not between monosyllabic adjectives and nouns. If *hěn* (very) is used, however, *de* should not be omitted.

yí ge hěn gāo de nánháizi	a very tall boy
piàoliang de dōngxi	pretty things

As noted above, an adjective can be modified by an adverb such as *hěn* (very).

Zhège píngguǒ hěn tián.	This apple is very sweet.

In Chinese equational sentences, adjectives are not linked to nouns with the verb "to be," as in English. Instead, a degree adverb such as *hěn* (very) is commonly used to link the noun and adjective, without adding any additional meaning.

Tā hěn gāo.	She is tall. (lit., She very tall.)

An adjective is made negative by placing the word *bú* (not) before it.

Tā bù gāo.	He is not tall. (lit., He not tall.)

f. Verbs

In Chinese, verbs are used to describe action, behavior, and emotion. They can be placed immediately after the subject or, in a manner quite different from English, they can come at the end of a sentence.

Wǒ zǒu.	I walk.
Tā xué Zhōngwén.	He learns Chinese.
Tā xǐhuan dòngwù.	She likes animals.
Wǒ kěnéng gēn péngyou yìqǐ qù.	I will probably go with my friends.

The negative form of a verb is obtained by placing the word *bù* (not) directly in front of it.

Tā bù xǐhuan kàn diànshì.	He does not like watching television.
Nǐ bú yìnggāi qù.	You should not go.

There are no verb conjugations in Chinese. A verb does not change its form depending on the subject. Verbs have the same forms when used with singular or plural pronouns. Furthermore, verbs do not change their forms to express the different tenses. Different tenses are expressed in Chinese by adding specific helping words to the verb.

g. Verb suffixes

The Chinese language uses verb suffixes to indicate the time sequence of an action. There are three verb suffixes: *le, zhe* and *guò*. *Le* is used to indicate a completed action; *zhe* is used to indicate an ongoing action or state of being; and *guò* is used to indicate a past action.

h. Adverbs

As in English, adverbs in Chinese are used to modify verbs and adjectives, as well as other adverbs. Their purpose is to clarify the words they modify by answering the questions how, when, where, or why.

The word *hěn* (very) is probably the most used adverb in the Chinese language. Like *zuì* (the most) and *tài* (too), it is placed immediately before the adjective it modifies. A typical example of its usage is:

Nǐ shuō de hěn hǎo.   You speak very well.

Adverbs used to modify verbs include *mǎshàng* (immediately) and *yìqǐ* (together). In general, they are placed in front of the verbs they modify.

i. Conjunctions

Chinese uses different conjunctions to link words, phrases and sentences.

píngguǒ hé xiāngjiāo	apple and banana
píngguǒ huòzhě xiāngjiāo	apple or banana
Wǒ yīnwèi bìng le, suǒyǐ (wǒ) bùnéng qù.	Since I am sick, (lit., therefore, so) I cannot go.
Wǒ xiǎng qù, kěshì wǒ tài máng.	I want to go, but I am too busy.

j. Prepositions

Prepositions relate a noun or a pronoun to another word, generally in regard to position, direction, space, or time. They usually precede a noun in Chinese. A commonly used locative preposition *zài* (at, in, on) is used in the following sentence:

Wǒ zài jiā lǐ.   I am at home. (lit., I at home inside.)

k. Particles

Particles are short invariable words that are very commonly used in the Chinese language.

De is used frequently and when placed after a pronoun, it makes the pronoun possessive.

Zhè shì wǒde shū.	This is my book.
Zhè jiā fàndiàn de cài hěn hǎo.	This restaurant's food is very good.

The particle *de* can also be used to form adverbial expressions. In this case, *de* is placed immediately after a verb and followed by an adjective.

Tā zuò de hěn hǎo.	He does it very well.

Note that three different Chinese characters correspond to the *pīnyīn* word *de*. They are three different words with different functions, but the same pronunciation.

The particles *ma* and *ne* are known as "ending particles" because they are placed at the end of sentences to create questions.

Nǐ hǎo ma?	How are you?
Nǐ ne?	How about you?

The particle *ba* is placed at the end of a sentence to make the sentence more polite.

Qǐng jìnlái ba!	Please come in!

l. Exclamation

Exclamatory words, such as *na, le,* and *ya,* are used to help express strong feelings, such as surprise, joy, or shock. They are used in combination with other words and are always placed at the end of sentences.

Tiān na!	My God! (lit., Heaven!)
Zāo le!	Darn it!
Zhēn zāogāo ya!	It's really bad! (lit., Really bad!)

m. Sound words

Sound words are used to express a speaker's personal emotions, including sorrow, happiness, or anger. They typically stand alone and are placed before an accompanying sentence.

Ai! Nà jiā lǚguǎn zài nǎli?   Oh! Where is that hotel?

Hāhā! Wǒ hěn gāoxìng!   Ha ha! I am very happy!

3. NUMBERS

a. Cardinal numbers 1 to 10

yī	one	*liù*	six
èr	two	*qī*	seven
sān	three	*bā*	eight
sì	four	*jiǔ*	nine
wǔ	five	*shí*	ten

b. Cardinal numbers 11 to 100

shí yī (10 + 1)	eleven	*shí qī* (10 + 7)	seventeen
shí èr (10+ 2)	twelve	*shí bā* (10 + 8)	eighteen
shí sān (10+ 3)	thirteen	*shí jiǔ* (10 + 9)	nineteen
shí sì (10 + 4)	fourteen	*èrshí* (2 x 10)	twenty
shí wǔ (10 + 5)	fifteen	*èrshí sān* (20 + 3)	twenty-three
shí liù (10 + 6)	sixteen	*sānshí* (3 x 10)	thirty

sìshí (4 x 10)	forty	*qīshí* (7 x 10)	seventy
sìshí jiǔ (40 + 9)	forty-nine	*bāshí* (8 x 10)	eighty
wǔshí (5 x 10)	fifty	*jiǔshí* (9 x 10)	ninety
wǔshí liù (50 + 6)	fifty-six	*jiǔshí jiǔ* (90 + 9)	ninety-nine
liùshí (6 x 10)	sixty	*yībǎi* (1 x 100)	one hundred

c. Cardinal numbers from 200 to 1,000,000,000

èrbǎi/liǎngbǎi	two hundred	*yìqiānwàn*	ten million
yīqiān	one thousand	*yíyì*	one hundred million
yíwàn*	ten thousand	*shíyì*	one billion
yìbǎiwàn	one million		

d. *Líng* is used to express "zero" in numbers.

yìbǎi líng sì	104	*yìqiān líng sānshí èr*	1,032
yìqiān líng sì	1,004	*yíwàn líng sì*	10,004
yìqiān líng wǔshí	1,050		

e. The word *yī* is added before *shí* in numbers ending in the numerals 10 through 19.

111	*yìbǎi yīshí yī*	312	*sānbǎi yīshí èr*
210	*èrbǎi yīshí*	519	*wǔbǎi yīshí jiǔ*

*Note that "ten thousand" is not expressed as *shíqiān* as expected.

f. *Èr* and *liǎng*

The number two is expressed in two different ways in Chinese. *Èr* is used for counting and numeric expressions, such as twelve *(shí èr)* or two hundred *(èrbǎi)*. *Liǎng* is used in combination with nouns.

g. More examples with numbers:

2,010	*èrqiān líng yīshí*
8,100,243	*bābǎi yīshíwàn líng èrbǎi sìshí sān*
987,654,321	*jiǔyì bāqiān qībǎi liùshíwǔwàn sìqiān sānbǎi èrshí*

h. Ordinal numbers

Dì is added to a cardinal number in order to form an ordinal number.

yī	one	*dì yī*	the first
jiǔ	nine	*dì jiǔ*	the ninth

4. NOUNS

There is no distinction in form between singular and plural nouns in Chinese. A number or a measure word can be placed in front of a noun to designate it as either singular or plural.

yí ge píngguǒ	one apple
liǎng ge píngguǒ	two apples

The ending *men* can be used to create plural nouns, but only if they refer to human beings. Adding *men* will also make the noun definite, i.e., referring to a specific group of people.

Háizimen ài chī tángguǒ.	The children love eating candy.
Lǎoshīmen jìnlái le.	The teachers came in.

When *men* is added to the noun *rén*, the resulting noun is indefinite and generic.

Rénmen ài tā.   People love him/her.

If a number or measure word precedes a noun, *men* cannot be used.

Correct	*liǎng ge háizi*	two children
Incorrect	*liǎng ge háizimen*	two children

5. PERSONAL PRONOUNS

a. Singular personal pronouns in Chinese are:

1st person	*wǒ*	I/me
2nd person	*nín (fml.)* *nǐ (infml.)*	you
3rd person	*tā* .	he, she, it/ him, her, it

There is no difference among the personal pronouns for "he," "she," and "it" in pronunciation. *Tā* is used for all. However, the Chinese characters for *tā* (he), *tā* (she) and *tā* (it) are different.

Chinese does not distinguish between subject and object pronouns. For example, the word *wǒ* means both "I" and "me."

Wǒ xǐhuan tā, tā yě xǐhuan wǒ.   I like him and he likes me, too.

b. Plural personal pronouns in Chinese are:

1st person	*wǒmen*	we/us
2nd person	*nǐmen*	you, all of you
3rd person	*tāmen*	they/them

Note that there is no special polite or formal form for the 2nd person plural pronoun *nǐmen*. Instead, phrases *nín liǎng wèi* (you two/both of you) or *nín jǐ wèi* (several of you) can be used.

Nín liǎng wèi qǐng zùo. You two (pl. fml.), please sit down.
Nín jǐ wèi yào dào nǎlǐ? Where do you (pl. fml.) need to go?

c. *Tā* and *tāmen*

Unlike in English, you never use *tā* as the subject of a sentence when talking about the weather.

Xiàyǔ. It is raining.
Qíng tiān. It is sunny.

However, *tā* (it) can be used to refer to an animal or an object.

Tā shì chǒngwù. It is a pet.
Wǒ zuì ài tā. I love it the most.

When *tā* (it) refers to an inanimate object, it is usually omitted from the sentence when it is understood.

Nà běn shū hěn hǎokàn. This book is very interesting.
Nǐ kàn guò méiyǒu? Have you read (it) yet?

In colloquial conversation, *tāmen* is not normally used to replace a plural noun for animals or objects. Instead, a plural demonstrative pronoun is used.

Zhè xiē shì chǒngwù. These are pets.
Wǒ zuì ài zhè liǎng běn shū. I love these two books most.

However, if a noun referring to animals is the object of a sentence immediately following another sentence in which these animals were identified as a species, *tāmen* can be used. This use of *tāmen* occurs rarely in Chinese.

Wǒ yǒu sān zhī māo. Wǒ hěn xǐhuan tāmen.	I have three cats. I like them a lot.

6. POSSESSIVE PRONOUNS

Possessive pronouns consist of personal pronouns followed by the particle *de*.

Singular		
1st person	*wǒde*	my/mine
2nd person	*nínde (fml.)* *nǐde (infml.)*	your/yours
3rd person	*tāde*	his, her, its/ his, hers, its

Plural		
1st person	*wǒmende*	our/ours
2nd person	*nǐmende*	your/yours
3rd person	*tāmende*	their/theirs

7. DEMONSTRATIVE PRONOUNS: *ZHÈ* AND *NÀ*

Chinese has two demonstrative pronouns: *zhè* (this) and *nà* (that). A measure word must be placed between a demonstrative pronoun and a noun that it modifies.

zhè běn shū	this book
nà běn shū	that book

In the plural, *xiē* is used: *zhè xiē* and *nà xiē*. No additional measure word is needed.

zhè xiē shū	these books
nà xiē shū	those books

The noun (but <u>not</u> the measure word) that follows *zhè* or *nà* can be left out if its meaning is clear from the context.

Zhè běn shū shì nǐde.	This book is yours.
Zhè běn shì nǐde.	This (one) is yours.

8. INDEFINITE PRONOUNS

There are several types of indefinite pronouns in Chinese. Indefinite pronouns such as "anyone," "anybody," "anything," or "anytime" consist of question words (who, what, when, where, why, etc.) + *yě/dōu*.

shéi + yě/dōu	anyone
shénme dōngxi + yě/dōu	anything
shénme shíhòu + yě/dōu	anytime
nǎli/nǎr + yě/dōu	anywhere
shénme rén + yě/dōu	anybody

Wǒ shéi yě bú jiàn.	I don't see anyone.
Tā shénme dōngxi yě chī.	He eats anything.
Nǐ nǎr yě bú zhù.	You don't live anywhere.
Nǐ xǐhuan shénme shíhòu lái yě kěyǐ.	Come over anytime you like.
Shénme rén yě kěyǐ qù.	Anybody can go.

When indefinite pronouns function as subjects, they can also be formed using *rènhé* (any) + *yě* as follows:

rènhé rén + yě	anyone
rènhé dōngxi + yě	anything
rènhé shíhòu + yě	anytime
rènhé dìfang + yě	anywhere
méiyǒu rén, shénme rén yě + negation with *bù* or *méiyǒu*	nobody

Rènhé rén yě kěyǐ qù.	Anyone can go.
Rènhé dōngxi yě huì biàn.	Anything can change.
Rènhé shíhòu yě kěyǐ.	Anytime is fine.
Rènhé dìfang yě kěyǐ.	Anywhere is fine. (lit., Anywhere can be.)
Méiyǒu rén lái.	Nobody came.

The indefinite pronouns "someone" and "somebody" are expressed with *yǒu rén,* while the indefinite pronoun "something" is expressed with *diǎn dōngxi.*

Yǒu rén zài zhèr.	Someone is here. (lit., There is person here.)
Yǒu rén zhǎo nǐ.	Somebody is looking for you.
Wǒ yǒu diǎn dōngxi gěi nǐ.	I have something to give you.

The indefinite pronouns "wherever," "whoever," and "whatever" are formed with *wúlùn* (no matter) + question words (who, what, where, etc.) + *yě.*

wúlùn . . . nǎli/nǎr . . . yě	wherever
wúlùn . . . shéi . . . yě	whoever
wúlùn . . . shénme . . . yě	whatever

Wúlùn nǐ qù nǎr, wǒ yě qù. — Wherever you go, I will go.

Wúlùn shì shéi, wǒ yě bú huì jiàn. — Whomever he/she is, I will not see him/her.

Wúlùn wǒ chī shénme, tā yě chī. — Whatever I eat, he/she eats.

9. MEASURE WORDS

When a noun is modified by a number word or a demonstrative pronoun, a measure word is needed between the number word or the demonstrative pronoun and the noun. Different nouns require the use of different measure words.

For example, the measure word *běn* needs to be added between *yī* and *shū* to form the complete expression *yì běn shū* "one book/a book."

The measure word changes according to the category to which the given noun belongs. There are different measure words for nouns denoting round objects, flat objects, items of clothing, people, etc.

Measure words are classified according to the following categories:

a. Nature of the object

Measure word	Category	Examples
zhī	animals[2]	yì zhī jī (one/a chicken) yì zhī māo (one/a cat) yì zhī niǎo (one/a bird)
zhī	utensils	yì zhī bēi (one/a cup/glass) yì zhī wǎn (one/a bowl) yì zhī guō (one/a pot)
tái	machinery	yì tái jīqì (one/a machine) yì tái diànnǎo (one/a computer) yì tái diànshì (one/a television)
jiàn	clothing (top)	yí jiàn chènshān (one/a shirt) yí jiàn fēngyī (one/a wind-breaker)
tiáo	clothing (bottom)	yì tiáo kùzi (one/a pair of pants) yì tiáo qúnzi (one/a skirt)

[2]Special measure words are used for the following three animals: yì tiáo gǒu (one/a dog), yì tóu niú (one/a cow), and yì pī mǎ (one/a horse).

Measure word	Category	Examples
bǎ	something with a handle	*yì bǎ cháhú* (one/a teapot) *yì bǎ yǔsǎn* (one/an umbrella) *yì bǎ shànzi* (one/a Chinese fan) *yì bǎ yǐzi* (one/a chair)
zuò	large and imposing objects	*yí zuò sān* (one/a mountain) *yí zuò dàlóu* (one/a building)
liàng	vehicles	*yí liàng chē* (one/a car)
jiā	families or enterprises	*yì jiā fànguǎn* (one/a restaurant) *liǎng jiā rénjia* (two families)
ge[3]	people	*yí ge rén* (one/a person) *liǎng ge lǎoshī* (two teachers)

[3]The polite form is *wèi*. For example: *yī wèi lǎoshī* (one/a teacher).

b. Shape of the object

Measure word	Category	Examples
zhāng	flat surface	*yì zhāng zhǐ* (one/a piece of paper) *yì zhāng bàozhǐ* (one/a newspaper) *yì zhāng zhàopiàn* (one/a photo) *yì zhāng chuáng* (one/a bed)
zhī	pointed and thin or like a branch	*yì zhī bǐ* (one/a pen) *yì zhī qiāng* (one/a gun) *yì zhī jūnduì* (one/a troop)
lì	granular	*yí lì mǐ* (one/a grain of rice) *yí lì zhǒngzi* (one/a seed)
kē	small and round	*yì kē yǎnlèi* (one/a tear drop) *yì kē hóngdòu* (one/a red bean)
tiáo	long and thin	*yì tiáo lù* (one/a road) *yì tiáo sījīn* (one/a silk scarf) *yì tiáo xiàn* (one/a string)

Measure word	Category	Examples
pán	something round and flat or shaped like a plate	*yì pán wéiqí* (one/a game of Chinese checkers) *yì pán cídài* (one/a tape)

c. Containers that function as measure words

Measure word	Category	Examples
bēi	cup	*yì bēi shuǐ* (one/a cup of water)
dài	bag	*yí dài píngguǒ* (one/a bag of apples)
pán	plate	*yì pán cài* (one/a dish)
xiāng	box	*yì xiāng lājī* (one/a box of rubbish)

d. Measure words denoting quantity

Measure word	Category	Examples
duì[4]	pair[5]	*yí duì xiézi* (one/a pair of shoes) *yí duì kuàizi* (one/a pair of chopsticks)
shuāng	pair	*yì shuāng wàzi* (one/a pair of socks) *yì shuāng yǎnjing* (one/a pair of eyes)
fù	pair	*yī fù yǎnjìng* (one/a pair of glasses)
qún	group	*yì qún yāzi* (one/a group of ducks) *yì qún rén* (one/a group of people)
dá	dozen	*yì dá jīdàn* (one/a dozen eggs)
chuàn	cluster	*yī chuàn pútáo* (one/a cluster of grapes)

[4]The measure word *zhī* is used instead of *duì* and *shuāng* when it is necessary to single out one object out of the pair, e.g., *yì zhī wàzi* (one/a sock).
[5]"A pair of trousers" is *yì tiáo kùzi* and "a pair of scissors" is *yì bǎ jiǎndāo* in Chinese.

e. Measure words *xiē*, *jǐ*, and *yìdiǎn(r)*

Xiē can combine with a demonstrative pronoun or the number word *yī* to signify an undetermined quantity of something. It is the equivalent of "some" or "a few" in English. "*Jǐ* + measure word" can be used to denote a smaller amount than *xiē*, while *yìdiǎn(r)* simply means a small amount of something.

nà xiē rén	those people
yì xiē shū	some books
jǐ ge rén	several people
yìdiǎn yán	a little salt

Xiē can be used with countable and uncountable nouns. *Yìdiǎn(r)* is only used with uncountable nouns and *jǐ* is only used with countable nouns.

f. Amounts or portions of things

Measure word	Category	Examples
kuài	piece	*yí kuài dàngāo* (one/a piece of cake)
dī	drop	*yì dī shuǐ* (one/a drop of water)
cè	volume	*yí cè shū* (one/a volume of a set of books)

g. Units of measurement

cùn	inch	*chǐ*	foot
yīnglǐ	mile	*gōngchǐ/mǐ*	meter
gōnglǐ	kilometer	*gōngjīn*	kilogram
jīn	catty[6]	*bàng*	pound

The table below shows the different units of measure used in mainland China, Taiwan, and Hong Kong.

Units of measure	Mainland China	Taiwan	Hong Kong
Length	*mǐ* (meter)/ *gōnglǐ* (kilometer)	*mǐ* (meter)/ *gōnglǐ* (kilometer)	*chǐ* (foot)/ *gōnglǐ* (kilometer)
Weight	*gōngjīn* (kilogram)	*gōngjīn* (kilogram)	*bàng* (pound)/ *gōngjīn* (kilogram)/*jīn* (catty)

h. The measure word *gè*

Gè (often written as *ge)* is the most extensively used measure word. It is used especially with those nouns that don't have particular measure words assigned.

| *yí ge píngguǒ* | one/an apple |
| *yí ge zhàoxiàngjī* | one/a camera |

---

[6]1 catty = 600 gr.

In addition, it is also used for abstract things, such as dreams and ideas.

yí ge xīngqī	one/a week
yí ge mèng	one/a dream
yí ge zhǔyì	one/an idea

i. As a general rule, each noun combines with one specific measure word. A few nouns can combine with more than one measure word.

| *yì tái diànnǎo* or *yí bù diànnǎo* | one/a computer |
| *yí ge diànyǐng* or *yí bù diànyǐng* | one/a film |

10. "VERB-OBJECT" VERBS

Special two-syllable verbs exist in Chinese that consist of verbs and their objects. For example, the verb *chīfàn* consists of the word *chī* (to eat) and *fàn* (cooked rice, meal). The object is usually not translated in English.

| *Wǒ chīfàn.* | I eat. (lit., I eat a meal.) |
| *Tā kāichē.* | He drives. (lit., He opens car.) |

Not all two-syllable verbs in Chinese are "verb-object" verbs. Most verbs, such as *jiǎnchá* (to examine), do not fall into this category.

This is an important distinction because "verb-object" verbs require special treatment under certain circumstances. When a "verb-object" verb is modified by an adverb or verb suffix, such as *le* or *guò*, the adverb or suffix can be placed between the verb and the object. But in the case of other two-syllable verbs, adverbs and suffixes are always added after the verb.

| *Wǒ chīle fàn.* | I ate. |
| *Wǒ jiǎnchá le.* | I examined. |

11. YǑU (TO HAVE)

a. *Yǒu* is used to indicate possession. The negative form of *yǒu* is *méiyǒu*.

Wǒ yǒu liǎng běn shū.	I have two books.
Nǐ yǒu sān tiáo gǒu.	You have three dogs.
Tā méiyǒu qián.	He does not have money.

b. The question forms of *yǒu* are:

Nǐ yǒu qián ma?	Do you have money?
Nǐ yǒu méiyǒu qián?	Do you have money? (lit., Do you have money or not?)

The positive and negative answers to these questions are:

Yǒu.	Yes, I do.
Méiyǒu.	No, I don't.

12. SHÌ (TO BE)

The use of the verb *shì* (to be) in Chinese is very different from its usage in English. The most striking difference is that, in Chinese, *shì* is never placed between a noun and an adjective in an equational sentence. For example:

Tā hěn gāo.	He is tall. (lit., He very tall.)

The uses of *shì* are as follows:

a. *Shì* is used between a subject noun and a predicate noun in an equational sentence.

Měiguó de shǒudū shì Huáshèngdùn.	America's capital is Washington.
Jīngyú shì yī zhǒng dòngwù.	The whale is one kind of animal.

b. *Shì* is used to indicate existence or a state of being. (Refer to Item 31 below.)

c. *Shì* is used between two identical nouns and then this pattern is repeated for two different nouns in the same sentence to indicate that the two nouns are not related and must not be mistaken for one another.

Nín shì nín, wǒ shì wǒ, qǐng nín bú yào hùn zài yìqǐ. You are you, I am I, please don't confuse the two.

d. *Shì* is used in compound sentences whose first half uses *shì* between two identical nouns, adjectives, or verbs to mean "although."

Hǎo shì hǎo, jiù shì guì le yīdiǎnr. Although it's good, it's a little bit expensive. (lit., Good is good, but expensive more a little bit.)

Rén shì hǎo rén, jiùshì tài shòu. Although he is a good person, he is too thin.

13. MODAL VERBS

There are three types of modal verbs in Chinese. They are used as follows:

a. To indicate possibility:

1. Among its many applications, *huì* can be used as a modal verb to mean "to be able" or "know how to."

Wǒ huì shuō Yīngwén hé Zhōngwén. I can (know how to) speak English and Chinese.

2. Another word that expresses possibility in Chinese is the modal verb *kěyǐ* (can). *Kěyǐ* must precede the main verb in a sentence, but does not need to be placed immediately before it.

Tā kěyǐ chī shí wǎn fàn. He can eat ten bowls of rice.

Wǒ kěyǐ gēn nǐ qù. I can go with you.

When used in questions, *kěyǐ* is placed after the main verb and separated by a comma. It can stand alone as a one-word answer, meaning "yes."

Nǐ míngtiān qù, kěyǐ ma?	Can you go tomorrow? (lit., You go tomorrow, can you?)
Kěyǐ.	Yes, I can.

b. To express desire or willingness:

Yào (to want) and *xiǎng* (to want/would like) are both used to express willingness. The first indicates a stronger sense of desire.

Wǒ yào zhù zài xuéxiào fùjìn.	I want to live near the school.
Wǒ xiǎng hē yì bēi kāfēi.	I would like to drink a cup of coffee.

c. To express necessity:

1. *Yīnggāi* (should) is placed before the main verb to show that an action is imperative. It can be separated from the main verb by an adverb that further qualifies the action.

Nǐ yīnggāi mǎshàng zuò fēijī qù Běijīng.	You should take the plane to go to Beijing immediately.

2. *Děi* (to have to/must) is widely used in colloquial language to show a sense of necessity. It is placed in front of the main verb, although sometimes it is separated from that verb by an adverb or adverbial phrase.

Nǐ děi zǎo yìdiǎn huíqù.	You have to go back earlier.

The modal verbs listed above can all be negated with *bù* except for the verb *děi*. The negative form of *děi* does not exist. Instead, one can say:

Nǐ yídìng bù kěyǐ chī.	You mustn't eat.

14. COMMANDS AND REQUESTS
a. Commands

The imperative form of a verb is simply formed by using the verb without any subject. However, the particle *ba* can be placed at the end of the sentence in order to soften the tone.

Zǒu!	Go! (Get out!)
Zǒu ba!	Go! (Go ahead, go.)

To formulate a negative command, *bié* is placed before the verb.

Bié shuì!	Don't sleep!
Bié zǒu!	Don't go!

b. Requests

Common phrases that are used to form requests include:

1. The expression *Nǐ kěyǐ . . . ?* (Can you . . . ?) is often used to begin a request.

Nǐ kěyǐ guān mén ma?	Can you close the door?

2. You can also add the word *duìbuqǐ* (excuse me) when making a request.

Duìbuqǐ, nǐ kěyǐ bāng wǒ ma?	Excuse me, can you help me?

3. *Máfan nǐ/nín* literally means "to bother you" but is often used in requests to mean "Could you . . ." or "May I trouble you . . ."

Máfan nǐ gěi wǒ yìxiē hújiāo.	Could you give me some pepper (please)?

4. One of the most important words to know when making a request is *qǐng* (please).

Qǐng gěi wǒ . . .	Please get/give me . . .

15. EXPRESSING A COMPLETED ACTION USING *LE*

The suffix *le* is put after a verb to indicate that an action has been completed or that something is different from the way it was in the past, including a change in seasons. Because *le* can also be used to refer to something that has not yet happened, its function is very different from the simple past tense in English.

Tā qùle Shànghǎi.	He went to Shanghai.
Qiūtiān láile.	Now it's autumn.
Fēijī kuài qǐfēi le.	The plane is about to take off.

16. EXPRESSING A PAST ACTION USING *GUÒ*

The suffix *guò* is placed after a verb to indicate that an action took place during a period of time from the past until now. It is usually translated as the present perfect tense in English.

| *Wǒ qù guò Zhōngguó.* | I have been to China. |

Here is how to form a question using *guò*:

| *Nǐ qù guò Zhōngguó méiyǒu?* | Have you ever been to China? |

The positive and negative answers to this question are:

Wǒ qù guò.	Yes, I have (been).
Wǒ hái méi qù guò.	No, I haven't been yet.
Wǒ méi (yǒu) qù guò.	No, I have never been before.

Note that the word "no," which is typically used at the start of a reply in English, is merely implied in Chinese.

17. EXPRESSING CONTINUOUS ACTIONS USING *ZÀI* AND *ZHE*

a. Use of *zài* to denote an ongoing action

The word *zài* is placed before a verb to indicate that an action is continuous and ongoing. It is equivalent to the present continuous tense in English.

| *Wǒ zài kàn shū.* | I am reading. |
| *Tāmen zài gōngzuò.* | They are working. |

b. Use of *zhe* to denote an ongoing state of being

Placing the word *zhe* after a verb also indicates continuous action, but refers to a state of being rather than a kinetic activity. Like *zài*, it is similar to the "-ing" form in English.

| *Tā zhàn zhe.* | He is standing. |
| *Nǐ ná zhe yì běn shū.* | You are holding a book. |

c. *Zài* vs. *zhe*

Note that the difference between *zài* and *zhe* is subtle. *Zài* refers to a continuous active motion, while *zhe* refers to a frozen action or state of events that continues in time.

| *Tā zài chuān yīfu.* | She is putting on clothes. |
| *Tā chuān zhe yí jiàn hóngsè de yīfu.* | She is wearing a red piece of clothing. |

18. EXPRESSING FUTURE ACTIONS USING *HUÌ*

Huì has different meanings in Chinese depending on how it is used. One of its uses is to express action that takes place in the future. When placed immediately before a main verb in a sentence, it is equivalent to both "shall" or "will" in English.

| *Wǒ míngtiān huì qù Shànghǎi.* | I shall go to Shanghai tomorrow. |
| *Tā děng yíhuìr huì gěi nǐ.* | He will give it to you in a while. (lit., He will give you in a while.) |

19. NEGATIVE PARTICLES *BÙ* AND *MÉIYǑU*

Bù and *méiyǒu* are used to negate sentences involving tense.

a. *Bù*

Bù is usually used in negative statements in the present, future, or continuous tense.

Wǒ bù hē jiǔ.	I don't drink alcohol.
Wǒ bú huì zǒu.	I won't go/leave.
Tā bú zài fàndiàn.	He is not in the hotel.
Huáng xiānsheng bú zài gōngzuò.	Mr. Huang is not working (at this moment).

b. *Méiyǒu*

Méiyǒu is used in negative statements denoting completed actions or actions that are translated using the present perfect tense in English. *Méiyǒu* is also the negative form of the verb *yǒu*.

Wǒ méiyǒu hē jiǔ.	I didn't drink alcohol.
Wǒ méiyǒu hē guò jiǔ.	I have never drunk alcohol before.
Wǒ méiyǒu liǎng wàn kuài.	I don't have twenty thousand dollars.

20. ADVERBIAL USE OF *DE*

In Chinese, the word *de* is placed between a verb and an adjective (verb + *de* + adjective) to form an adverbial expression that describes how an action is done. *De* is always placed immediately following the verb for this purpose.

Tā chī de hěn kuài.	He eats very fast.
Nǐ shuō de hěn hǎo.	You speak very well.

If the verb has an object, then the verb has to be repeated and the object must be placed between the twin verbs.

Wǒ shuō Zhōngwén shuō de	I don't speak Chinese very well. (lit., I
hěn bù hǎo.	speak Chinese not very well.)

Note that, in Chinese characters, *de* (得) differs from the possessive *de* (的), although both have the same pronunciation.

21. MANY, SOME, ALL, EVERY

a. The words *hěn duō* and *bù shǎo* are used to signify "many/a lot of/quite a few," while *yìxiē* is used to signify "some" in Chinese.

They all precede the noun they modify.

Wǒ yǒu bù shǎo gǒu.	I have many dogs.
Zhōngguó yǒu hěn duō rén.	There are a lot of people in China.
Tā yǒu yìxiē wèntí.	He has some questions.

Please note that no measure word is used between *hěn duō/bù shǎo* or *yìxiē* and the nouns they qualify.

b. *Quánbù* is "all" and *měi* is "every/each."

It is not necessary to add a measure word between *quánbù* and a noun it modifies. However, you do need to add a measure word between *měi* and a noun.

Quánbù rén dōu sǐ le.	All people died.
Měi ge rén dōu sǐ le.	Everyone died.
Wǒ měitiān shàngxué.	I go to school every day.

Note that in the last example, it is not necessary to add a measure word between *měi* and *tiān*, since *tiān* itself can function as a measure word. The same rule applies to the expression *měinián* (every year). However, it is necessary to add a measure word when saying *měi ge xīngqī* (every week) and *měi ge yuè* (every month).

c. "All" and "every" can also be expressed using duplicate measure words and *dōu*.

Gègè rén dōu xǐhuan tā.	Everyone likes him. (lit., All the people like him.)
Běnběn shū dōu hěn guì.	Every book is expensive./All books are expensive.

22. USE OF *DŌU*

The word *dōu* means "all" or "both" when it is placed before the main verb in a sentence containing more than one subject.

When the subject refers to two individuals, *dōu* means "both." When the subject refers to more than two individuals, *dōu* means "all." It also means "all" when referring to uncountable and nationality nouns.

Huáng xiānsheng hé Huáng tàitai dōu bú zài.	Both Mr. Huang and Mrs. Huang are not here.
Bob, Bill hé Susie dōu shì xuésheng.	Bob, Bill, and Susie are all students.
Māo, gǒu hé zhū dōu shì dòngwù.	Cats, dogs, and pigs are all animals.
Wǒmen dōu shì Měiguórén.	We are all American.

23. COMPARISON
a. Comparative adjectives

The properties of two nouns can be compared using the grammatical structure "A *bǐ* B + adjective," which means "A has a property greater than B."

Wǒ bǐ nǐ dà.	I am older than you. (lit., I am bigger than you.)
Zhè běn shū bǐ nà běn shū guì.	This book is more expensive than that one.

To express the exact degree of difference between two properties, words specifying age or amount are placed immediately after the comparative adjective.

Wǒ bǐ nǐ dà sān suì.	I am three years older than you.

b. Comparative adverbs

Two adverbial expressions can be compared using the structure "A + verb + *de bǐ* + B + adverb," which means "A is doing something to a greater degree than B."

Wǒ zǒu de bǐ nǐ kuài.	I walk faster than you do.

c. Similarity

There are two ways to express similarity between the properties of two objects.

1. You can use the expression *yǒu . . . zhème/nàme* (as . . . as) as follows.

Wǒ yǒu nǐ nàme gāo.	I am as tall as you.

2. Another option is to use the grammatical structure "A + *hé* + B + *yíyàng* + adjective."

Wǒ hé nǐ yíyàng gāo.	I am as tall as you. (lit., I and you are the same height.)

d. Superlative

The superlative form of an adjective is formed by placing the word *zuì* immediately before it.

Zhè jiā fàndiàn zuì hǎo.	This hotel is the best.
Tā de chē zuì kuài.	His car is the fastest.

24. OR

Huòzhě and *háishì* both mean "or" in Chinese. *Huòzhě* is used in statements, while both *huòzhě* and *háishì* can be used in questions, although with differences in meaning. *Háishì* indicates that there is a preference while *huòzhě* indicates that there is no preference or control over the choices.

Both *huòzhě* and *háishì* can be placed between nouns or noun phrases.

Wǒ huì qù Shànghǎi huòzhě Běijīng.	I'll go to Shanghai or Beijing.
Nǐ hē huòzhě wǒ hē dōu kěyǐ.	Either you or I can drink it. (lit., You drink or I drink, both are fine.)
Nǐ xǐhuan wǒ háishì tā?	Do you like me or him?
Càidān yǒu mǐfàn huòzhě miàntiáo ma?	Is there rice or noodles on the menu?

25. HÉ AS A CONJUNCTION WORD

a. *Hé* is equivalent to the word "and" in English, but its usage is much more limited. It can only be used to connect nouns or noun phrases.

Wǒ xǐhuan qù lǚxíng hé kànshū.	I like traveling and reading.
Wǒ hé tā yìqǐ zuò huǒchē.	He and I take the train together.

Note that in Chinese, *wǒ* (I) can precede other pronouns in a group, as in *wǒ hé tā* (I and he).

b. *Hé* can also be used as the equivalent of the English preposition "with."

Wǒ hé Huáng xiānsheng chǎojià.   I quarrel with Mr. Huang.

26. FORMING SIMPLE QUESTIONS
a. *ma*

There are three types of simple questions in Chinese. The first type of simple question is formed by placing the particle *ma* at the end of a sentence. Note that the word order of a simple question with *ma* is the same as the word order of the answer to that question.

Nǐ qù ma?	Do you go?
Wǒ qù.	Yes, I do (go).
Zhāng xiānsheng zhù zài zhèr ma?	Does Mr. Zhang live here?
Tā zhù zài zhèr.	Yes, he does.
Tā pǎu de kuài ma?	Does he run fast?
Tā pǎu de kuài.	Yes, he does.

b. *bú*

The second type of simple question is formed by placing the word *bú* between the two elements of a reduplicated verb or adverb. The question particle *ma* is not needed.

Nǐ qù bú qù?	Do you go or not?
Wǒ qù.	Yes, I do.
Tā pǎu de kuài bú kuài?	Does he run fast?
Tā pǎu de kuài.	Yes, he does.

c. *ne*

The particle *ma* is typically used at the end of a sentence to ask a simple question, while *ne* is usually used to succinctly ask the same question without repeating it.

Nǐ xǐhuan hē chá ma?	Do you like drinking tea?
Wǒ xǐhuan. Nǐ ne?	Yes, I do. How about you?

27. YES-NO ANSWERS

How the answers "yes" and "no" are expressed in Chinese depends on how questions are asked. Generally speaking, these answers require a repetition of the verb used in the question.

a. Example 1

Nǐ shì Zhāng xiǎojiě ma?	Are you Miss Zhang?
Wǒ shì.	Yes, I am.
Wǒ bú shì.	No, I am not.

b. Example 2

Nǐ huì shuō Yīngwén ma?	Do you know how to speak English?
Wǒ huì.	Yes, I do.
Wǒ bú huì.	No, I don't.

c. Example 3

Nǐ qù ma?	Do you go?
Wǒ qù.	Yes, I do.
Wǒ bú qù.	No, I don't.

d. Negative answers

Normally, the particle *bù* (not) is placed before the verb in negative answers. This rule holds true for most but not all verbs. The verb *yǒu* (to have) is an exception.

e. Answering negative questions

Here is an example of a negative question using *méiyǒu:*

Nǐ méiyǒu qián ma?	Don't you have money?

The positive and negative answers to this question are:

Bú shì. Wǒ yǒu.	Yes. I have (money). (lit., No. I have money.)
Shì. Wǒ méiyǒu.	No. I don't (have money). (lit., Yes. I don't have money.)

Note that, in the first example, "no" in Chinese is equivalent to "yes" in English because the reply in Chinese expresses disagreement with the question asked and implies a rejection of the idea that the person questioned may not have any money.

In other words, fully stated, the first reply reads as follows in Chinese: "No, that's not true. I do have money." In English, this translates as: "Yes, I have money." A similar situation occurs in the second example, where the answer "yes" in Chinese is equivalent to the answer "no" in English. In this case, the reply reads as follows in Chinese: "Yes, you are right. I don't have money." In English, this translates as: "No, I don't have money."

28. QUESTION WORDS

shénme	what
shénme shíhòu	when
nǎlǐ/nǎr	where
nǎ + measure word *(sg.)*	which
nǎ + *xiē (pl.)*	which
shéi	who/whom
duōshǎo qián	how much (money)
duōshǎo/jǐ + measure word	how many
duōshǎo	how much

zěnme (yàng)	how
wèishénme	why

Nǐ jiào shénme míngzi?	What is your name? (lit., What name are you called?)
Nǐ shénme shíhòu qù Zhōngguó?	When do you go to China?
Huǒchēzhàn zài nǎlǐ/nǎr?	Where is the train station?
Nǎ běn shū shì nǐ de?	Which book is yours?
Nǎ xiē shū shì nǐ de?	Which books are yours?
Tā shì shéi?	Who is he/she?
Shéi shì Huáng xiānsheng?	Who is Mr. Huang?
Zhè jiàn yīfu duōshǎo qián?	How much is this clothing?
Nǐ yǒu duōshǎo xuésheng?	How many students do you have?
Nǐ yǒu jǐ ge xuésheng?	How many students do you have?
Nǐ yǒu duōshǎo lìliàng?	How much strength/power do you have?
Tā zuìjìn zěnme yàng?	How is he recently?
Nǐ wèishénme bú qù?	Why don't you go?

29. USE OF *SHÌ . . . DE*

The grammatical structure *shì . . . de* is used to place emphasis on specific elements in a sentence. Generally, the word that follows *shì* is the one that is emphasized.

a. In sentences that answer questions about where, when, how, or for what purpose an action takes place, the word *shì* comes immediately in front of the verb and *de* usually comes at the end of the sentence.

Tā shì cóng Běijīng lái de.	He is from Beijing. (emphasis on location)
Wǒ shì lái mǎi nǐ de chē de.	I've come to buy your car. (emphasis on purpose)

b. When emphasis is on the subject, *shì* is placed immediately in front of it.

Shì wǒ chī pínguǒ de.   I'm the one who ate the apple.
                                 (emphasis on "I")

c. When emphasis is on the object, *shì* comes before the verb and *de* is placed in front of the object rather than at the end of the sentence.

Wǒmen shì hē de chá.   We drank tea.
                                 (emphasis on "tea")

30. USE OF THE PREPOSITION *ZÀI* AND OTHER LOCATION WORDS

a. The preposition *zài* (at, in, on) is used to specify location.

Wǒ zài xuéxiào (lǐ).   I am in school.
Tā zài Měiguó.   He is in the U.S.

b. Location words

A number of auxiliary words are also used in Chinese to specify additional information about location. These words are positioned following a place name or a place word in a sentence.

qiánbiān	in front of
hòubiān	behind
shàngbiān	above
xiàbiān	under
zuǒbiān	on the left
yòubiān	on the right
póngbiān	beside

zhōngjiān	between
lǐ(biān)	inside/in
wàibiān	outside

Wǒ de shū zài zhuōzi de xiàbiān.   My book is under the table.

The positioning of *zhōngjiān* is different from that of other location words. It requires the following sentence structure: "A *hé* B *de zhōngjiān,*" where A and B are separate place names or words.

31. THERE IS/ARE: *YǑU* AND *SHÌ*

There are two ways to indicate existence in Chinese. One is to use *yǒu* (there is/there are) in a sentence, usually following this word order: place word + location word + *yǒu* + subject.

Xuéxiào (lǐ) yǒu hěnduō *xuésheng.*   There are a lot of students in the school. (lit., School inside there are lots of students.)

Gōngyuán lǐ yǒu yì tiáo gǒu.   There is a dog in the park. (lit., Park inside there is a dog.)

The other way to indicate existence is to use *shì* in a sentence with the following word order: place word + location word + *shì* + place word. Note that the object here must be singular.

Gōngyuán de hòubiān shì *xuéxiào.*   There is a school behind the park. (lit., The back of the park is school.)

32. TELLING TIME

The following sentence is used to ask about the time.

Xiànzài shì jǐdiǎn?   What time is it now?

The answer to this question takes the following form:

Xiànzài shì . . .   It's . . . now.

a. Hours

Each hour is expressed with a numeral + *diǎn* (o'clock).

yī diǎn	1:00	one o'clock
liǎng diǎn	2:00	two o'clock
shí diǎn	10:00	ten o'clock

b. Minutes

Fēn means "minute" in Chinese. Minutes on the clock are expressed as follows:

| *yī diǎn shífēn* | 1:10 | ten past one (lit., one o'clock ten minutes) |
| *liù diǎn líng yī fēn* | 6:01 | one minute after six (lit., six o'clock one minute) |

Chinese has the following expressions for the half hour and the quarter hour.

sān diǎn yíkè	3:15	a quarter past three (lit., three o'clock a quarter)
jiǔ diǎn bàn	9:30	half past nine (lit., nine o'clock half)
wǔ diǎn sānkè	5:45	a quarter to six (lit., five o'clock three quarters)

You can also say:

chà yíkè liù diǎn	5:45	a quarter to six (lit., a quarter less than six)

c. AM and PM

The following expressions can be added to the time specified: *zǎoshang* (early morning), *shàngwǔ* (morning), *zhōngwǔ* (noon), *xiàwǔ* (afternoon), *wǎnshang* (night/evening), or *bànyè* (middle of the night, midnight).

These words have to be put before the hour in a sentence and can be used with the following time periods:

bànyè	after midnight *(bànyè* is also the word for "midnight")
zǎoshang	before 10 am
shàngwǔ	after 10 am
zhōngwǔ	12:00 pm
xiàwǔ	before 6 pm
wǎnshang	after 6 pm

zǎoshang qī diǎn	7:00 am (lit., morning seven o'clock)
shàngwǔ shí diǎn bàn	10:30 am (lit., morning ten o'clock)
bànyè liǎng diǎn	2:00 am (lit., middle of the night two o'clock)
wǎnshang jiǔ diǎn	9:00 pm (lit., night nine o'clock)

33. DATES

a. Year: cardinal numbers (0–9) + *nián* (year)

èr líng líng wǔ nián	2005 (lit., two zero zero five year)
yī bā qī èr nián	1872 (lit., one eight seven two year)
yī qī qī liù nián	1776 (lit., one seven seven six year)

jīnnián	this year
qùnián	last year
qiánnián	year before last
míngnián	next year
hòunián	year after next

b. Month: cardinal number of month (1–12) + *yuè* (month)

yī yuè	January
èr yuè	February
sān yuè	March
sì yuè	April
wǔ yuè	May
liù yuè	June
qī yuè	July
bā yuè	August
jiǔ yuè	September
shí yuè	October

shí yī yuè	November
shí èr yuè	December

zhè ge yuè	this month
shàng ge yuè	last month
qián ge yuè	month before last
xià ge yuè	next month
xià xià ge yuè	month after next

c. Week: *xīngqī/lǐbài* (week) + cardinal number of the day (1–6)

Note that Sunday is an exception. Sunday is *xīngqī/lǐbài + tiān*, not *xīngqī/lǐbài + qī* (7).

Monday	*xīngqī yī/lǐbài yī*
Tuesday	*xīngqī èr/lǐbài èr*
Wednesday	*xīngqī sān/lǐbài sān*
Thursday	*xīngqī sì/lǐbài sì*
Friday	*xīngqī wǔ/lǐbài wǔ*
Saturday	*xīngqī liù/lǐbài liù*
Sunday	*xīngqī tiān/lǐbài tiān*

this week	*zhè ge xīngqī*
last week	*shàng ge xīngqī*
week before last	*qián ge xīngqī*
next week	*xià ge xīngqī*
week after next	*xià xià ge xīngqī*

d. Day: cardinal number (1–31) + *hào/rì*

yī hào/yī rì	1st day of the month
wǔ hào/wǔ rì	5th day of the month
sānshí yī hào/sānshí yī rì	31st day of the month
sān yuè èrshí hào	March 20th

jīntiān	today
zuótiān	yesterday
qiántiān	day before yesterday
míngtiān	tomorrow
hòutiān	day after tomorrow

Note that both *hào* and *rì* mean "day of the month." *Hào* is more colloquial and *rì* is more formal.

e. The order of words in dates is: year, month, day, and weekday.

yī qī qī liù nián qī yuè sì hào	July 4, 1776 (lit., 1776 year, July 4th)
èr líng líng wǔ nián shí èr yuè	Friday, December 25, 2005 (lit., 2005
èrshí wǔ hào xīngqī wǔ	year, December 25th, Friday)

34. EXPRESSIONS OF TIME AND PLACE

When combined with the preposition *zài*, words that express time or location usually precede the main verb in a sentence. When both time and location expressions are used in a sentence, the location expression usually precedes the time expression.

Wǒ zài túshūguǎn děng nǐ.	I'll wait for you in the library.
Wǒ zài Měiguó niànshū.	I study in America.
Tā měitiān qī diǎn shàngbān.	He goes to work at seven every day.
Wǒ xīngqī sān zài huǒchēzhàn děng nǐ.	I'll wait for you at the train station on Wednesday.

35. MONEY EXPRESSIONS

The name of the currency used in China is *rénmínbì* (RMB). The basic unit is called *yuán* (dollar). One *yuán* contains ten *jiǎo* (ten cents, or dimes). One *jiǎo* contains one hundred *fēn* (cents). Colloquially, *yuán* is pronounced as *kuài* and *jiǎo* is pronounced as *máo*.

To ask about the price, use the expression *Duōshǎo qián?*, where *qián* means "money."

Zhè ge (yào) duōshǎo qián?	How much is this one? (lit., This one needs how much money?)

To answer the above question, say:

Zhè ge sānshí kuài qián.	This costs thirty dollars.
Zhè ge sānshí kuài wǔ máo.	This costs thirty dollars and fifty cents.

In colloquial language, *qián* is often eliminated after *kuài* in the answer.

Zhè ge sānshí kuài.	This one costs thirty dollars.

Máo or *fēn* can also be dropped.

Zhè ge sānshí kuài wǔ.	This one costs thirty dollars and fifty cents.

36. BASIC FACTS ABOUT CHINESE CHARACTERS

Chinese does not have an alphabet where each character corresponds to a sound in the language. Instead, characters denote individual words. For example, the character 花 is pronounced *huā* and means "flower." The shape and structure of some characters are associated with pictures derived from an ancient form of Chinese writing. For example, 人 is the character for "man" in Chinese. It is reminiscent of a person standing with his two legs apart.

Chinese characters fall into many different meaning categories. Sometimes, it is possible to tell the category of a character from its root symbol, called "a radical," even if you are not familiar with the character itself. For example, when the radical 艹 is written on top of a character, the character is associated with plants, as in 草 *cǎo* (grass). When the radical 冫 is written on the left side of a character, the character is associated with ice, as in 冰 *bīng* (ice). If the radical 氵 is written on the left side of a character, the character is associated with water, as in 河 *hé* (river).

There are over 10,000 Chinese characters. A well-educated Chinese person knows about 5,000 characters. Characters can either stand alone or combine with one another to form compound vocabulary words, or word units. The meaning of these compound words can be very different from the meanings of the individual characters they contain, which makes written Chinese a highly complex and difficult system to master. For example, the word 电脑 *diànnǎo* contains the characters 电 *diàn* (electricity) and 脑 *nǎo* (brain) and means "computer." Another example is 地铁 *dìtiě*, where 地 *dì* means "earth" and 铁 *tiě* means "iron," but the compound word means "subway."

Chinese characters are written in strokes and according to a set pattern of rules that govern the direction and sequence of the strokes. Just as writers of English follow specific rules of penmanship and develop individualized handwriting, so the Chinese spend much time practicing their characters and personalizing their style of writing until, for many, it becomes an art form, known as calligraphy. An average Chinese starts learning how to write characters as early as at the age of three and is encouraged to perfect his or her handwriting since good penmanship is regarded as a gauge of character throughout China.

Here is a list of the one hundred most essential Chinese characters:

	Character	Pronunciation	Meaning
1.	一	*yī*	one
2.	二	*èr*	two
3.	三	*sān*	three
4.	四	*sì*	four
5.	五	*wǔ*	five
6.	六	*liù*	six
7.	七	*qī*	seven
8.	八	*bā*	eight
9.	九	*jiǔ*	nine
10.	十	*shí*	ten
11.	百	*bǎi*	hundred
12.	千	*qiān*	thousand
13.	万	*wàn*	ten thousand
14.	大	*dà*	big
15.	中	*zhōng*	middle

16.	小	*xiǎo*	small
17.	车	*chē*	car
18.	电	*diàn*	electricity
19.	云	*yún*	cloud
20.	雨	*yǔ*	rain
21.	火	*huǒ*	fire
22.	水	*shuǐ*	water
23.	山	*shān*	mountain
24.	上	*shàng*	on, above
25.	下	*xià*	under
26.	左	*zuǒ*	left
27.	右	*yòu*	right
28.	前	*qián*	in front of
29.	后	*hòu*	behind
30.	书	*shū*	book
31.	菜	*cài*	dish, vegetable
32.	鸡	*jǐ*	chicken
33.	鸭	*yā*	duck
34.	牛	*niú*	cow
35.	羊	*yáng*	sheep
36.	猪	*zhū*	pig

37.	鱼	*yú*	fish
38.	酒	*jiǔ*	wine
39.	笔	*bǐ*	pen
40.	字	*zì*	character
41.	是	*shì*	to be
42.	几	*jǐ*	several
43.	美	*měi*	beautiful
44.	国	*guó*	country
45.	高	*gāo*	tall, high
46.	低	*dī*	low
47.	不	*bù*	not
48.	没	*méi*	not to have
49.	有	*yǒu*	have, there is/ there are
50.	也	*yě*	also
51.	了	*le*	(verb suffix)
52.	东	*dōng*	east
53.	南	*nán*	south
54.	西	*xī*	west
55.	北	*běi*	north
56.	人	*rén*	people, person

57.	今	*jīn*	at present
58.	我	*wǒ*	I, me
59.	你	*nǐ*	you
60.	他	*tā*	he
61.	她	*tā*	she
62.	来	*lái*	come
63.	去	*qù*	go
64.	们	*men*	(plural particle)
65.	做	*zuò*	do
66.	元	*yuán*	dollar
67.	两	*liǎng*	two
68.	再	*zài*	again
69.	见	*jiàn*	see
70.	刀	*dāo*	knife
71.	分	*fēn*	separate, minute, cent
72.	到	*dào*	until, reach
73.	力	*lì*	strength
74.	加	*jiā*	plus
75.	又	*yòu*	also
76.	口	*kǒu*	mouth

77.	门	*mén*	door
78.	叫	*jiào*	call
79.	名	*míng*	first name
80.	和	*hé*	and
81.	茶	*chá*	tea
82.	在	*zài*	in, on, at
83.	坐	*zuò*	sit
84.	报	*bào*	report, newspaper
85.	外	*wài*	outside
86.	内	*nèi*	inside
87.	天	*tiān*	sky
88.	太	*tài*	too (excessive), very
89.	好	*hǎo*	good, well
90.	姓	*xìng*	last name
91.	学	*xué*	learn
92.	文	*wén*	written language
93.	家	*jiā*	home, family
94.	写	*xiě*	write

95.	对	*duì*	correct
96.	老	*lǎo*	old
97.	年	*nián*	year
98.	月	*yuè*	month, moon
99.	日	*rì*	day, sun
100.	从	*cóng*	from

Important signs in Chinese characters:

Character	Meaning
男	Men
女	Women
卫生间 or 厕所 or 洗手间	Lavatory, Toilet, Restroom
有人	Occupied (lit., there is person)
无人	Vacant (lit., there is no person)
不准抽烟	No Smoking
不准进入	No Admittance
敲	Knock
铃	Ring, Bell
私人	Private
查询	Inquire Within

停! or 止步!	Stop!
去!	Go!
小心!	Look out!
危险!	Danger!
慢走	Go slowly!
绕道	Detour
警告	Caution
保持右走	Keep to the Right
桥	Bridge
不准停车	No Parking
衣帽间	Check Room
兑换	Money Exchange
资料	Information
等候室	Waiting Room
不要伸出窗外	Don't Lean Out (of the Window)
飞机场	Airport
铁路	Railroad
快车	Express (lit., fast car)
慢车	Local (lit., slow car)
站	Stop (bus, train, etc.)

不可张贴	Post No Bills
修理中	Under Repair
入口	Entrance
出口	Exit
配家具房子	Furnished Rooms
房子	House
油漆未干	Wet Paint
十字路口	Crossroads
肉店	Butcher
饼店	Bakery
牛奶	Dairy
裁缝店	Tailor Shop
鞋店	Shoe Store
理发店	Barber Shop
菜市场 or 市场	Grocer, Market
药房 or 药店	Pharmacy, Drugstore
糖果店	Confectioner, Candy Store
文具店	Stationery Store
信箱	Mail Box
酒吧	Bar, Tavern
公安局	Police Station

酒	Wines
油站	Gas Station
书店	Bookstore
市政府	City Hall
点心 or 小吃	Refreshments, Snacks
(冷)水	(Cold) Water
(热)水	(Hot) Water

Dialogues in Chinese Characters

Below are the first four conversations from this course written out in Chinese characters.

LESSON 4 (CONVERSATIONS)
Conversation 1

马丽： 您好吗？
Mali: **Nín hǎo ma?**
Mary: *How are you?*

海： 我很好。谢谢。
Hai: **Wǒ hěn hǎo. Xièxie.**
Hai: *I'm very well. Thank you.*

马丽： 您是老师吗？
Mali: **Nín shì lǎoshī ma?**
Mary: *Are you a teacher?*

海： 我不是老师。 我是学生。
Hai: **Wǒ bú shì lǎoshī. Wǒ shì xuésheng.**
Hai: *No, I'm not. I'm a student.*

马丽： 对不起。
Mali: **Duìbuqǐ.**
Mary: *Sorry.*

海： 不要紧。 你也是学生吗？
Hai: **Búyàojǐn. Nǐ yě shì xuésheng ma?**
Hai: *That's okay. (lit., It doesn't matter.) Are you a student too?*

马丽: 我不是学生，我是老师。

Mali: Wǒ bú shì xuésheng, wǒ shì lǎoshī.

Mary: I'm not a student. I'm a teacher.

海: 请问您贵姓？

Hai: Qǐngwèn nín guìxìng?

Hai: May I ask your last name?

马丽: 我姓张，中文名字叫马丽。 你呢？

Mali: Wǒ xìng Zhāng, Zhōngwén míngzi jiào Mǎlì.
Nǐ ne?

Mary: My last name is Zhang. (My) Chinese first name is
Mali. How about you?

海: 我姓王，叫王海。

Hai: Wǒ xìng Wáng, jiào Wáng Hǎi.

Hai: My last name is Wang. I'm called Wang Hai.

马丽: 再见。

Mali: Zàijiàn.

Mary: Goodbye.

海: 再见。

Hai: Zàijiàn.

Hai: Goodbye.

CONVERSATION 2

海: 张老师，早安。

Hai: Zhāng lǎoshī, zǎo'ān.

Hai: Good morning, teacher Zhang.

马丽: 您是…？

Mali: Nín shì…?

Mary: You are…?

海： 我是王海。
Hai: Wǒ shì Wáng Hǎi.
Hai: I'm Wang Hai.

马丽： 对不起，王海。
Mali: Duìbuqǐ, Wáng Hǎi.
Mary: Sorry, Wang Hai.

海： 不要紧。 张老师，请问您是哪国人？
Hai: Búyàojǐn. Zhāng lǎoshī, qǐngwèn nín shì nǎguórén?
Hai: No problem. Teacher Zhang, may I ask what nationality you are?

马丽： 我是美国人。 您呢？
Mali: Wǒ shì Měiguórén. Nǐ ne?
Mary: I'm American. How about you?

海： 我是中国人。
Hai: Wǒ shì Zhōngguórén.
Hai: I'm Chinese.

马丽： 他们也是中国人吗？
Mali: Tāmen yě shì Zhōngguórén ma?
Mary: Are they also Chinese?

海： 不是。 他们是日本人。
Hai: Bú shì. Tāmen shì Rìběnrén.
Hai: No. They're Japanese.

马丽： 你几岁？
Mali: Nǐ jǐ suì?
Mary: How old are you?

海： 我二十岁。
Hai: Wǒ èrshí suì.
Hai: I'm twenty.

LESSON 8 (CONVERSATIONS)
CONVERSATION 1

海: 杰西，早安！
Hai: Jié Xī, zǎo'ān!
Hai: Good morning, Jess!

杰西: 王海，早安！
Jess: Wáng Hǎi, zǎo'ān!
Jess: Good morning, Wang Hai!

海: 杰西，你有兄弟姐妹吗？
Hai: Jié Xī, nǐ yǒu xiōngdìjiěmèi ma?
Hai: Jess, do you have any siblings?

杰西: 没有，我的家只有三口人。我，爸爸和
妈妈。王海，你家有几口人？
Jess: Méiyǒu, wǒde jiā zhǐyǒu sān kǒu rén. Wǒ,
bàba hé māma. Wáng Hǎi, nǐ jiā yǒu jǐ kǒu
rén?
*Jess: No. My family has only three people: (my) father, (my)
mother, and myself. Wang Hai, how many people are
there in your family?*

海: 我家有五口人。爸爸，妈妈，姐姐，
弟弟和我。
Hai: Wǒ jiā yǒu wǔ kǒu rén. Bàba, māma, jiějie,
dìdi hé wǒ.
*Hai: My family has five people: (my) father, (my) mother,
(my) older sister, (my) younger brother, and myself.*

杰西: 啊，你的家真热闹。
Jess: Ā, nǐde jiā zhēn rènao.
Jess: Oh, your home is really bustling.

海: 我们还有一条小狗和两只猫。

Hai: Wǒmen háiyǒu yì tiáo xiǎogǒu hé liǎng zhī māo.

Hai: *We also have a puppy and two cats.*

杰西: 我家没有狗，也没有猫，只有三条鱼。

Jess: Wǒ jiā méiyǒu gǒu, yě méiyǒu māo, zhǐyǒu sān tiáo yú.

Jess: *My family doesn't have a dog or cat. We only have three fish.*

CONVERSATION 2

海: 请坐！

Hai: Qǐng zuò!

Hai: *Please sit down.*

杰西: 王海，你的家很漂亮！有几个卧房？

Jess: Wáng Hǎi, nǐde jiā hěn piàoliang! Yǒu jǐge wòfáng?

Jess: *Wang Hai, your home is very pretty! How many bedrooms do you have?*

海: 我们的公寓太小了，只有三个卧房和一个浴室。我和弟弟用一个房间。

Hai: Wǒmende gōngyù tài xiǎo le, zhǐyǒu sān ge wòfáng hé yí ge yùshì. Wǒ hé dìdi yòng yí ge fángjiān.

Hai: *Our apartment is too small. We only have three bedrooms and one bathroom. (My) younger brother and I share (lit., use) a room.*

杰西: 那是你们的照片吗？

Jess: Nà shì nǐmende zhàopiàn ma?

Jess: *Is that your (family's) photo?*

海： 是，那是我们的照片。

Hai: Shì, nà shì wǒmende zhàopiàn.

Hai: Yes, that's our photo.

杰西： 这是你的姐姐吗？

Jess: Zhè shì nǐde jiějie ma?

Jess: Is this your older sister?

海： 不是，这是我妈妈。

Hai: Búshì, zhè shì wǒ māma.

Hai: No. This is my mother.

杰西： 对不起。

Jess: Duìbuqǐ.

Jess: Sorry.

海： 不要紧。 我妈妈是老师。

Hai: Búyàojǐn. Wǒ māma shì lǎoshī.

Hai: That's alright. My mother is a teacher.

杰西： 她很年青。

Jess: Tā <u>hěn</u> niánqīng.

Jess: She looks very young.

The **best-selling** language course
Completely revised and updated!

Words, phrases, sentences, conversations: speak a new language with confidence right from the start with our simple four-step building block approach. Designed to be effective in a short period of time, these comprehensive courses have everything you need—pronunciation, vocabulary, grammar, culture, and practice.

Each course package includes:
- A coursebook with 40 step-by-step lessons
- 4 audio CDs with all the essential course content
- An extensive grammar reference section
- Supplemental sections on e-mail and internet resources
- A learner's dictionary or a reading and writing guide

Available In:

**4 CDs/Coursebook/
Reading and Writing Guide**
$29.95/$34.00 Can.

Arabic: 978-1-4000-2408-7

Reading and Writing Guide
$8.99/$9.99 Can.

Arabic Script: 978-1-4000-0924-4

---

4 CDs/Coursebook/Dictionary
$29.95/$34.00 Can.

Chinese:	978-1-4000-2426-1
[Mandarin]	
French:	978-1-4000-2410-0
German:	978-1-4000-2412-4
Inglés:	978-1-4000-2414-8
Italian:	978-1-4000-2416-2
Japanese:	978-1-4000-2418-6
Portuguese:	978-1-4000-2420-9
Russian:	978-1-4000-2422-3
Spanish:	978-1-4000-2424-7

Coursebook Only
$10.95/$12.50 Can.

Arabic:	978-1-4000-1992-2
Chinese:	978-1-4000-2525-4
[Mandarin]	
French:	978-1-4000-2409-4
German:	978-1-4000-2411-7
Inglés:	978-1-4000-2413-1
Italian:	978-1-4000-2415-5
Japanese:	978-1-4000-2417-9
Portuguese:	978-1-4000-2419-3
Russian:	978-1-4000-2421-6
Spanish:	978-1-4000-2423-0

Dictionary Only
$7.95/$9.95 Can.

Chinese:	978-1-4000-2452-0
[Mandarin]	
French:	978-1-4000-2444-5
German:	978-1-4000-2445-2
Inglés:	978-1-4000-2446-9
Italian:	978-1-4000-2447-6
Japanese:	978-1-4000-2448-3
Portuguese:	978-1-4000-2449-0
Russian:	978-1-4000-2450-6
Spanish:	978-1-4000-2451-3

In-Flight Chinese

Wondering how to make use of all that spare time on the plane? Between your in-flight meal and in-flight movie, brush up on your Chinese! This 60-minute program covers just enough Chinese to get by in every travel situation.

CD Program
978-0-609-81074-3 • $13.95/$21.00 Can.

Ultimate Chinese [Mandarin] Beginner-Intermediate

Our most comprehensive program for serious language learners, business-people, and anyone planning to spend time abroad. This package includes a coursebook and eight 60-minute CDs.

CD Program
978-1-4000-2103-1 • $79.95/$110.00 Can.

Coursebook Only
978-1-4000-2102-4 • $18.00/$26.00 Can.